Strap on your seat belt and get ready to learn everything you want to know about newsletters...

"*Marketing With Newsletters* fills a very big gap: I've never come across anybody who made as much sense of the promotional aspect of the newsletter as a medium—and said so, four-square."
Jan V. White, author
Editing by Design

"If newsletters figure anywhere in selling your ideas, products or services, you simply *must* read *Marketing With Newsletters.*"
Gordon Burgett, author
Empire Building by Writing & Speaking

"The new *Marketing With Newsletters* is one-third larger but contains ten times as much information. You follow your own advice and make every page so readable! The inclusion of the duck as a cross reference is *terrific.*'"
Murray Raphel, owner
Raphel Marketing, Atlantic City, NJ

"I've read a lot about newsletters. In fact, I received my B.A. in public relations at a time when PCs were not available. I find your work keeps me updated with ideas and technology better than other sources."
Tina Mitchell, owner
Common Sense Marketing, Waterford, MI

"Wow! What a great book. It's packed with useful information and is so reader-friendly."
Sam Horn, author and speaker
Tongue Fu! and Concrete Confidence

"*Marketing With Newsletters* bulges with practical information."
Jack Gillespie, editor
communication briefings, Alexandria, VA

"You've done it again! *Marketing With Newsletters* covers everything an editor could need... an amazing collection of tips and techniques."
Lyn Dahl, newsletter trainer
SkillPath, Mission, KS

"I have been in sales and marketing most of my adult life and have found many good ideas in your book *Marketing With Newsletters.* It is most informative and helpful."
Robert E. Bowman
Las Vegas, NV

"I began reading your book as soon as I unwrapped it, and I am already amazed by the useful information in it. Your thoughts on newsletters are going to be a terrific addition to my stack of notecards—and ultimately to my thesis."
Lisa I. Micklin-Rouh, graduate student
Mantua, NJ

"*Marketing With Newsletters* is the best I've read on the subject. Lots of good information, well organized, attractive, easy to read and enjoyable. It's well worth the price."
Sue Simmons
Beacon Insurance Co., Columbus, OH

"Elaine Floyd has forgotten more about newsletters than most people know."
Lew Williams, direct mail copywriter
Dallas, TX

"Your book was very helpful in aiding me during my creation of the newsletter I provided for the support staff. Once I began it, I enjoyed doing it so much that I plan to launch another from my home-based business. Thanks."
    Daronda McDuffie, editor

"I will surely keep *Marketing With Newsletters* in mind when talking to people about newsletters. What a resource for our students."
    Don Ranly, Ph.D., professor
    University of Missouri, Columbia, MO

"WOW! *Marketing With Newsletters* is designed so enticingly that even the skimmers like me will be hooked on what you have to say. We'll keep coming back to nibble more bits of knowledge until we've read *Marketing With Newsletters* from cover to cover. Then we'll start over again. Your book is one of those rare treats: a reference book that's fun to read."
    William E. Stroupe, editor
    Tarheel Banker, Raleigh, NC

"*Marketing With Newsletters* holds the answers to every conceivable question a newsletter publisher could face. Not only that, you provide a list of resources in the back of others who can do things for me. Congratulations on a wonderful book."
    Jim Cathcart, author and speaker
    La Jolla, CA

"Well-written, thorough, educational and entertaining."
    Paul Swift, editor
    Newsletter Clearinghouse, Rhinebeck, NY

"*Marketing With Newsletters* packs in practical marketing-oriented advice which goes far beyond most general 'how to write' competitors."
    Midwest Book Review

"You're a helluva writer and a major contributor to the world of guerrilla marketers. Thank you for doing what you're doing, Elaine."
    Jay Conrad Levinson, author
    Guerrilla Marketing

3rd edition

Marketing with Newsletters

with

How to boost sales,
add members & raise funds
with a print, fax, e-mail,
Web site or postcard newsletter

Elaine Floyd

**Also by Elaine
Floyd:**

**Quick and Easy
Newsletters**
(EFG)

**The Newsletter
Editor's Handbook**
(EFG, co-authored with
Marvin Arth and Helen
Ashmore)

**Making Money
Writing Newsletters**
(EFG)

**Marketing Your
Bookstore with a
Newsletter**
(EFG)

**Creating Family
Newsletters**
(EFG)

Marketing With Newsletters: How to boost sales, add members and raise donations with a print, fax, e-mail, Web site or postcard newsletter.

Copyright © 2002 Elaine Floyd

Acknowledgements. This book continues to help busy marketers thanks to the help it received early on from my newsletter mentors—Mark Beach, Robert Bly, Lyn Dahl, Howard Penn Hudson, Jack Lim, Ronnie Lipton, Terri Lonier, Roger Parker, Polly Pattison, Lawrence Ragan, Kathleen Ryan, Marlon Sanders, Sarah Stambler, Jill Thomas, Bob Westenberg and Jan V. White.

ISBN: 1-950300-11-4

Third Edition. First Printing.
Printed and bound in the United States of America.

EFG, Inc.
SAN 297-4541
St. Louis, MO

www.newsletterinfo.com

Distributed to the trade and art markets in North America by:

Writer's Digest Books
an imprint of F&W Publications, Inc.
4700 East Galbraith Road
Cincinnati, OH 45236
(800) 289-0963

Hey, You Book Surfers Out There

This will just take a second... Since much of this book is dedicated to communication with skimmers of newsletters, it would be rude to ignore you book skimmers. There's just one thing you need to know.

Throughout the book, selling through newsletters is illustrated by leading readers through four stages, collectively called NEWS.

Name: Telling people who you are, where to find you and what you provide.

Enticement: Drawing people to your news by showing that you can provide what your prospects want and that you're an expert.

Written Words: Giving specific reasons why your prospects should choose you over your competitors.

Sell: Telling readers what action to take—visit your Web site, return the reply card, call your toll-free number or send in an order or donation.

To see me in action, see page 19.

One other skimming feature—from time to time you'll see a surfer in the margin telling you about additional information on another page. His job is to further aid your skimming experience. Okay, now you can skim, skip, and flip at your leisure.

What's Inside:

Overview:

Launch an Effective News Campaign

A friend of mine shared some great news the other day. He is launching a series of free breakfast seminars for his target market. The seminars are filled with valuable content and also include a free workbook and DVD presentation. My friend proudly showed me the four-color newsletter that he was going to mail soon to his list of 1,000 people. His goal was that 100 of these folks would sign up for the event.

With value-packed content and a high-quality giveaways and even *food*—mailing out one news announcement should be enough to fill the room. Right?

From Newsletters to Newscasting

Those of you who have been in my friend's shoes are out there moving your heads from left to right about now.

You know the amount of repetition it takes to make sure that everyone is aware of your current news, products and offerings. It's not that people don't like what you're doing. They are just busy, overwhelmed, forgetful... you name it.

Luckily, you have many different options for reach your audience with your news—traditional newsletters, postcards, e-mail, Web sites, fax, news announcements at events and news listings in other publications.

Take One!

For strategic news, use a variety of media to repeat it to your audience in a variety of ways. Only then can you be assured that they are aware of what you're doing.

Here is how newscasting works:

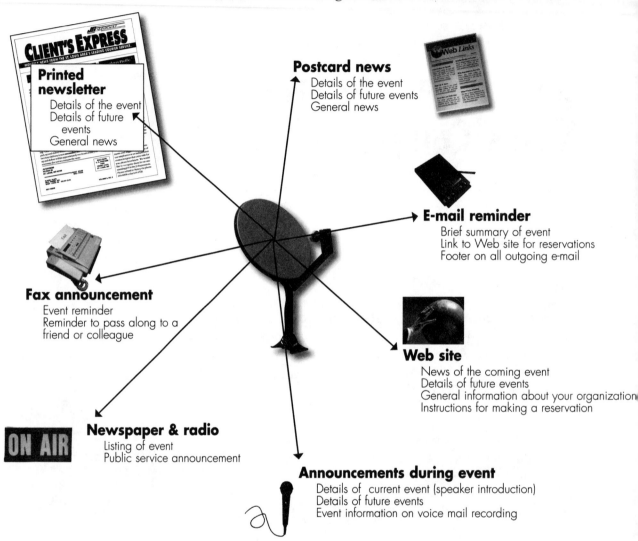

Printed newsletter
Details of the event
Details of future events
General news

Postcard news
Details of the event
Details of future events
General news

E-mail reminder
Brief summary of event
Link to Web site for reservations
Footer on all outgoing e-mail

Fax announcement
Event reminder
Reminder to pass along to a friend or colleague

Web site
News of the coming event
Details of future events
General information about your organization
Instructions for making a reservation

Newspaper & radio
Listing of event
Public service announcement

Announcements during event
Details of current event (speaker introduction)
Details of future events
Event information on voice mail recording

NewsCast Marketing Using News Tools

Simulcasting news of an upcoming event to several different media greatly increases the chances that your target audience will see and remember your news.

Create a NewsWave™ with a Campaign

The key to strategic newscasting is to create all of your news elements at the same time but time their release so that they all appear on the radar screen of your target market at the same time.

If you've ever been frustrated by a competitor who seems to have their name "everywhere," you now hold in your hands everything you need to know to do this, too. Every effort has been made to provide tips that help you organize the project so that you reap maximum benefit in the least amount of time.

The three elements of campaigns are:

1. Identify your most important products, services or events and define your desired outcome.

2. Decide on a time line so that the campaign has a beginning and an end (this way you can evaluate effectiveness, have the feeling of an accomplishment and move on to the next campaign.)

3. Create all of the pieces at the same time and plan for their release.

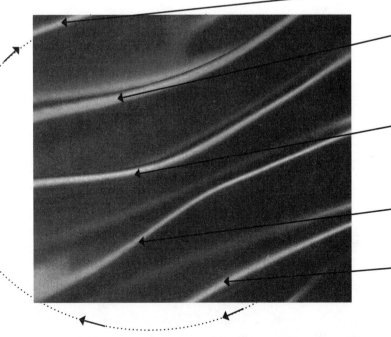

2 to 6 months prior:

List as upcoming event in newsletter

Announce as a coming event at meetings

1 month to 3 weeks prior:

Mail out print newsletter

Send news release to newspapers

2 to 3 weeks prior:

List details on Web site

Send news release to radio and TV stations

1 week to 1 day prior:

Send out fax and e-mail reminders

At the event:

Preview next event

You Need This Book!

Regardless of the final form of your newsletter, this book shows you how to maximize its promotional value. It contains practical information for editors with all levels of experience.

This book helps you:

❑ discover sales and marketing methods you can immediately put to work in your newsletter

❑ learn skills that make newsletter editing and production run smoothly

❑ find out how to put it all together into targeted news that promotes your products, services and ideas

I hope the information you need is easy to find, fun to learn and immediately applicable to the successful promotion of your organization. Your news is good news, so let's get it out there.

Elaine Floyd
St. Louis, June 2002

Chapter 1:

Combat the "Out of Sight, Out of Mind" Syndrome

O ne of the key benefits of producing a newsletter is that your name will regularly cross the desktops of your best customers, prospects or supporters. Every salesperson knows that you must stay in front of your customers or they will forget about you.

Effective newsletters function like personal sales calls. They remind your best prospects of your existence. They also tell your target audience about all of your new and existing products, services, causes or events. This helps you combat another marketing syndrome—the "I-Didn't-Know-That-You-Did-That Syndrome."

In this chapter:

- what newsletters are good for

- how you know they're working

- how to "sell" through news

- reflecting your image and look

- what to write about

- generating reader response

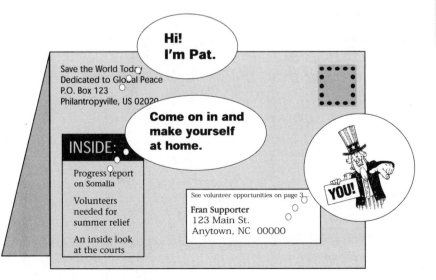

Signs of Newsletter Success

All newsletters promote specific goals. Association and church publications strive to gain new members and retain existing ones. Customer newsletters provide service while selling additional products. Charities use newsletters to increase donations or volunteer time.

In general, newsletters are a good way to:

- ❑ bring in new supporters
- ❑ keep in touch with existing customers
- ❑ sell more to existing customers
- ❑ drive traffic to your Web site
- ❑ reinforce your specialty

Humorist Terry Braverman markets his speaking and consulting through his fun-loving *News to Amuse*. The newsletter name reinforces his specialty from the beginning.

- ❑ establish expertise and credibility
- ❑ spur word-of-mouth referrals
- ❑ inform and educate
- ❑ save selling time
- ❑ attract volunteers and members
- ❑ bring back lost customers
- ❑ win support
- ❑ boost donations
- ❑ publicize your organization to the media
- ❑ network with industry allies and vendors
- ❑ unify a "community" of readers

However, in order to achieve these goals, newsletters have to be read. Successful promotional newsletters get people to read not only what interests them, but also what the publisher wants them to read. Successful promotional newsletters keep sight of two things:

- ❑ the readers' interests
- ❑ the publication's goals

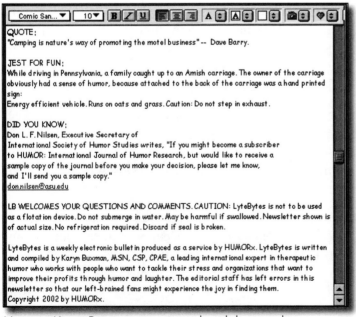

www.humorx.com

Humorist Karyn Buxman stays in touch with her speaking and consulting clients with an e-mail newsletter, *LyteBytes*.

Tried & True Do's & Don'ts

At newsletter seminars throughout the world, people mention the same items that they like and don't like to see in newsletters.

Readers Like:
- interesting subjects
- short articles
- good visuals
- easy-to-skim designs
- bulleted lists
- content telling how to make money, save time
- clear organization
- calendars
- offers, benefits

Readers Don't Like:
- intimidating pages
- disorganized information and links
- long e-mails, continuing articles
- overly frequent sendings
- irrelevant content
- impersonal tone
- receiving multiple copies
- chaotic page design
- too many pages or screens

How Newsletters Sell

One of the factors affecting the benefits gained from newsletter publishing is the degree of "reader interaction" you achieve. Reader interaction techniques can be broken down to coincide with four levels of promotion. Combine these levels, and you'll be marketing with NEWS.

Here are the four steps to NEWS:

❑ **Name.** Your prospects need a basic awareness of your organization before they can do business with you. Tell them who you are, where to find you, and, in general, what products or services you provide. Keep your name in front of prospects in the hope that they'll remember you.

❑ **Enticement.** You must project a professional image. In the initial stages of a purchasing decision, your prospects carefully evaluate your organization. Why should they place an order, make an appointment or give a donation to you instead of someone else? Prove that you run a credible operation.

❑ **Written Words.** Your prospects and customers want more information on why they should support you. Show that you're an expert. Give specific features, Drive traffic to your Web site where you have further information and resources.

❑ **Sell.** Without a call to action, there can be no sale. Once your prospects are ready to act, tell them what to do. Cast your vote this Tuesday. Visit this Web site now. Call this toll-free number. Send $25 to help feed a family.

The four levels of NEWS—name, enticement, written words and sell—show how promotional newsletters market your organization. The next section takes you through each promotional level in detail and shows the news elements used to sell at each level.

Skipping Steps

Readers often move from "enticement" directly to "sell" and give you the response you want. It happens simply because you've established your name in their minds as a reputable organization.

Name: The Introduction

Most readers enter at the mailing panel—the front door of your newsletter. They glance at the mailing label containing their name, your return address and anything else close by. At this point, your newsletter will unobtrusively remind people of your existence. It can help them recall an upcoming event or a brochure you previously sent. Your name enters your prospects' minds as soon as they glance at the return address.

Place information that spurs interest in your organization on the mailing panel. Use any of these:

- ❑ your organization's logo
- ❑ your slogan
- ❑ a location map or your Web address
- ❑ a list of your products and services
- ❑ a highlight of the volunteer of the month
- ❑ an advertisement for a monthly special
- ❑ teasers to encourage recipients to open the newsletter
- ❑ the date of your next meeting
- ❑ a message line on the label above the person's name
- ❑ a box listing the content of the newsletter

Don't Throw Me Away!

Your job in designing your mailing area or e-mail subject box is to convince your readers to open the newsletter. You only have a few seconds.

You must convince recipients that the newsletter includes timely information they should read now. Because almost everyone will look at the mailing area, place the one thing you want everyone to know here.

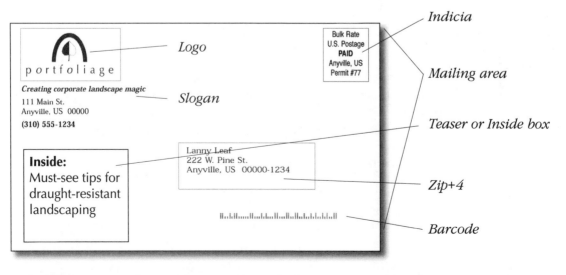

Mailing list broker's successful nameplate. The name, *Direct Success*, tells the reader what benefits the newsletter offers. The tagline gives another benefit and the subject, "Quarterly tips & techniques for profitable direct mail marketing."

Enticement: The First Impression

The next thing most readers do is open to the front page or top of the screen and glance at the nameplate area. The nameplate signals the starting place for the newsletter content. Through the nameplate, you can catch readers' interest with:

- ❑ a newsletter name explaining the benefits of reading
- ❑ a tagline that says your newsletter is written just for them
- ❑ a nameplate design telling more about what you do

A charity's newsletter for prospective volunteers and donors is called *Making a Difference*. The tagline tells readers the result of their support—"How your time and donations are improving the lives of the homeless."

The name and the tagline come together in the design of the nameplate (see illustration below). For an e-mail newsletter, the name and tagline may be followed by a contents listing that encourages readers to scroll on.

Once people look at the name, they begin skimming the headlines and illustrations. This gives them a feel for the type of information you're providing. (What they're really doing is looking for an excuse not to read the newsletter.)

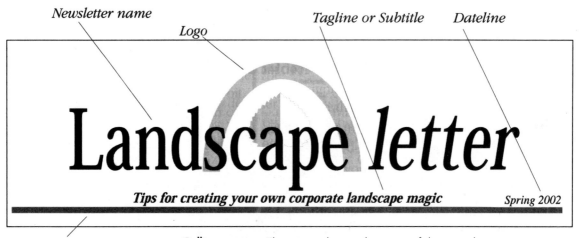

Newsletter name

Logo

Tagline or Subtitle

Dateline

Landscape *letter*

Tips for creating your own corporate landscape magic

Spring 2002

Rule or line

Calling names. The nameplate is the area of the newsletter containing the newsletter's name.

You have about 15 seconds to grab their attention through:

- ❑ intriguing or emotional photographs or headlines
- ❑ illustrations or charts that condense your message
- ❑ captions that pull readers into the article
- ❑ fun cartoons illustrating your promotional message
- ❑ concise, easily removed calendars
- ❑ headlines telling the benefits of reading an article
- ❑ subheads that list your main ideas at a glance
- ❑ pull quotes that intrigue readers
- ❑ the "emotional" elements of paper, color and design

See examples of attention-getting graphics on pages 193-196.

Kicker

Headline

Deck

Drop or initial cap

Pull quote

End mark

Illustration or Clip art

Caption

Bulleted list

Ogilvy on Editorial

According to advertising expert David Ogilvy, editorial material is three times more persuasive than advertising. While Americans have developed negative attitudes toward most advertising, they've developed positive attitudes toward informative editorial.

More Inside... ☞

Turn over. The goal of a local association's newsletter is to draw its members to monthly meetings and events. They use an oversized postcard newsletter with the area near the address label listing facts about upcoming meetings. The opposite side summarizes other association news.

When people glance through your news, reading headlines, examining photos and scanning for content, they absorb your image. If you've used effective promotional tactics, the reader will learn the type of service you offer. If the contents are worthwhile, you have a good chance of convincing your reader to read on and maybe even to call you or click through to your Web site.

Written Words: The Content Makes the Sale

The graphics, headline, contents and link techniques described earlier provide readers with "points of entry." Points of entry are places for readers to start gathering more specifics. Provide other options for a reader who may not be interested in the first article. Remember, you only have about 15 seconds to capture a reader.

Most readers are front- and back-page minglers. They scan the pages, searching for a place to stop and "chat." Invite them to join several "conversations" by providing at least three articles on the front page. In a print newsletter, this is the entry point for 85% of readers.

If your newsletter includes long articles, place these on the inside pages or toward the end (but not on the back page). Use links for long online articles. The back page needs short articles, too. This is the entry point for the other 15% of readers.

Use the content in the specifics stage to:

- ❑ introduce new products and services
- ❑ tell your success stories in case histories
- ❑ recognize top members, donors, employees or customers
- ❑ report on trends and statistics
- ❑ show your involvement in lively editorials
- ❑ give "how-to" information
- ❑ provide technical advice in question and answer columns
- ❑ share inside information

Select and write all of these articles to reinforce your promotional message to clients and prospects.

Editorial

Lead

Head shot or Mug shot

Body copy, Text or Articles

Newsbrief

Feature

Byline

Bluegrass Should be Blue & Other Observations

Lorem ipsum dolor sit amet, con secteteur adipiscing elit, sed diam nonnumy nibh euismod tempor inci dunt ut labore et dolore magna ali quam erat volupat. Ut wise enim ad minim veniam, quis nostrud exerci tation ullamcorper suscipit laboris nisl ut aliquip ex ea commodo con sequat. Duis autem vel eum irure dolor in henderit in vulputate velit esse consequat.

Vel illum dolor eu feugiat mulla facilsi at vero eos et accusm et ius to odio dignessim qui blandt prae sent luptatum zzril delenit aigue duos dolore et mosestias exceptur sint occaecat cupidtat not simil pro vident tempor sunt in culpa qui oficia desrunt

Alex Todorov is president and green-ery expert at Portfoliage. He can be reached at

Landscape letter
Landscape letter is filled with ideas for creative landscaping and published quarterly by Portfoliage, Inc., 123 W. Main St., Leaf City, MO 63000.

Please feel free to call (314) 000-0000 with any questions or to be added to the list.

Editor, Joe Johnson

ECOLOGY ACROSS THE WORLD:

Using Resources Wisely

Japan Junks Incinerator Plan

Lorem ipsum dolor sit amet, con secteteur adipiscing elit, sed diam nonnumy nibh euisnod tempor inci dunt ut labore et dolore magna ali quam erat volupat. Ut wise enim ad minim veniam, quis nostrud exerci tation ullamcorper suscipit laboris nisl ut aliquip ex ea commodo con sequat. Duis autem vel eum irure dolor in henderit in vulputate velit esse consequat.

Vel illum dolor eu feugiat mulla facisi at vero eos et accusm et ius to odio dignessim qui blandt prae sent luptatum zzril delenit aigue duos dolore et mosestias exceptur sint occaecat cupidtat not simii pro vident tempor sunt in culpa.

Fertilizer Fails in Finland

ui officia desrunt mollit aniom ib est abor un et dolor fuga. Et harumd dereud facilis est er expedit distint. Nam liber tempor cum solu ta nobis eligent option congue nibil impediet domìng id quod maxim plecat facer possum omnis voluptas assumenda est, mnis repel lend.

Temporibud auteui quinsud et aur offik debit aut tum rerum necessit atib saepe eventi ut er mosit non reusand. Itaque earun rerum hic ten tury sapiente delectus au aut perfer zim ednbis dolorib asperiore repellat. Hanc ego cum

Paraguay Plans Petunia Party

eme senteniam, quid est kur verear ne ad eam non passing accommodare nost ros quos tu paulo ante cum emmorite tum etia ergat. Nos amice et nbevol, olestias access potest fier ad augent ascum consci ent to factor tum poen legum odio qu civiumda. Et tamen in busdam negque nonor imper.

Nos amice et memorite tum etia ergat mbevp. Pestoas aces est foer ad augend ascum consci ent to factor tum ppoen legum odio que civiuna. Et tamen in busdam neque as minim veniam, quis nostrud exerci tation ullamcorper suscipit laboris nisl ut aliquip ex ea commodo sonsequat. Dues atuem velit esse mol estie consequat.

Lorem ipsum dolor sit amet, con secteteur adipsicing elit, sed diam nonnumy nibh euisnod tempor inci dunt ut labore et dolore magna ali quam erat volupat. Ut wise enim ad minim veniam, quis nostrud exerci tation ullamcorper suscipit.

Mulch Mixes in Mexico

ui officia desrunt mollit aniom ib est abor un et dolor fuga. Et harumd dereud facilis est er expedit distint. Nam liber tempor cum solu ta nobis eligent option congue nibil impediet domìng id quod maxim plecat facer possum omnis voluptas assumenda est, mnis repel lend.

Temporibud auteui quinsud et aur offik debit aut tum rerum necessit atib saepe eventi ut er mosit non reusand. Itaque earun rerum hic ten tury sapiente delectus au aut perfer zim ednbis dolorib asperiore repellat. Hanc ego cum

Botswana Buys Bougianvilleas

eme senteniam, quid est kur verear ne ad eam non passing accommodare nost ros quos tu paulo ante cum emmorite tum etia ergat. Nos amice et nbevol, olestias access potest fier ad augent ascum consci ent to factor tum poen legum odio qu civiumda. Et tamen in busdam negque nonor imper.

Nos amice et memorite tum etia ergat mbevp. Pestoas aces est foer ad augend ascum consci ent to factor tum ppoen legum odio que civiuna. Et tamen in busdam neque as minim veniam, quis nostrud exerci tation ullamcorper suscipit laboris nisl ut aliquip ex ea commodo sonsequat. Dues atuem velit esse mol estie consequat.

Ireland Eyes Ivy

ui officia desrunt mollit aniom ib est abor un et dolor fuga. Et harumd dereud facilis est er expedit distint. Nam liber tempor cum solu ta nobis eligent option congue nibil impediet domìng id quod maxim plecat facer possum omnis voluptas assumenda est, mnis repel lend.

CUSTOMER FEATURE:

ABC Corporation Proves That

by Susan Shrubbery

Lorem ipsum dolor sit amet, con secteteur adipiscing elit, sed diam nonnumy nibh euisnod tempor inci dunt ut labore et dolore magna ali quam erat volupat.

Ut wise enim ad minim veniam, quis nostrud exerci tation ullamcorper suscipit laboris nisl ut aliquip ex ea commodo con sequat. Duis autem vel eum irure dolor in henderit in vulputate velit esse consequat.

From weeds to wisteria
Vel illum dolor eu feugiat mulla facils at vero eos et accusm et ius to odio dignessim qui blandt prae sent luptatum zzril delenit aigue duos dolore et mosestias exceptur sint occaecat cupidtat not simil pro vident tempor sunt in culpa qui oficia desrunt mollit aniom ib est abor un et dolor fuga. Et harumd dereud facilis est er expedit distint. Nam liber tempor cum solута nobis eligent option congue nibil impediet dom ing id quod maxim plecat facer possum omnis voluptas assumenda est, mnis repel lend.

Temporibud auteui quinsud et aur offik debit aut tum rerum necessit atib saepe eventit ut er mosit non reusand. Itaque earun rerum hic ten tury sapiente delectus au aut perfer zim ednbis dolorib asperiore repellat.

Not too contrary
Hanc ego cum tene senteniam, quid est kur verear ne ad eam non passing accommodare nost ros quos tu paulo ante cum emmorite tum etia ergat. Nos amice et nbevol, olestias access potest fier ad augent ascum consci ent to factor tum poen legum odio qui civiumda. Et tamen in busdam negque nonor imper.

Nos amice et memorite tum etia ergat mbevp. Pestoas aces est foer ad aigend ascum consci ent to factor tum ppoen legum odio que civiuna. Et tamen in busdam neque as minim veniam, quis nostrud exerci tation ullamcorper suscipit laboris nisl ut aliquip ex ea commodo sonsequat. Dues atuem velit esse mol estie consequat.

Hanc ego cum tene senteniam, quid est cur verear ne ad eam non possing accommodare nost ros quos tu apule ante cum memorite tum etia ergat.

Chemical-free maintenance
Facile erricerd possit duo conetud notier si effercerit, et opes bel fortuanag vel ingen liberalitat magis convenniunt, da but tuntung ben evolent sib concilliant, et aptis sim est ad qute.

Vel illum dolor eu feugiat mulla facils at vero eos et accusm et ius to odio dignessim qui blandt prae sent luptatum zzril delenit aigue duos dolore et mosestias exceptur sint occaecat cupidtat not simil pro vident tempor sunt in culpa qui oficia desrunt mollit aniom ib est abor un et dolor fuga. Et harumd dereud facilis est er expedit distint. Nam liber tempor cum soluta nobis eligent option congue nibil impediet dom ing id quod maxim plecat facer possum omnis voluptas assumenda est, mnis repel lend.

Growing like weeds without the weeds
Vel illum dolor eu feugiat mulla facils at vero eos et accusm et ius to odio dignessim qui blandt prae sent luptatum zzril delenit aigue duos dolore et mosestias exceptur sint occaecat cupidtat not simil pro vident tempor sunt in culpa qui oficia desrunt mollit aniom ib est abor un et dolor fuga. Et harumd dereud facilis est er expedit distint. Nam liber tempor cum soluta nobis eligent option congue nibil impediet dom ing id quod maxim plecat facer possum omnis voluptas assumenda est, mnis repel lend.

▶ **Tips for Great Growing this Spring**

- Lorem ipsum dolor sit amet
- Con secteteur adipsicing elit
- Sed diam nonnumy nibh euisnod
- Tempor inci dunt ut labore
- Dolore magna ali quam erat volupet.
- Ut wise enim ad minim veniam.
- Quis nostrud exerci tation ullamcorper
- Suscipit laboris nisl ut aliquip ex ea.
- Lorem ipsum dolor sit amet
- Con secteteur adipsicing elit
- Sed diam nonnumy nibh euisnod
- Tempor inci dunt ut labore
- Dolore magna ali quam erat volupet.
- Ut wise enim ad minim veniam.
- Quis nostrud exerci tation ullamcorper

Masthead

Alley

Gutter

Folio

Signature line

Subhead

Sidebar

See more about content in Chapter 6, starting on page 109.

OUTLOOK

Epilepsy Outlook

Targeted content starts with targeted name. Pay special attention to your newsletter name and tagline. Avoid general newsletter names like "News" or "Update." Tell readers about your specialized content right away.

6 Types of Newsletter Content

1. **News articles**. New product articles fulfill the "news" requirements of a newsletter, while also marketing your products. When you develop a new product or service, or embark on a new cause, write up the details of your project in the newsletter. Let prospects know when a new product or service is available. If you're launching a new fund drive, tell prospects exactly how they can participate. List volunteer jobs available. Give starting dates and deadlines for participation.

   In addition to your own news, include news of your industry. Summarize all of the top trends and news items. You'll provide your readers with a time-saving benefit while also promoting your expertise.

2. **People stories**. After your new product, service or program is in use, write about its success. Success stories are an important part of promoting your organization. In addition, recognize key customers, members and donors. People donating their time and money usually do so because they support your cause. But chances are, they support other causes as well. Keep their attention by giving them yours.

3. **Educational information**. Many organizations promote their products by providing expertise in the form of "how-to" information. Choose a subject that creates a need for your products or services. For example, a household accessory maker could show readers how to organize their homes in eight easy steps by using their products.

4. **Events**. Include calendars and event listings. Be sure to include times, RSVP information and links to Web sites that contain further information.

5. **Humor and motivation**. Humor or motivational quotes are both great ways to slow down the skimmers.

6. **Response**. An effective newsletter is a two-way communique. Provide ways to reach you, offers, links, e-mail addresses and reply cards.

Sidepage:

What Am I Going to Write About?

This is one of the first questions people ask when setting up a promotional newsletter. The next is, "Do I have enough to say on an ongoing basis?"

Fast Track to Finding Content

When choosing your newsletter's content, first look at the hard news you have for supporters and prospects—new services, special events and so on. Then search for information that keeps readers involved and interested in your subject—"how-to's," other people's products, worksheets, calendars, etc. These increase your newsletter's value and keep prospects reading time after time.

Musical Interests

For instance, the owner of a violin shop is interested in starting a newsletter but isn't sure what to include. The store receives new products frequently but not often enough to devote an entire newsletter to them. Should the proprietor abandon the project? Not just yet.

The shopkeeper should be providing promotional information that goes beyond just new product releases. The information can include anything that keeps prospects interested in music—new classical music on compact disc, announcements of symphony performances, a list of area music teachers, maintenance tips for violins, muscle strengthening exercises, the importance of posture, etc.

Learn about writing reply cards on page 161.

Sell: Generating the Desired Response

Once your newsletter has a prospect's attention, offer specific ways to respond to your offer. Tell readers what action you want them to take and how to take it. This is done by providing:

- ❑ a self-mailing reply card
- ❑ a link to a downloadable coupon
- ❑ the e-mail address to send a letter to the editor or how to submit articles or other content
- ❑ ordering information listed at the end of an article
- ❑ a contest in which readers can send in photographs or suggestions on how to use your products
- ❑ a readership survey that generates content suggestions
- ❑ a telephone number to call
- ❑ hours of operation when prospects can stop by
- ❑ an advertisement telling how to buy a specific product
- ❑ the date of an event
- ❑ a product list that includes an order form readers can use to order immediately

---

SURVEY/COUPON

Complete this short survey and we'll send you a free 5-foot interior plant.

Which of the following services do you presently use or need:

Indoor plant maintenance	❑ use	❑ need
Interior design with plants	❑ use	❑ need
Lawn/landscape maintenance	❑ use	❑ need
Landscape renovation	❑ use	❑ need
Custom design for exterior landscape	❑ use	❑ need

Hurry. Offer expires 5/15/03. Please e-mail, mail, fax or call.

Name: _____
Company: _____
Address: _____
City/State/Zip: _____
Phone: _____

p o r t f o l i a g e
123 W Main St. • Leaf City, US 63000
(314) 000-0000 • FAX: (314) 000-0001
www.portfoliage.com

Repeat services. By asking readers to check off the information they need on a reply card, you're repeating your organization's complete list of products or services. Even if they aren't interested in all of your services, readers see them one more time. If the need ever arises, the reply card helps remind prospects that you offer something they need. In addition, the responses you receive tell you which subjects your readers are interested in reading about.

You'll receive several types of response to your newsletter. Some people just want more information. For those who feel more comfortable writing than calling, provide reply cards and coupons. For those who'd rather visit you online, list your Web site and specific links to order forms and articles. List your phone number and hours of operation. For diehard shoppers, list your store hours and a location map.

For those ready to order now, include an order form. Encourage people to e-mail, phone or fax in their order.

Reap Maximum Benefit Through Your Response

Most communication experts agree that you must repeat the same information at least four different times in four different ways before you can assume people are aware of your message. Some marketing consultants go even further. Some believe you must connect at least seven times within an 18-month period.

As a direct response tool, newsletters can add to your marketing plan. By providing another place to repeat your message, your newsletter offers prospects another opportunity to respond.

To make your newsletter successful, you must be sure to follow up on all responses. Most of your respondents are going to buy someone's product or support someone's cause soon. Make it yours.

Can you visualize your prospects shouting, "I want to join," "I'd like to place an order," "Here's my donation for," or "I want more information"?

It's time to see if we can get them moving. The next two chapters help you set realistic expectations for your newsletter, based on the resources you have available.

Sidepage:

Keeping Your Customers in the "Tub"

Anyone who doesn't use your services is a prospect. Current customers not using all of your services are *better* prospects.

This is the universal rule of "80/ 20"—80% of your sales, volunteer time, billings or donations come from 20% of your customers, members, patients or donors. So, if you're trying to expand your customer base (i.e. get more customers in the "tub"), keep all customers from going down the drain while you also pour in new business.

Higher Response Rates

By concentrating on current customers for new business, you get more for your marketing dollars. Marketing to existing customers is five times less expensive than winning new ones. Your response rate is higher, because you know who your customers are and your customers know you.

Keep customers in mind as prime prospects for additional sales. For instance, the couple delivering their firstborn at your hospital are now prospects for your other family services. You can provide them information on exercise programs, infant nutrition classes and any number of other family-oriented services. Because the couple is familiar with your hospital, they are much better prospects than people who have never used your facility.

Looking for New Faces

While it's important to keep your existing clients, you need to replenish your customer base with new faces. Even the best-run organizations suffer some attrition. Members and volunteers move out of town, businesses close down. It happens.

Chapter 2:

Jump Start With a Marketing Plan

Every newsletter is published with the hope of generating a flood of responses. But before you can achieve your dreams, you must first set up your marketing goals.

These goals will give you the direction you need when choosing newsletter format, content, design, mailing lists and other elements. This chapter shows you how to set specific goals that can be achieved within the pages or screens of your newsletter. It also shows you how to streamline the promotional efforts of your newsletter with your other marketing projects.

Set Performance Goals

In general, all marketing materials seek to:

- ❑ increase awareness of the organization
- ❑ sell products, services, ideas and causes
- ❑ maintain contact with clients, members, volunteers, employees or supporters
- ❑ contact prospects
- ❑ reinforce other advertising campaigns

Your newsletter's goals may encompass the general ones listed above, but they also include specific goals unique to your newsletter. You may be trying to maintain or increase membership of

**Jump Start
Your Brain**

Doug Hall, marketing
master and author of
Jump Start Your Brain,
explains these three
steps for increasing
your number of usable
ideas by 500%:

Total Immersion:
Concentrate on col-
lecting information
through facts as well
as other stimuli—play
with your product, visit
your customers, read
magazines, go shop-
ping, look at other
people's ideas.

*Eureka! Seed
Explosion:* Use
your experience
from immersion to
spark ideas that are
unabashed. Anything
goes during this
stage and a setting of
unconditional creativ-
ity is vital.

InterAct Inventing:
Assemble the seeds,
sort out the good ones
and concentrate on
the practical.

your association. Perhaps you're lobbying an issue to legislators or community leaders. If you provide a service, such as accounting, you may be trying to find clients fitting a certain profile.

If your newsletter is being used to promote your existing products and services, use the 80/20 rule discussed on page 26. Include your existing support base in your promotional goals, so that jobs from current clients continue to come in while you're converting other prospects.

Many publishers think only of existing supporters and exclude prospects. In fact, some organizations send newsletters only to their current donors and volunteers. But your news should also be sent to community members who are not already supporting the organization.

Think about your specific goals. Why are you interested in publishing a newsletter? What do you expect it to do for you?

What Every Editor Must Know

A newsletter's objective is stated in its mission statement or statement of purpose. The editor must know the following:

- ❑ what direction(s) are we expanding into?
- ❑ what are our long-term goals?
- ❑ how do we currently reach customers and clients?
- ❑ how do customers and clients want to be reached?
- ❑ why do customers buy?
- ❑ what is the average time to make a sale?
- ❑ how well are we known in the market?
- ❑ what are we selling?
- ❑ how are we different from competitors?

The answers to these questions ultimately lead to the:

- ❑ newsletter name
- ❑ tagline
- ❑ content
- ❑ response mechanisms
- ❑ layout decisions
- ❑ distribution methods

It's important that the goals of your newsletter be in line with your organization's current short-term and long-term plans.

Determining Your Promotional Level

Let's look further at the specific ways your newsletter helps you achieve your promotional goals. The NEWS promotional levels help you determine which newsletter elements to use to achieve your goals. For example, if you want to tell prospects about a new service, you'd do one or all of the following:

Name: place a teaser on the mailing panel

Enticement: show the product in a photograph along with a caption

Written Words: detail the features of the product in an article

Sell: include a unique Web site link for requesting information about the new product

Your choice depends on the promotional level of your newsletter. In general, most newsletters promote at all of the levels. One recipient may only look at the subject line or your e-mail and then delete it. Another reader may read it from cover to cover and then call you for more information.

Concentrate on the promotional levels you need to achieve the goals of your newsletter. If an image newsletter is right for you, you should pay special attention to image techniques. However, that doesn't mean you shouldn't provide any specifics or ways to respond. A response mechanism can be as basic as listing your phone number, Web site address and store hours or as elaborate as a postage-paid reply card offering a gift to respondents.

To determine which level to use, look closely at how the following factors relate to your organization. The NEWS promotional levels are used in a variety of ways depending on:

❑ how well you're known
❑ the complexity of what you're promoting
❑ why people enlist your services or support your cause

Let's examine these factors.

5 Steps to Marketing Plans

According to Illise Benun's guide, *Making Marketing Manageable*, marketing plans are made up of five steps.

Step 1: Set your objective based on your goals

Step 2: Target your market and find a list

Step 3: Determine the marketing tools you will use

Step 4: Devote time and money to each project

Step 5: Set a weekly timetable for each step

How Well Do Readers Know You?

Look at the average characteristics of your targeted readers. The mix of customers and prospects tells you how well you are known. Your existing customers should recognize your name, as should some of your prospects. But not everyone knows you. It depends on how long you've been around and how active you've been at promoting yourself in the past.

Well-established organizations worry little about name recognition. Industry leaders like IBM can assume most of their prospects have heard of them. They are more concerned with image and distributing information.

Newcomers, however, face a different challenge. Not only do they have to gain name recognition, they often must work within a small budget. Newcomers usually give the most attention to name recognition and image techniques, because their reader base consists primarily of prospects.

Have We Been Introduced?

A computer parts manufacturer sent out a newsletter with pictures and descriptions of three new products. Since there was little competition and great demand for the products at the time, it received hundreds of replies, just by letting buyers know it had the products they needed. The design and quality of the newsletter were professional. This kept buyers from faltering because they didn't recognize the company's name.

Worksheet: How Well You're Known

		Concentrate on:
❑	New to my market	Name
❑	Name becoming established, products or services not yet known	Enticement
❑	Name, products, and services known; need way to inform and educate on features or specifics	Writing
❑	All information known; need more response and feedback	Sell

---

What You're Promoting

The more complex the product, the more information people need before they can buy. As a general rule, newsletters offering content are good for any organization that has to educate buyers and supporters in order to promote its products and services. Enticement newsletters are ideal for simple products and services. But sometimes, there's more to the puzzle. Other

Sidepage:

Reflect Your Marketing Strategy

Every printed piece produced by Animal Attractions targets people who treat their pets as family and spend as much on them as the average parent spends on a child. The "where pets are people too" slogan is reflected in the logo design, in the newsletter name and throughout the operation.

The newsletter content continues this theme. A past article, "A Day in a Dog's Life at Animal Attractions," used a timeline structure to explain how dogs spend the day when they are dropped off to be groomed. (After all, any parent with children in day care knows what it's like to worry about them.)

Raining Cats & Dogs

The company's fine-tuned marketing efforts have paid off. The business made a profit within a few months of opening its doors and has continued to grow over the last three years.

The newsletter keeps new clients coming in. "It's being passed along to friends and relatives," says owner Regina Huggins. "We keep these pass-along readers in mind and include a location map and squeeze in contact information whenever possible."

In addition, brochures are inserted into each newsletter that list the complete grooming services

(continued on page 2)

pieces include competition and the rate of change within your organization.

Enticement newsletters are valuable for products and services with little competition. Often, winning a supporter is just a matter of letting prospects know you have the product or service they need.

Writing and content-rich newsletters are ideal for industries with rapid changes and scarce information. By providing prospects with needed information, organizations can differentiate themselves from their competitors.

Image-building enticement newsletters are often shorter and easier to write. Because they don't have to provide as much information as content-heavy newsletters, they contain less text and more graphics. You can usually publish an enticement newsletter at a lower cost.

Some products and services can be sold through enticement alone, while others have to go through the longer process of explaining specific information to prospects.

How Long It Takes to Close a Sale

The complexity and price of your products usually determines the average time it takes to convert a prospect to a customer. Usually, the more expensive and complex the product and long-term the relationship, the longer it takes your prospect to make a purchasing decision.

For expensive products, most people need more time. They want to see the product demonstrated, spend time on your Web site, take a brochure home and study it, see a review and read about it in the newsletter. Over 90% of industrial buyers prefer seeing some type of printed literature before they purchase.

Some services and causes also have sales cycles. For example, a voter making a decision on a candidate needs time and information. People not only want to know where the candidate stands on all of the major issues, they also want to know about the candidate's background.

Knowledge Turned to Action

"Remember, knowledge is not power. Knowledge turned into action is power. This action is started by developing a specific, detailed plan for implementing your goals."

Walter Hailey
multimillionaire and owner of Planned Marketing

On the other hand, retail shoppers are making a decision that will cost them between $20 and $100. Usually, the decision is made in a matter of seconds—based on a desire for the product.

Worksheet: Time Needed to Convert a Prospect

Concentrate on:

❑ Purchasing decision made on impulse   Name

❑ Product purchased or support given
based on special need (little competition) Enticement

❑ Products purchased or support given
only after lengthy gathering of all
of the facts   Writing

❑ Prospects ready to act now;
need incentive   Sell

This brings us to the purchasing decision itself. The better you know your prospects, they more you can influence their decision to buy, join, donate or vote.

Why People Buy From You

In order to provide information that promotes your products, you have to know what has made people support you in the past. You also have to know their common questions or problems and why some won't buy from or support you.

The answers to these questions aren't always simple. It's also not necessarily the same for every prospect. Even so, you can spot some trends, and this information will help you develop effective visuals and article content.

In Chapter 4, you'll be given methods of surveying your customers. For now, make your own estimation by looking at the ways you've been attracting customers or supporters.

A retailer sends sales postcards and e-mails event notices to current customers and advertises sales and special events in the

See more about marketing surveys on pages 81-82

newspaper. Why does this work? A quick guess is that the events and products advertised were of interest to their customers and prospects. Once the prospects knew that the store carried interesting items, they came in to get more information.

Many professional services such as doctors, lawyers and accountants get business through referrals. Prospects like getting a recommendation from someone else, because it makes it a "safe" choice. It also saves them the time they might have to spend to find a good service. People giving money to charities want to know more about the people their money will help. They also want to know that their donations will be spent effectively.

Worksheet: Why Prospects Buy

Concentrate on:

❑ Because they've heard of your
organization   Name

❑ Because your organization has a
good reputation   Enticement

❑ Because you offer exactly what
they need   Writing

❑ Because they were ready to respond
and received the incentive   Sell

The answers from the previous three worksheets will give you a direction for the type of newsletter you should consider.

Sidepage:

What You're Promoting

© Music Man

© Bluebird Cafe

Content-Rich News Works for Music Man

Music Man sells high-priced computerized keyboards and synthesizers. Before starting a newsletter, the owner had trouble keeping musicians updated on new products and events. For Music Man, publishing a newsletter was an efficient way to consolidate mailings and still inform customers of new products and upcoming events in a timely fashion.

Nightclub's Success With Enticement Newsletter

The Bluebird Cafe is a nationally-known nightclub for songwriters. At first, the owner published a bi-monthly news-letter featuring interviews with some of the performers.

The newsletter took too much time and the bi-monthly calendar insert was quickly outdated. Instead, the calendar insert was published as a monthly flier.

Types of Marketing Newsletters

There is no such thing as a "typical" newsletter. Your newsletter should follow your objectives, not other standards. Here are some different types of newsletters to consider, based on the promotional level you're aiming for.

Letter-style newsletter: *Client's Express*. This is a simple format, one- or two-page newsletter that's quick and easy to put together, inexpensive to print, and quick for buyers to read.

E-mail news briefs:
All About Memories
NEW *NEW*
NEW. The scrapbook retailer keeps her best customers informed of all of the new products arriving weekly.

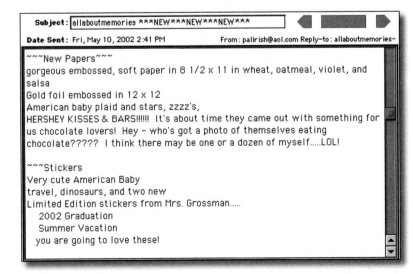

MarketBeat

Home buying and selling tips for the Garden District   Fall 2002

WHAT'S SELLING?

The summer season was one of the most active in the last five years. All sellers received within 1% of listing price.

6243 Magnolia	$289,950
4141 Tulip Ln.	$272,500
4255 Rosebud	$217,500
4156 Daisy Dr.	$157,900
3900 Lilac Ln.	$239,900
4118 Petunia	$294,900
4239 Carnation	$319,900

For more information about each of these home sales, including specifications of the properties, visit garden-realty.com/sales.htm.

WHO'S BUYING?

Buying trends from west to east

Most of the buyers for our district are moving in from west coast states including California, Arizona and Oregon.

See census.gov for more information.

FREE CONSULTATIONS

What to renovate first?

The average Garden District homebuyer spends $25,000 in home improvements during the first three years in their home. If you're getting ready to renovate and want to make sure that you get the most home equity for your investment, give us a call for a free home renovation consultation.

Call Susan at 555-1212.

FREE FALL SEMINAR

Summer seminar was standing room only!

Join us on Tuesday, September 15 at the Park Complex, 125 W. Main Street. The 90 minute presentation is guaranteed to save you at least $1,000 when selling or buying.

To make sure you get a seat, RSVP with Tom at 555-1212.

Garden Realty
The source for Garden homes
123 W. Main St.
Floral Park, US   00001
(800) 555-1212
Sell-it@gardenrealty.com
www.gardenrealty.com

ADDRESS CORRECTION REQUESTED

Free Seminar: Home Selling and Home Buying in the Garden District. See www.gardenrealty.com or turn over this card for more information.

Postcard newsletter: *MarketBeat.* Real estate professionals need to be in visible year-round. Busy homebuyers and sellers have time for these quick newscards.

Designed Image: *The Compendium*. The design elements of this newsletter are noticed before the content. This type of newsletter works well for products sold with emotion, such as clothing, music, art and events.

The Informer: *The Raphel Report*. This is a traditional, four-page newsletter packed with information. It may even be given a cover price (but still distributed for free) to further reinforce the value of the information.

Inserts: *Publishing Pointers*. The newsletter for self-publishing expert Dan Poynter is mailed along with other offers for books and mailing lists. Each of the sheets is letter-folded and mailed in a #10-sized envelope.

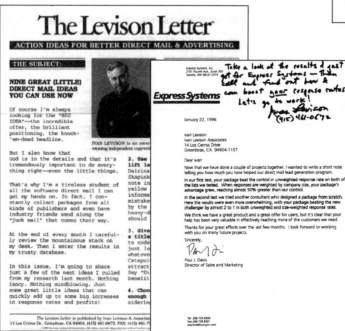

Testimonial Letters: *Levison Letter*. Copywriter Ivan Levison includes a letter from a satisfied client along with every issue of his newsletter. He handwrites a note at the top of the letter telling the reader that he can produce the same results again.

Mix and Match Your News Broadcasts

Your newsletter is a vital part of your marketing plan—but it's still only a part. To be reasonably sure that people remember your marketing messages, they have to see them seven to ten times. This means that your sales, new products and special events must appear in at least seven different places.

Your newsletter can be the backbone of your new product launches. Readers see the product mentioned again and again in a variety of interesting ways, and the repetition helps sell more of each product.

For example, your new product would be promoted in a:

- ❑ preview in the newsletter
- ❑ e-mail announcement
- ❑ news write-up in the newsletter
- ❑ postcard mailing
- ❑ press release
- ❑ sales letter
- ❑ reminder from sales staff
- ❑ announcement in the newspaper
- ❑ calendar in the newsletter
- ❑ case history in the newsletter or on your Web site of someone using the product

Tradeshow Tip

You may be able to get otherwise reluctant people to give you their business card and e-mail address at a tradeshow by offering a free subscription to your newsletter. Make a poster of your newsletter, along with the offer for a free subscription.

Good & Bad Times to Mail and E-Mail

When choosing the timing for your most interesting promotional material, plan around the times of year your customers usually buy, join or donate. Avoid the times when your prospects are overwhelmed with things to do.

For retailers, a Federal Reserve study showed the months of consumer spending from highest to lowest as: December, November, October, September, May, April, June, August, March, January, July and February. Look at the revenue trends for your specific organization and use them in your planning.

Sidepage:

Other Marketing Tools to Consider

Advertisements—Paid ads that announce a sale, event, offer or other information about your organization.

Annual reports—Promote your organization's achievements and future plans to stockholders, vendors, customers, supporters and employees.

Booklets—Give customers and prospects useful information and "how-to" advice, so they'll save the piece and have your organization's name in mind.

Brochures, product or service—Explain how a product or service works; highlight benefits and uses.

Brochures, company—Explain the capabilities and philosophy of the organization.

Case histories—Tell success stories of customers who have used your products to solve specific problems.

Catalogs—Provide prospects with complete list of products and services along with specific information.

Direct mailings & circulars—Give people a special deal with a deadline.

Postcard campaigns—Announce a sale or special.

Public relations—Provide the industry with news of new products, services or offers; inform of organizational changes.

Sales calls—Meet prospects for a discussion of their needs and explanation of how your products or services solve them.

Sales letters—Explain new offers or products in a personalized, friendly way.

Seminars—Enhance your image as an industry expert.

Telemarketing—Speed up response; qualify prospects.

Trade shows—Meet customers and prospects in one central location; give hands-on demonstrations of services.

For print newsletters, you should also consider the times when people pay more attention to direct mail. Studies by the Direct Marketing Association show that people read and respond to direct mail the most in September, October, November, January and February. It makes sense, since these are periods when vacation season is over, children are back in school and people have returned to work.

For example, the nursery business is seasonal. One nursery publishes a four-page newsletter once during the summer, fall and winter. The newsletters provide seasonal information, such as summer watering tips, fall tree planting, and frost protection. Because business is best in the spring, it publishes a two-page newsletter every other week for the first two months of the spring planting season. This increased frequency keeps the nursery on the minds of its prospects who are waiting for the first sign of good weather to go out and buy some plants.

July is a slow month for many types of businesses. But not for a dealer of swimming pool supplies. January would most likely be the month their newsletter would be ignored—while people might like to dream about warmer days, they're unlikely to want to stock up on chlorine.

Your top months for sales may depend on:

- ❑ holidays
- ❑ the academic year
- ❑ the seasonality of your specific industry
- ❑ your company's sales cycle

Frequency: How Often Should You Mail?

Most newsletters are mailed monthly, every other month or quarterly. E-mail newsletters are broadcast daily, weekly, monthly or as news breaks.

The ideal frequency is at least monthly. Daily newsletters, for example, run the risk of being ignored because they arrive too frequently. However, as a creative marketer, you have alternatives to traditional monthly or quarterly frequencies. Let your marketing goals drive your publication dates.

Springing into Action

A gardening center could use monthly theme issues during the spring and early summer. (Each issue would arrive at the time when seedlings are started, bulbs tended, flowers planted and so on.) The size could be kept small enough to be easy to write. Or, with a bit of planning, the newsletters could be written during the winter months when the marketing manager is twiddling her green thumbs.

Say you publish a quarterly newsletter and send it to manufacturers involved in the automotive industry. If you distribute your newsletter in January, April, July and October, one of your newsletters will basically be ignored. Why? The auto industry re-tools its factories for the next year's models in July. Nothing is happening that will help your sales.

If your business has strong buying cycles like this, consider an "irregular" schedule for your newsletter. Every industry has its own sales cycles and periods of strong sales activity. A newsletter mailed frequently during these times will boost sales. During a business' slower months, a newsletter will be fighting the sales cycle and may even be completely ignored.

Traditionally, most publishers try to avoid vacation seasons. December is a bad time to mail a newsletter. January is strong. The last few weeks of August are slow, as many families take vacations (or move) during this time.

A quick note of caution: You must know your sales cycle in depth. Often, buyers make purchasing decisions well in advance of when the purchase is actually made. For example, January may be your top sales month, but September and October are the months when budgets are submitted and purchases approved. In this instance, you'd be better off increasing the frequency in the fall than in the winter.

Special greeting. Although December is one of the lowest response months, it's the ideal time to say "thank you" to your clients and members. Many organizations plan a special message for this issue.

TIP: Arrive early.
To avoid having your publication buried under someone's mail stack over the holidays, try to get it into the reader's hands before the middle of December.

See how to fax special editions on page 251.

When to Use Special Editions

Many publishers who want stay on their regular schedule of quarterly or bi-monthly publish special editions during busy times in their sales cycle. Special editions work well to announce a new product or service, attract attention, react quickly to a controversy, or provide a handout for a trade show or special event.

Keep the design of the special edition the same as that of the regular newsletter. But add a word signaling immediacy to the nameplate design, such as "briefing," "special edition," "alert," or "update."

```
==================== Good Experience - 23 May 02 ====================
                    By Mark Hurst
                <www.goodexperience.com>
=====================================================================

Thursday, May 23, 2002

This is a special issue of Good Experience, announcing the launch of
a new report, which is now available for downloading.

Download the report, "Managing Incoming E-mail":
<http://www.goodexperience.com/reports/e-mail>
```

Special e-dition: Good Experience. If you have your e-mail distribution list set up, it's easy to send out special broadcasts as needed.

Breaking news. If your newsletter is published quarterly, consider a special edition for that news that can't wait three months for your next publication.

Editorial Calendar Coordinates Other Promotions

Combine your newsletter with your yearly marketing plan by creating an editorial calendar for the newsletter. Depending on how quickly your industry or organization changes, it can be difficult to plan for everything. However, many events are announced well in advance. Examples include seminars, annual conventions, elections, annual fund-raising events, special issues of trade magazines and new product launches.

As you go through the year, update the calendar to include new products and advertising campaigns. To reinforce an advertisement or direct mailing, you may even want to insert the same promotional literature into your newsletter.

A newsletter should be just one of your marketing tools. If you coordinate it with your other marketing strategies, your marketing efforts will be more effective and less expensive, because they will reinforce each other.

Up to this point, you've seen all of the ways newsletters can be used to promote. You know whether or not you should publish a newsletter. The next step is to determine if you can publish a promotional newsletter on your own or whether you'll need to find outside help.

© Mid South Marine

Newsletter article

Recognition guaranteed. A marine parts distributor used a newsletter to help launch a new campaign (called "Delivery Guaranteed") telling customers that it delivered parts faster than its competition.

The company placed stickers on its packaging, distributed a brochure detailing the program, instructed salespeople to tell all of their customers and included an article in the newsletter. The newsletter article appeared first and explained the program in detail. When prospects received the brochure and began seeing stickers on every box, they were reminded again about the benefits of the program.

Sticker

Brochure

Chapter 3:

Stretching Your Budget & Finding Help

It's time for the "reality chapter." News broadcasts do take time and money. This chapter helps you push the edges of these limits to make the most of your time and money and helps you find people who will do the parts that you don't want to do.

Take a few minutes to ask yourself:

- ❑ which parts of the newsletter you want to do yourself?
- ❑ which parts you want to find other people to do for you?

To help you plan your time, resources and budget, this chapter includes several checklists. They are designed to help you create a great newsletter. If you find you need help, newsletter subcontractors are listed, along with how to find them. Setting and stretching your budget are covered toward the end of the chapter. Lastly, you'll find out how to coordinate the project to meet your schedule with a minimum amount of energy.

Keep the Promotional Pulse Pounding

Promotional newsletters are created in two steps. First, you set up all the things that stay consistent from issue to issue. Second, for each new issue, you write news, collect links and find illustrations.

In this chapter:

- what's involved in putting together a newsletter
- finding help through vendors and volunteers
- finding sponsors
- saving money and making money on newsletters
- budget-friendly designs
- how often newsletters should be sent
- scheduling your newsletter so it comes out on time

Get a feel for the steps involved and think "promotion" during each one. Subsequent chapters cover the exact "how-to's" for doing each one.

When you first develop your newsletter, you must do the following things:

❑ **Set promotional goals for your newsletter.** Your promotional goals help you measure your success. Your goal might be to increase donations or revenue by 10% within six months. It could be to spur referrals by 25 names.

❑ **Identify prospective readers and set up a distribution list**. Add your current customers or members, top prospects and all others who can influence your success, including your vendors and your staff. If needed, collect fax and e-mail addresses if you need them.

❑ **Research audience interests**. To attract the attention of your readers, find out what they want to read.

❑ **Develop content**. The content of your newsletter serves two purposes. It captures the attention of your prospects, it encourages readers to open your messages every time you send them and it motivates them to respond to your promotional message. Assure year-round success by setting up an editorial schedule.

❑ **Set a budget**. Plan for the amount of time and money required. Study ways to save time through subcontracting. Look into reducing costs by publishing a smaller newsletter and mixing e-mail broadcasts and postcards.

❑ **Name your newsletter**. The name and tagline of your newsletter define its subject, include a benefit of reading and target the reader.

❑ **Decide on format and frequency**. The more frequently the newsletter comes out, the better it works for your marketing. The shorter the newsletter, the better the chance of its being read.

❑ **Create a design**. The design of your newsletter is the first thing your reader sees. In essence, it's your "calling card." Match your newsletter's style to your organization's image.

As you develop each issue of the newsletter, follow these steps:

- ❑ **Plan content**. Begin with the timely information you have. Add other attention-getting content that achieves your goals

- ❑ **Collect information**. Find people willing to help you gather interesting content. Interview, research other publications and find sources within your organization. Choose facts and features that enhance your marketing message and interest your readers.

- ❑ **Find visuals**. Find or create photographs, clip art and charts that tell your story. Visuals not only attract skimmers, they reinforce your promotional message.

- ❑ **Write articles, headlines and captions**. In a concise writing style, present the information your prospects need. Include news summaries and blurbs. Write skimmable headlines and captions that include benefits.

- ❑ **Edit and proofread**. Assure correct spelling and accurate information to increase your newsletter's quality.

- ❑ **Put it together**. Combine the text with visuals on the page or screen in a way that leads readers to what you want them to see.

- ❑ **Print**. Choose a printer who can give you the quality you want and a timely turnaround.

- ❑ **Label and mail or broadcasts**. Find the most cost-effective and appropriate method of mailing. Follow all mailing regulations to assure expeditious delivery of each newsletter to maximize your reach.

- ❑ **Follow up**. Thank contributors and vendors involved with each issue. Immediately follow up on the responses your newsletter generates. Evaluate your work and start planning for the next issue.

Depending on the type of promotional newsletter you choose, you may be concerned with only part of the list. For example, if you're printing postcards from your laser printer, you won't have to worry about finding a printer.

> **Save Time with an Editorial Calendar**
>
> You can make planning each issue and collecting information easier by having a yearly editorial calendar.

Support From Within Your Organization

The best way to save time, while meeting your newsletter's goals, is to have an internal support team. While many newsletters are produced using outside vendors, the internal team keeps the publication on its promotional track. The managing editor is the leader of the team and an editorial board is the support.

Managing editor's responsibilities. The managing editor oversees the preparation of the newsletter. The editor is in charge of setting deadlines; writing or finding writers for the chosen articles; editing copy; and monitoring the production and distribution.

Because your newsletter deals with news, trade issues and trends as they relate to your targeted audience, the managing editor must know the subject well. Enthusiasm for the project, the capacity to control the promotional tone of the piece, and most importantly, the ability to motivate vendors, staff, volunteers and readers are all essential attributes of a managing editor.

Editorial board's responsibilities. The editorial board is responsible for keeping the marketing functions of the news broadcast in focus. The group typically critiques each issue and provides new article ideas. The team also sets up the long-range marketing plans for the publication, including the editorial schedule.

The board can consist of as few or as many people as needed to get the job done. The size of the board will also depend on the size and structure of your organization. It might include sales representatives, board members, technical experts, senior partners, marketing experts, your Web master, public relations experts, fund-raising staff, writers and members of your production team.

Each member of the board is responsible for suggesting, checking and reviewing a specific part of the news. An engineering manager may be asked to check for technical accuracy and suggest articles on certain product features. The president, CEO or board members scrutinize the news broadcast for consistency with the organization's image and policies.

While your board can be made up of several representatives, it's important to keep it lean. Educate all board members on the promotional aims of the newsletter. Give everyone a style sheet (a list of acceptable abbreviations, etc.) For the benefit of your sanity, thoroughly define the responsibilities of each person and make sure they give the newsletter top priority during its production.

With fax, e-mail, phone bridges and video conferencing, it's not necessary for the board to meet around the same conference table. For organizations spread across the country or the world, article suggestions can be given over the phone, wording and layout approved by faxing or e-mailing files.

The time it takes you to produce each newsletter depends on how much of the work you do yourself, the amount of experience you have, and the page size, length and frequency of the newsletter.

The Benefits of Doing Your Own Newsletter

If you have the capabilities, or are interested in cultivating them, there are advantages to doing your own newsletter. Many editors value the opportunities it gives them to talk with customers and other important people in the industry. One editor commented that newsletter production keeps her up-to-date on the market and the needs of her clients. She sees the results in increased sales.

The skills you develop while producing a newsletter are also useful for other marketing projects. They're so handy, it may be worth the investment of time and money to get professional training. You can attend seminars for Web publishing, newsletter editing, design and desktop publishing (see listing in the Resources Section). To improve your writing, you might take a news reporting class at a community college. The skills you use to write powerful editorial copy can also be used for press releases.

A relatively inexpensive investment in computer equipment and training allows you to create your news broadcasts yourself. With the same equipment, you can produce e-mailings, Web content, proposals, manuals, catalogs and brochures.

Canary Corrections

"I always thought that most people only noticed my newsletter's design and layout. I knew it was important to proofread, but I didn't always have the time. Then, one day my boss brought in a copy of the newsletter that had been returned by our best donor. All of the errors were highlighted in yellow. The page looked like a canary shed on it! I added a proofreader to my production team on the next issue."

—An Anonymous Editor

Chances are, your organization has a lot of hidden talent you can draw on to help with other steps in newsletter production. An amateur photographer can take photographs at an industry convention; an illustrator may be able to create professional-looking cartoons. Others may be willing to proofread. The more of your staff you involve, the greater the support and awareness of the publication within your organization.

Advantages of Finding People to Do It for You

One problem people in many organizations face is their lack of time, especially those in small businesses. In the U.S., 85% of businesses have fewer than 20 people. These small businesses need ways to free their employees' time for day-to-day business.

If you have more money than time, hiring subcontractors to write and produce your newsletter may be the path to choose. Even if you're strapped for cash, you may still save money and end up with a more effective sales piece.

One of the benefits of using subcontractors is that, over time, you may get better work at a lower cost than you'd get by doing it yourself. With hourly charges of $20 to $100, this may be hard to believe at first glance, but a professional can often do the same job in a fraction of the time it would take you. This gives you more time for other marketing tasks, easily adding enough to your bottom line to cover the subcontractor's fee.

The best part of working with subcontractors is that they rely on regularly published or broadcasted newsletters for their income. That means you have people on your production team with an incentive to complete each issue and get the next one in the works.

Where to Find Talented Help

Finding good subcontractors can be tricky. Ask friends and associates for suggestions. When a newsletter, Web site or e-mailing catches your eye, call the publisher and ask who handles the individual production tasks. Seek out local communication associations (see Resources Section). Look in the Yellow Pages. Or

Editorial Experts

"We used to subcontract the writing of our newsletter. Every month, the writer would talk with industry experts, interview our clients and pore over stacks of trade journals. As a result, she was as up-to-date as the marketing, sales and public relations people in our firm. Through her expertise, she was able to write a successful publication for our company. Then we started to think of how her insight could help with other marketing projects. We hired her full-time."

—An Anonymous Editor

find a vendor who can refer you to others. For example, your printer—especially one who prints a lot of newsletters—can refer you to capable designers, photographers, newsletter specialists, and mailing services. And remember that subcontracting your promotional newsletter production isn't an all-or-nothing proposition. You can match your in-house capabilities with those of the subcontractors.

Here is of how each subcontractor can help you:

Marketing consultant. A good consultant can help you with your newsletter project by looking at your goals and available resources, then pointing you toward other specialists for the parts of the project you're unable to do in-house.
Locating: The best place to find a good consultant is a referral from an organization with successful marketing.

Advertising agency or newsletter production shop. These specialists have either internal resources or subcontractors for every step of your newsletter's production. They have already spent the time and trouble to find vendors who are reliable, affordable and quality-conscious.
Locating: Seek referrals from printers, Internet service providers, desktop publishing firms, marketing consultants and mailing services.

Designer. Artists can design your nameplate, page layout, color combinations, typeface choices and any other graphic elements used to make newsletters inviting to read. Some designers will provide a template you can use on your own computer.
Locating: Advertising agencies have lists of independent designers they may share with you. Designers can also be referred by freelance writers, marketing consultants, printers, mailing services or Internet service providers.

List management service. This service sets up your mailing list on their computers and can add, remove and change addresses and other information to your list. List management services already have basic database structures and can set up a sophisticated list with much more information than just the mailing address. They can also provide the list to you on disk so you can access customer, donor or member information from your own

Proof Is in the Printing, Not the Pricing

"I thought I was so shrewd. One day a man called on me and gave me a great price on my newsletter—almost 50% less than I was paying. I gave him my next newsletter job. When he didn't show up on the day it was due, I called the print shop. It turns out that this man was an independent rep and they hadn't seen him in a few days. They knew nothing about my job. It took days to get my artwork back. I took it to my tried and true printer. The issue was two weeks late. I questioned low prices from then on."

—An Anonymous Editor

See how to find fax broadcasting services on page 257.

office. If you decide to hire a service to label your newsletters, find one that also provides list storage and maintenance. Many list companies provide this service.

Locating: Look in the Yellow Pages under "mailing list management." List management services are also handled by mailing services and secretarial services.

Writer. Professional writers research and write your newsletter. They understand how to collect information and turn it into the attention-getting copy needed to draw readers into an article. For best results, find a writer with experience in your particular industry. These writers require less briefing and can offer fresh suggestions by bringing experiences from businesses similar to yours. You can give your writer a general outline of a story assignment, or you can give them rough notes or a first draft to be reworked into a professional piece.

Locating: Ask designers, desktop publishing services, marketing consultants, printers and typesetting services. In the Yellow Pages, look under "editorial services" or "writers."

Desktop publishing service. These services take your typed newsletter content and newsletter design and produce your newsletter layout at a reasonable price. For high-quality promotional newsletters, their work can be output on high-resolution typesetting equipment. Many desktop publishing services can also design your newsletter.

Locating: Look in the Yellow Pages under "desktop publishing" and also under "typesetting." These services can also be found through printers, writers, marketing consultants and mailing services.

Proofreader. Increase your overall quality by hiring a professional or finding a skilled volunteer to proofread your work. The need for proofreading can't be stressed enough. Nothing adds to a professional newsletter more than accurate facts, perfect spelling and proper grammar.

Locating: Ask your desktop publishing or writing service. To find volunteers, look for detail-oriented people who are meticulous in their work.

Sidepage:

Vendor Dud Checklist

☐ **Review samples of work**. Take plant tours. Look at random samples of the work they're creating. (Remember that the samples in the portfolio are their best jobs.) Look for organization and cleanliness.

☐ **Check references**.

☐ **Request price quotes**. Ask about realistic turnaround times. Make sure they fit with your needs.

☐ **Establish final deadline**. Involve subcontractors in planning realistic schedules.

☐ **Question low prices**. Find out how the vendor is set up to do this. A low price may mean lower quality.

☐ **Consider new vendors**. Some vendors just starting out in the market may be offering more competitive rates. This is a good opportunity for you to get good work while helping a fellow entrepreneur. However, make sure the vendor is committed to the new business.

☐ **Look for hardware and software compatibility**.

☐ **Find vendors who are set up for**, and want, the kind of work you have.

☐ **Don't give someone work just because you like the person**. Make sure that your rep has a hand in quality control and production.

☐ **Give small test projects**. Gradually work into your involvement with the vendor as they prove themselves. Don't rely on a new vendor for a time- or quality-critical project.

☐ **Do press checks**. Let the printer know you'll be there for the press run.

Cost of Design Depends on Whom You Hire

According to Board Report, a newsletter for graphic designers, the average cost of having a nameplate designed depends on whom you hire to design it. The following prices were for three design concepts and the finished art on the one selected: $770 from a graphics design firm, $577 from a home business, $1,085 from an ad agency, and $741 from a company art department.

For monthly production of a four-page newsletter with all the photos and a double-spaced typed manuscript provided, the price was $640 from the design firm, $394 from the home business, $1,925 from the ad agency, and $347 from the company art department.

Printer. Your printer is one of your most important subcontractors. Although it's tempting to choose a printer based on price only, quality, turnaround time and service will affect your overall "price" as much as the actual bottom line. Find a printer that has full-time salespeople to follow up on any problems and to pick up and deliver artwork, proofs and finished printing. Make sure to gather several bids when you begin your newsletter project. In addition to requesting firm prices, request a guaranteed turnaround time.

Locating: Find a wholesale printer. Seek the referral of a designer, desktop publishing service, writer, newsletter editor, mailing service, marketing consultant, advertising agency, local business or typesetting service. You can also look in the Yellow Pages under "printers."

Photocopy service. For simple designs, you can use standard photocopying machines to duplicate your newsletter onto standard paper or pre-printed letterhead. If your list has only a few hundred names, the quality and price may be just right for you. Some copy services also have printing presses for higher quantity jobs.

Locating: As quality may vary, ask for a referral from a designer, desktop publishing service, writer or typesetting service. Since there are usually several in each town, look for one convenient to your office. You can also check the Yellow Pages under "copying services."

Mailing service (also called a lettershop). A mailing service affixes labels and postage onto your printed newsletter, sorts the pieces into zip code order and delivers them to the post office. A good service keeps up with changing regulations and can advise you on the most cost-effective methods of mailing. Find an automated mailing service that can take your database on disk or via modem. They will sort it, remove duplicates and correct addresses, using data provided by the post office. Then they can print it onto Cheshire (paper) labels, saving you the cost of pressure-sensitive labels. This frees up your computer's printer and saves you money by preventing you from mailing to outdated addresses.

Tip: Many mailing services have printing presses. If your newsletter isn't too complicated, your mailing service may be able to print it for you.

Locating: Mailing services can be referred by designers, desktop publishing services, writers, list management services, marketing consultants, advertising agencies, printers and typesetters. Look in the Yellow Pages under "mailing services."

E-mailing service. Since this technology changes so quickly, look online for services. Search under keywords "e-mail" and "lists" and "broadcasting" and "newsletters."

Remember that it takes time to orient subcontractors to you, your newsletter, organization and industry. Before you invest this time, take special care to choose the right vendors. Once you get them going, you'll spend a decreasing amount of time on each project.

Tip: Look for a one-stop shop—like a printer who can take your disk and print it out on their typesetting equipment. This saves you time by not having to take your disk to a service bureau first. Many experts predict that soon your printer will be able to take your computer file and make printing plates directly without first printing it on special paper or film.

Many printers can also address and mail out your newsletter. Some have ink jet printing capabilities that access database information and address your newsletters automatically. These same capabilities can be used to add personalized messages within the newsletter.

Finding In-Kind Service Donations

For many nonprofit organizations, hiring subcontractors is too expensive. Donations by services such as printers can greatly offset the costs of publishing. Ask for service—as opposed to cash—donations. Depending on the extent of your newsletter's distribution, a mention in the masthead may be an excellent advertising source for newsletter vendors.

To find service donations, try sending a special mailing to printers, editors and designers soliciting help. Follow it up with

---

Overtaken by Printer Noise

"Printing out our 5,000-name mailing list every month tied up our printer, made a lot of noise, and required someone to monitor the process. While visiting us one day, our mailing service representative suggested that he take over that part of the operation. Since the service could take our list and print the names on Cheshire labels (which could be affixed using automated equipment) our mailing prices went down."

—An Anonymous Editor

Donations on Paper

"I extended the budget for my nonprofit organization's newsletter by finding a paper distributor to donate all of the paper for our newsletter. The distributor gives us the leftovers from the large rolls. Not all of the paper matches exactly, but the newsletters are never seen side by side and, on their own, they look great."

—An Anonymous Editor

Volunteer Tip

The editor of Chesapeake, the Sierra Club newsletter for the Potomac area, noticed several would-be journalists within his group. He turned this desire into an effective ad soliciting volunteers. The headline read, "Didn't get that job you wanted with the Washington Post?"

phone calls. Be sure to give full information on your organization, just as you would to any other potential donor. You may be surprised at the support you get for your efforts.

Be prepared to give volunteer subcontractors some extra turn-around time, but don't lower your quality standards. You want to produce a piece that everyone will be proud of.

Tips for Recruiting, Keeping & Motivating Volunteers

To find volunteer help either within your organization or from outside volunteers, do the following.

- ❑ **Publish a list of people you need**. Define the specific jobs or tasks you need done. Break jobs down into smaller commitments. Give volunteers a chance to test working with you without making a long commitment.

- ❑ **Add value to the experience**. Set up a mentor system. Give each new volunteer an experienced person to turn to with questions for additional training.

- ❑ **Give people a view of the big picture**. Show prospective volunteers past issues of the newsletters and tell them about the effects they have had.

- ❑ **Provide precise, written instructions**. Develop a style guide and give all contributors a copy. Plan the schedule for each issue in detail and give all volunteers a copy.

- ❑ **Give people credit for their work**. Praise much, criticize little and make the job fun. List the byline of all contributing reporters. Most editors use "reported by."

In general, a talented pool of volunteers and "mentors," combined with a high-quality newsletter, makes it easy to find additional volunteers.

Costs to Consider

The costs of publishing a newsletter can be broken down into one-time fees, on-going fees and costs for producing extras, such as special edition broadcasts, inserts and reply cards.

Setup costs. Your investment of time and money will peak when you first set up your newsletter. You will be going through some of the planning discussed in the previous section and may even be going to the expense of hiring professionals to create the design for the newsletter.

These initial setup costs can include:

- ❑ consulting fees
- ❑ newsletter design
- ❑ mailing list setup

Once you've decided on which steps to subcontract and chosen your vendors, collect firm quotes for each step.

Ongoing costs. Once your newsletter is underway, you'll have the same expenses for each issue. These may include:

- ❑ writing
- ❑ photography
- ❑ illustrations
- ❑ editing
- ❑ proofreading
- ❑ layout
- ❑ Web site updates
- ❑ monthly maintenance fees
- ❑ color proofing (If printing in four-color)
- ❑ newsletter printing
- ❑ domestic postage
- ❑ foreign postage (if any)
- ❑ phone calls
- ❑ mailing list maintenance
- ❑ rush charges
- ❑ tax

The $14 Apiece Newsletter

A regional bank decided it needed a newsletter and called in its advertising agency. Without budgeting the project, they went through design after design. They drew artwork for each article, extensively rewrote all copy and printed the newsletter on an oversized heavy paper. The result: a bill that averaged $14 a newsletter!

The editor quickly regrouped. He decided articles would be written by the bank and given to the agency for final editing. The newsletter was reduced to a standard size and the paper changed to a commonly stocked grade. They used the same creative elements but made other changes that reduced the cost per newsletter to under $1 per piece.

Other costs, such as printing a year's worth of envelopes or fees for bulk rate permits and business reply numbers, will be incurred yearly.

Inserts and response cards. If you choose to insert an advertising piece or a reply card, budget for the additional cost. Include the cost of printing, additional mail house charges for insertion, additional writing and design, and return postage if you use business reply mail.

*This form is **budget.pdf** on the CD.*

Budgeting Worksheet

1st Choice:	Size:	Paper:	Qty:	# Issues/Yr.:	Other:
2nd Choice:	Size:	Paper:	Qty:	# Issues/Yr.:	Other:
3rd Choice:	Size:	Paper:	Qty:	# Issues/Yr.:	Other:

Description	Cost/Issue 1st Choice	Cost/Issue 2nd Choice	Cost/Issue 3rd Choice
Editing, Proofreading			
Paper			
Printing			
Mailing List Printing			
Labeling & Sorting			
Postage			
Other Expenses Address labels Envelopes			
Web & e-mail service fees Other			
Total:			
Total Cost/Year: (Total x # Issues/Yr.)			

Start with the size, paper type, quantity for each printing and number of issues you'd like to mail per year. List these specifications under "1st Choice" above. Collect prices for this choice and list them in the first column. If the cost is to high, go back under 2nd choice and change the specifications.

If your project is too expensive, see the previous page for ideas for saving money on newsletters. Also, see the section on e-mail newsletters on page 92.

From **Quick & Easy Newsletters**, by Elaine Floyd. www.newsletterinfo.com and www.paperdirect.com

As you're budgeting and looking for ways to cut costs, keep the following concepts in mind. Some costs are independent of the quantity you print and mail. For example, fixed fees like subcontractors' charges and production supplies are the same no matter how many newsletters you print. If you were to assign these fees as costs per newsletter, the cost per piece would decrease as you printed more newsletters. Printing charges aren't fixed. However, most printers charge you less per piece for 2,000 newsletters than for 200, for example. Other costs, such as postage, are fixed per piece and are independent of the number you mail.

Set up your newsletter's budget before you begin. This ensures that you know what you're getting into and can make any necessary changes before the first bill comes.

How to Cut Any Budget by 25%

Sales tax. Nonprofit organizations should apply for tax-exempt status to avoid being charged tax.

Mailing permits. You can avoid paying yearly permit fees by using the services of a mail house. Some will let you print their number on your pieces as long as you use their services to handle the mail.

Postage costs. If you regularly send other information to your mailing list, consider adding your newsletter to the mailing. This is called "piggybacking."

Rush fees. When using subcontractors, you may be faced with rush charges if you cause the project to fall behind schedule. With careful planning and scheduling, you can avoid these fees.

Minimize the time your project takes. Give subcontractors work in the most final form you can. For example, if you have written articles on your computer system, submit the articles to your layout service on disk.

Involve subcontractors in cost-reduction programs. They know the best ways to save you money.

Bulk mailing. Depending on the timeliness of the content, promotional newsletters can be mailed bulk rate. The advantage is

Swap Ads for Favors, Goodwill

According to Inc. magazine, two companies are strategically using ads in their newsletters. In California, San Luis Sourdough gives away ad space to good customers. In New Hampshire, Empire Video Superstore swaps ads in return for advertising space in area merchants' stores. The trades are effective in getting 50,000 to 100,00 pieces of promotion into potential customers' hands.

a savings of 33% over first-class. Non-profit organizations qualify for even greater discounts.

Keep pieces under one ounce. One important design note: for first-class mailings, unlike standard mailings, you pay by the ounce, so you may want to design your newsletter to weigh under an ounce. Be sure to include the weight of an envelope if used. Standard mail pieces can weigh up to 3.3667 ounces without additional charges. If the pieces weigh more, the mailing goes to a per pound rate.

Sign yearly contracts. Contracts with vendors, such as printers, can cut your bills by up to 30%.

Shop around. Printing prices vary. Specialties vary. Know the area of expertise and competitiveness of each vendor.

Set a budget and stick to it. Audit costs line by line.

Selling Ads in Your Newsletter

For many organizations, support from sponsors and advertising sales can help stretch a newsletter budget.

Some newsletter publishers sell small advertisements to offset costs. The best type of advertising is from vendors of hard-to-find supplies or items that directly interest your targeted readers.

Paid ads work well for:

- ❑ nonprofit organizations
- ❑ associations
- ❑ vendors of hard-to-find items or specialized sites
- ❑ classified ads
- ❑ ads swapped with other organizations

Paid ads don't work for:

- ❑ most marketing newsletters
- ❑ publications without an advertising manager

Concentrate on Content

If your newsletter is the exclusive source of crucial information, your publication could be scribbled on note paper and photocopied onto napkins... it will be read. Obviously, a well-designed newsletter filled with hot tips and exclusive information will be the best choice.

See an effective use of advertising in the example on page 225.

Sidepage:

Spin Off a Classified Section as Part of Your Newsletter

When Twigg Musique in Montreal, Canada, developed its first newsletter, *The Bullhorn*, the idea was to publish it a few times a year and use it to promote the store's new products and services.

Sprinkled through the newsletter were ads from the store's suppliers. Says editor Colin Murray, "We didn't have a formal system for selling these ads. I'd just call up our suppliers and ask them if they wanted to place an ad. Most of the time they'd go ahead and buy one."

The newsletter also included a one-page classified listing called *The Band Exchange*. This advertising page was so popular that it took on a life of its own.

The Band Exchange lists band instruments that people want to sell or buy. Due to the number of ads people wanted to buy, it's now published monthly and mailed to subscribers. It is also available on the company's fax-on-demand system.

The Band Exchange fax-on-demand also can send people interested in placing an ad the listing form to complete and return by mail or fax.

© Twigg Musique

If you sell ads in your newsletter, you need a rate card. Include the following on the card:

- ❑ mission statement of the publication
- ❑ reader profile or demographics
- ❑ circulation or hits
- ❑ ad sizes available
- ❑ format of publication (paper, page size)
- ❑ cost
- ❑ frequency discounts
- ❑ form of artwork advertisers should submit
- ❑ publication dates and deadlines
- ❑ rules and regulations

Publication Profile

The *Multiuser PC News* is the only publication focused on the use of microcomputers in a true multiuser environment. This bi-monthly publication supplies the reader with first hand information on new hardware and software products; sales, marketing, and distribution information; dealer profiles and editorial opinion. Each issue of the *Multiuser PC News* has a circulation of at least 5,000.

Rates

1/6 Vertical	$90
1/3 Vertical	$175
Jr. Page	$225
1/2 Horizontal	$250
Full Page	$425

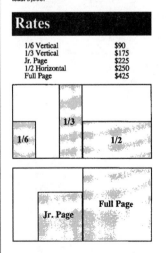

Printing Specifications

Camera-Ready

Camera-ready copy required. Please don't send original mechanical or negative. Sorry, no bleeds. If additional specifications are needed call (615) 254-0646.

	depth (in.)	width (in.)
1/6 Vertical	4 5/8	2 3/8
1/3 Vertical	9 1/2	2 3/8
Jr. Page	6 1/4	5
1/2 Horizontal	5 1/8	7 1/2
Full Page	10 1/4	7 3/4

Credit Terms

Credit is available for repeat advertisers. Invoices are payable upon receipt.

Cancellations

Any cancellations must be received by closing date. Cancellations after closing date will be invoiced for full amount.

Jan./Feb.	July/Aug.
Closing: Jan. 1	Closing: July 1
Mailing: Jan. 15	Mailing: July 15
March/April	**Sept./Oct.**
Closing: March 3	Closing: Sept. 1
Mailing: March 17	Mailing: Sept. 15
May/June	**Nov./Dec.**
Closing: May 1	Closing: Nov. 3
Mailing: May 15	Mailing: Nov. 17

Reader Service (Bingo) Card

Bingo card responses are provided as a free service to all advertisers.

Mailing Instructions

send all material to:

Multiuser PC News
Advertising Manager
476 Woodycrest Ave.
Nashville, TN 37210

Publisher's Policies

Please do not send original artwork. The publisher assumes no responsibility for damage to non-replaceable ads. Please notify publisher if you would like any materials returned.

Rates are subject to change on notice from publisher and become effective for all advertisers with the stated specific issue and all issues thereafter.

All advertising is subject to publisher's approval. The publisher reserves the right to reject or cancel any advertising for any reason at any time.

The publisher is not liable for delay in delivery as a result of an Act of God or any other abnormal event that results in an interruption of production or delivery schedules.

The advertiser assumes liability for the entire content of advertising printed, and also assumes responsibility for any claims arising therefrom made against the publisher.

Finding Deep-Pocketed Sponsors

An alternative to advertising is to locate a sponsor for all or part of your newsletter. Some nonprofit organizations are able to find sponsors to donate the cost of producing an entire issue.

Retail businesses often have co-op advertising money available from the manufacturers of the products they sell. A newsletter might qualify for these funds. Before relying on the assistance of your suppliers, send them a proposal, along with a sample of your newsletter. Show how you want to present their products or services. Be specific about the financial support you are seeking from the supplier. Make an offer, and send a contract.

For example, a financial consulting firm was able to underwrite most of the cost of its newsletter by charging a sponsorship fee. Various securities firms paid to publish informative articles on their products. The publisher achieved its goals while reducing expenses, since the information in the articles was precisely what the firm wanted to provide its customers.

What About Charging Subscription Fees?

Although subscription fees may help offset the costs of publishing a newsletter, they will also discourage readership and reduce the goodwill generated by a promotional newsletter. With a free newsletter, you can change or discontinue with minimal repercussions. It's different when you've collected money from subscribers.

One reason for charging a nominal fee is to offset the stigma of being pure advertising matter. To some audiences, a free newsletter implies the content is worthless. Charging for the newsletter may imply value. If your readers think this way, be creative. Give your free newsletter apparent value by printing a per-issue price on the cover or an annual subscription price in the masthead. Then you can offer free subscriptions to attract prospects and charge those who aren't good prospects but who request the newsletter.

Some newsletters start as free publications and grow into profit centers. One consultant launched a business brokerage newsletter to help market his services. The newsletter became so successful that he began to charge a subscription fee for it and soon gave up his other business to work full time on the newsletter. Many associations start free publications that turn into subscription pieces. *Psychology Today* is one example. If you have something valuable to say, people are willing to pay for it.

Quick & Easy Designs for Small Budgets

Any size budget can be used to produce a promotional newsletter. The trick is to determine what you want and what you can afford. A newsletter can be as simple as a typewritten publication on your letterhead or as formal as a four-color publication that looks almost like a magazine.

If you're on a tight budget, the key is to start out simple. At the beginning, all it takes is access to a writer/editor, computer and copier. As the project proves itself, you can expand to professional graphics and more expensive printing.

See other quick and easy examples on pages 201 and 215.

Doesn't get much quicker than this. This happy newsletter is printed on a postcard.

Consider the following:

❑ printing a letter-style newsletter on your company letterhead to give the feeling of personal communication

❑ printing a special version of your stationery (perhaps with the newsletter name), and photocopying black text onto it

❑ purchasing colorful pre-printed papers designed by stationery companies specifically for newsletters

❑ printing on a postcard

❑ designing a letter-sized newsletter and printing on the front only or front and back

❑ printing front only or front and back on a legal-sized sheet

❑ using a word processor to produce a simple format

❑ photocopying black text onto white or colored paper

Little-Known Secrets of Shorter Newsletters

Spending more money on a newsletter is not always the best way to guarantee effectiveness. Quick and easy newsletters tend to have increased readership. This is probably because the arrival of the daily mail brings a bombardment of information. People throw lengthy publications in their "to be read" stack, along with magazines and long reports. If you have such a stack, you know you don't always get around to reading everything. Quick and easy newsletters can be read in just a few minutes, as readers look through their mail.

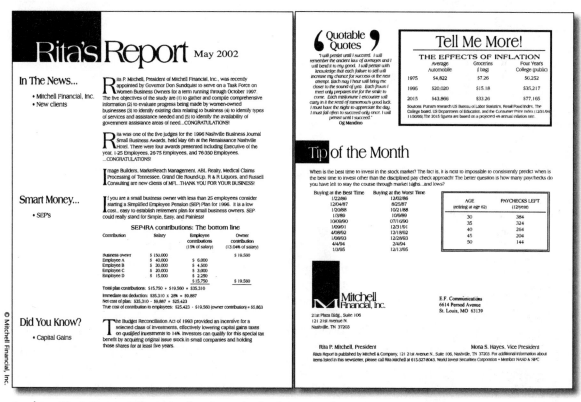

Look at Rita's Report. This is a level at which almost anyone can do a newsletter. The monthly one-page, two-sided newsletter costs its publisher only $40 to print and mail 100 copies. The important thing is that it works just as well as a more expensive newsletter. As part of leafing through their mail, Rita's customers can pause for three minutes to read the investment newsletter. The newsletter offers ideas for investments and has resulted in increased business for its publisher.

Another example is the Marketing Observer.
A marketing consultant uses this newsletter to promote his products and services. The newsletter is a legal size, one-page, two-sided mailer; the bottom section serves as a tear-away reply card. The consultant pays only 50¢ each, including mailing. (The reply card requires the respondent to add a stamp.) The brevity of the articles and the helpful information keeps readers looking forward to receiving the newsletter and has also caused many to respond to its offers. The project more than funds itself from respondents' purchases and also helps with the firm's long-term marketing plans.

Effects of Frequency & Length on Your Budget

Information, time and costs are factors in determining the frequency and length of your newsletter. If it comes down to a choice of frequency or length, it's usually best to publish more frequently, whether this means publishing only an e-mail broadcast, sending photocopied news on letterhead, using internal staff or cutting down on paper quality and photographs. As with any type of advertising, repetition is important. A short newsletter sent once a month is preferable to a long one every quarter.

> "A newsletter should be long enough to say what you need to say and short enough to be read on the way to the wastebasket."
>
> — Mark Beach

In addition, the more frequently the newsletter comes out, the more timely the information. If your company or industry is prone to rapid change, you could have problems using a quarterly publication as a news source. If a major change takes place, it could be three months before you can get the news to your readers.

One solution is to use special editions, which are usually devoted to one topic. Occasions for special editions include trade shows, major changes, seminars or a special new product launch. The less frequently your newsletter is published, the more useful special editions can be.

Getting It Out on Time

Whether your targeted publication schedule is weekly, quarterly or monthly, you should try to publish your newsletter on a regular basis. However, some people know from the beginning that they may have trouble with regular production.

Does haphazardness in your publication schedule show a lack of commitment to your readers? Will an irregularly published newsletter hurt rather than help your image?

I've never known anyone to be hurt by publishing just one promotional newsletter. Even if they only published their message once, they got the attention of some of their readers. The disadvantage is that they didn't stick with the project long enough to reap the benefits of longevity.

While publishing on a regular basis requires greater resources, you'll see the results faster. Every issue builds on the marketing efforts of the last newsletter. Within reason, the more issues or broadcasts your prospects see, the greater the promotional effects.

Sometimes you just may not have enough information to fill an entire issue. Many organizations e-mail news as it occurs. Or, you can publish a smaller newsletter.

The best way to ensure fast turnaround on your newsletter and increase your chance of publishing on a regular basis is by developing a schedule. The schedule helps eliminate surprises by letting vendors and editorial board members know when the work is coming. Careful planning also saves you time and money.

© Sou-wester Books

Only for special occasions. Publish your newsletter at least quarterly and preferably bi-monthly or monthly. If you feel unable to make a commitment to regular publication, admit it. One bookstore even calls its newsletter "The Occasional."

Two Sets of Books

Depending on the people you work with, you may want to keep "two sets of books." The first schedule would include inflated deadlines and the second schedule your actual deadlines. If you do this, don't let your contributors ever find out.

Scheduling Your Newsletter

The most vital planning tool is the schedule you set for each issue. Developing and sticking to your schedule not only helps increase the quality of your publication, it also saves you time and makes it easy to meet deadlines. You will have time to proofread the text, lay out the pages and doublecheck critical marketing information. These crucial steps are often bypassed or rushed when articles and other types of content are late.

From a promotional viewpoint, your schedule is used to implement your editorial calendar and your marketing plan. Use the plans you set down in the last chapter and combine them into your scheduling.

Scheduling your first issue. Scheduling your first issue is a bit of a shot in the dark. If you haven't produced a promotional newsletter before, it's hard to know how much time each step will take.

To get started, look at the steps listed on pages 48 and 49. Note the turnaround times quoted by your subcontractors or volunteers. (If timing is crucial, you may want to shop for writers, printers and mail houses for turnaround time as well as pricing.) Allow extra time for articles to be approved.

Next to each step, write down the estimated completion time. For your first issue, multiply this time by two.

Use this list and estimated schedule to prepare a calendar. As you complete each production stage, pencil it in on the calendar. Note any forgotten steps or discrepancies in time estimates and save the calendar, in order to make your next schedule more accurate.

Re-adjust your schedule to keep it realistic if your newsletter misses deadlines. If the schedule can't be changed, don't expect outside services to make up for your delays without an increase in price. Also realize that even if they don't charge you more, you're still paying a price. The next time you give your vendor a schedule, they may not budget time for you until they actually receive your materials.

Letting go of the first issue. Although not without reward, the production of your first issue can be grueling. One editor produced his first newsletter on a new desktop publishing system under a tight schedule. The 16-page newsletter was written and produced in five days in order to distribute it at a computer industry trade show. Still feeling exhausted, the editor met a former editor of *Time* magazine at the show. He asked how *Time* was produced under a weekly deadline.

Time's editor said that it was simple. "You just learn when to let one go and always try to make the next one better."

With this in mind, publish the first issue of your newsletter as soon as possible. Once you've proofread carefully and checked that you've eliminated any major errors, send it to the printer or broadcast it online. Don't wait until everything else is perfect. You can refine the publication along the way. It's better to publish a slightly imperfect newsletter regularly than a flawless one erratically.

Scheduling additional issues. When scheduling your next edition, start by evaluating the appearance and writing of your last one. Look at it critically. What was good about it? What do you think you could do to improve it? Carefully check the quality of the printing. Look at the condition of the piece after going through the postal service or online distribution (be sure to add your name to your list). See if the address label was put on straight. Read each article for clarity and completeness. Look at the layout and the overall design.

List the articles and important news that you want to include this time. If you have regular features—market briefs, an editorial, personnel or member profiles—include them in your list. Decide who is going to be responsible for each article and set the deadlines. Once you have your schedule, post it close by. If you check off each item when it's completed, you'll be able to spot any potential bottlenecks.

Tips for Staying on Schedule

Try to avoid unpleasant surprises. Make sure the people who approve copy are going to be available when needed and those scheduled to be interviewed are still available. If possible, have backups for all vital functions and spaces. Check vacation, trade show and travel schedules. Carefully note holidays and make sure to mark them on your schedule.

Project Schedule

Newsletter: _____

Issue/Date: _____

Task	Assigned To	Time Needed	Begin Date	Proof Date	Final Deadline
Finalize Content					
Approval					
Collect Information					
Write Articles					
Find/Create Graphics					
Edit Articles					
Approval					
Layout					
Proofread					
Print Final or Save to Disk					
Approval of Proof					
Print					
Run Mailing Labels (if mailing)					
Mail/Distribute/E-Mail/Upload					
Follow-up					
Other					

If you're announcing a special event in your publication, the newsletter should arrive no earlier than four to six weeks prior to the event and no later than one week before. Regularly scheduled events, such as monthly meetings, should be announced no earlier than two weeks prior to the event.

Scheduling each issue can be simplified by developing a yearly editorial calendar. By planning most of your content in advance, you can benefit from the economies of scale. Often, when you're researching one topic, you'll find information on a future topic as well. Rather than having to retrace your steps next time, you'll have the information already on file.

From reading these first three chapters, you now know what you want your newsletter to accomplish. But in order for it to meet your goals, it must also meet the needs of your readers. Just as you have analyzed your own needs, take a moment to study those of your readers.

Check Those Vacation Schedules

"I was scrambling to meet a deadline and had only one crucial interview left. Then I called the interviewee and found out she had just left for a three-week European tour."

—An Anonymous Editor

Sidepage:

How to Save on Postage

❑ **Add zip+4 to your list**. The zip+4 eliminates redundant sorts at the process sites resulting in faster delivery.

❑ **Convert zip+4 codes to PostNet barcodes**. Mailing service bureaus and/or off-the-shelf computer software can take a zip+4 code and convert it into a barcode that postal machines can read. The postal system offers generous discounts for pre-barcoded mail.

❑ **Clean your mailing list**. The post office confesses that an average of 33.1% of bulk mail is immediately trashed because of improper and/or incomplete addressing. A mailing service bureau or off-the-shelf software can correct addresses electronically.

❑ **Use meter stamps**. Stamps do not generally increase response rates significantly enough to justify the added application cost.

❑ **Avoid bulk mail permit fees**. Use a lettershop's permit or share the cost with other businesses.

❑ **Mail more for less**. Letter-size mail sent third-class can weigh up to 3.3 ounces for the same discount as a one-ounce letter.

❑ **Use an automated lettershop**. State-of-the-art equipment can process at speeds far greater than by hand.

❑ **Rent lists on diskette instead of labels**. Electronically combine lists, remove duplicates, sort and add PostNet barcoding.

❑ **Mail to dense zip code pockets**. The best bulk postal rates are attained by mailing a large volume to a specific zip code.

❑ **Don't mail postcards third-class**. The rates are about the same as for first-class.

Resource: Markus Allen, MailShop/USA, Newtown Square, PA; www.markusallen.com

Chapter 4:

Pinpointing Readers' Interests

Understanding your readers' likes and dislikes is the only way to create a newsletter targeted to them. If you know your readers' hot buttons, you know the type of content that will attract them. If you know demographic data, such as their ages, where they live, their education level and so on, you know the design techniques and writing styles that will appeal to them.

Anything less is a shot in the dark. Yes, you might connect a time or two but only by pure chance. This chapter covers how to find out more about your readers by surveying them, as well as how to use ongoing reader feedback to keep your newsletter on track.

Ask yourself three questions when designing your survey:

1. Whom am I going to survey?
2. What am I going to ask?
3. How am I going to ask it?

It's time to do some scouting.

In this chapter:

- easy ways to collect information about your readers

- types of surveys

- ideas for questions to ask

- using the results for more than just the newsletter

- fax and online surveys

- tips for increasing response rate

MYOB

Sensitivity can be a problem when asking demographic questions. If you ask your readers about their marital status or age, you may find the question goes unanswered. Or you may receive the comment, "None of your business."

If this information is truly important to your promotions, look for other ways to ask it. To ask a person's age, place the possible answers into broad categories, such as "29 to 40," "41 to 55."

Respect respondents' sensitivities by assuring them that answers are kept confidential.

Find Those in the Know

The first step on your scouting mission is to find out what information is already available. Your trade association or an industry magazine should have demographic data such as age, sex and buying authority for your particular audience. Your fund raisers may already know the top five reasons why people support your cause. Even if a formal survey hasn't been performed, top promoters can give you a general idea. This may be all you need. Your marketing department may know the publications people read. Going on a few sales calls, answering customer e-mails, or working in the booth at your next trade show is a great way to a fast start. You can also ask for feedback from salespeople.

Don't underestimate informal methods. A person who has spent hours face-to-face with your supporters has knowledge that no survey in the world can assess.

Once you find out what's available and what's not, concentrate on whether or not you need to conduct a survey. Surveys are useful as you develop your newsletter, as well as for making changes as you go along.

The most frequently asked question regarding marketing newsletters is, "Do they work?" Along with setting measurable goals, a readership survey can help answer this question.

Surveys allow you to:

- ❑ learn which parts of the newsletter are the most read
- ❑ find out what people want to read more of
- ❑ fine-tune your promotional content
- ❑ measure sales effectiveness
- ❑ generate marketing information about your readers
- ❑ show readers that you care
- ❑ see who wants to continue to receive the newsletter
- ❑ justify the project's budget
- ❑ assure accurate mailing addresses

Creating a Sign-Up Card or Online Form

A simple form of an ongoing survey is to create a sign-up card or online screen. This gives you a general idea of who your readers are—their everyday concerns, what makes them laugh, and so on.

If promoting to companies, ask for your prospects' titles. From this you can determine what type of information readers require (technical, managerial, etc.) You may also be able to determine their buying authority and budgets.

Rent More of the Same

Useful data on your readers' organization includes the number of employees, the industry and the type of equipment they own or are considering for purchase. This information also helps you when renting mailing lists. For example, if you find a large number of your prospects involved in a particular industry, you could rent a mailing list from that industry. Then you could select only the portion with the common job titles you've found from readers.

MAILING LIST REGISTRATION FORM

We will include your name on our mailing list if you fill out this form. Any ideas you have that will improve our services to you are appreciated. Thanks for mentioning our store to your friends!

— CHECK EACH APPLICABLE BOX —

- ☐ Parent
- ☐ Teacher
- ☐ Student
- ☐ Grandparent
- ☐ Other _____
- ☐ Kindergarten
- ☐ Grades 1-3
- ☐ Grades 4-6
- ☐ Grades 7-12
- ☐ Pre-School
- ☐ Librarian
- ☐ Homeschooler
- ☐ Student Teacher
- ☐ Media Specialist

Remarks: _____
_____

— PLEASE PRINT —

Name _____
Home Address _____
City _____ State _____ Zip _____
Phone (_____)_____ Date _____

WE WELCOME YOUR SCHOOL PURCHASE ORDERS!

☐ **YES**, I will recommend that our school sends you its purchase orders!

RETURN THIS FORM TO YOUR EDUCATIONAL SUPPLY STORE

CRAFTMASTERS OF SIKESTON
114-116 W. Front Street
Sikeston, MO 63801

CRAFTMASTERS — Sikeston, MO

THANKS FOR YOUR PATRONAGE!

© Craftmasters, Inc.

Sign me up. This sign-up form gives Craftmasters, a supplier of educational materials, additional information about its readers. The information can then be used to send targeted direct mailings as well as gain a greater understanding of the newsletter's readers.

Dewey Defeats Truman

In a famous picture, a smiling Harry Truman holds a copy of a freshly printed Chicago Tribune newspaper reading, "Dewey Defeats Truman." The newspaper wanted to be the first to report the election results. What better way to find out who's going to win than by conducting a survey of voters?

Their survey found overwhelming support for Dewey among readers. Their oversight was that very few Truman supporters read their journal. Hence, the survey was biased toward support for Dewey. Of course, Dewey never made it to the White House, and we have a good example of what can go wrong when you survey the wrong people.

One way to spot active readers is to ask how they currently seek out information. If they read other journals, newsletters or e-mail newsletters, they'll probably read your news.

On the other hand, if your prospects prefer going to conferences, talking with colleagues, watching educational videos or listening to cassette tapes, you may want to explore alternatives to a printed newsletter.

Once you find out how prospects receive their information, consider subscribing to the publications, visiting the Web sites or attending the events your readers list. This will give you sources of information for news articles that have a good chance of interesting your readers.

Why the Pros Survey Fewer People

When conducting any type of printed and mailed survey, do not send it to your entire list. The U.S. Census, conducted every 10 years by the government, is one of the few surveys in which all of a given population is surveyed. Most surveys select a portion of a group to be studied and survey only this "sample." After the sample is chosen, everything possible is done to get each person selected to respond.

Here is why sampling is so important. The people you want to reach in your newsletter survey are not only those who are reading it from cover to cover. You also want to reach those who don't read your newsletter. You want to know the characteristics that differentiate readers from mere recipients.

If you send your survey to your entire list, the people who respond will be the same people who attend meetings, volunteer to respond or are convenient to poll. Your results will be skewed and will not help you reach the other people... and these people have something valuable to tell you.

The best type of sample is a random sample, which means everyone in your entire readership has a chance of being selected. For readership surveys, organizations with elaborate computer database programs can run a function in which the computer selects a given number of names at random. An example of a simpler system is to print out your mailing list by alphabetical order and select every fifth name. Or, if you have 1,000 names and want 100 for a sample, select every tenth name.

Your choice of sample size ultimately boils down to the amount of money and time you have to conduct the sample. A basic rule is this: the larger the sample, the more reliable the results. Also, the smaller your readership base, the higher percentage you want to sample. If you're conducting a telephone survey, you won't be able to contact as many as you would if you were mailing out a written survey. Choose the number based on the time you have. Then strive for a response from every person in your sample.

How to Conduct Your Survey

The type of survey you need depends on the accuracy of information you want. Many surveys are conducted to get a general sense of people's feelings. Readership surveys can be as informal as calling a few readers from time to time, or as formal as embarking on a full-scale research effort.

Types of surveys:

- ❑ mail-back
- ❑ telephone
- ❑ fax-back
- ❑ focus groups
- ❑ informal
- ❑ online

When designing your survey, you'll need to balance your desire for the ideal survey with cost, convenience, space and time.

Questions That Solicit Usable Answers

In any survey, you can ask two types of questions: open-ended or close-ended.

An open-ended question lets respondents answer in their own words. It gives them a great deal of freedom in answering the question. A close-ended question presents respondents with a

Presenting Appropriate Information

Facts like readers' age, education, gender and title determine how you will present your information in your newsletter. For example, hospital surveys have shown that women are more likely to seek health information than men. However, men are more likely to make an appointment with a doctor based on a newsletter article. Knowing the gender mix of their audiences allows health newsletter publishers to concentrate on motivating prospects to either read or respond.

list of choices, asks them to pick one or more, and leaves space for comments and suggestions. Close-ended questions have the advantage of providing answers that are easily summarized. For example, a hospital might survey patients and ask why they chose the facility.

The question can be presented as:

Why did you come to this hospital?
[ ] Convenient location
[ ] My doctor recommended it
[ ] You offered a special test or service
[ ] Other _____

The results from this type of question can be easily summarized such as, 32% mentioned location, 27% mentioned doctor recommended, 37% mentioned special service, and 4% listed other.

If the question was presented in a open-ended format, it would appear as: Why did you choose this hospital?

_____

The answers could range from "because my uncle works there," to "reputation." Getting a wide range of answers isn't necessarily bad. The difficulty starts when you begin to summarize the survey findings. You'll have to decide whether "reputation" means the same thing as "well-qualified staff" or "you're okay." This is a major disadvantage.

However, consider the following situation. A hospital asked an open question for their survey and was surprised to find "good reputation" as the top answer. If they had asked the closed question shown above, they might have led the respondents by the first three options and not have gotten as strong a response for "reputation."

Check all the questions on your survey for clarity and wording. The best way to do this is to pretest the questionnaire on four or five people before sending it out. Pretesting tells you if there are problems with any of the questions and helps you estimate how long it takes to complete the questionnaire. Pretesting with open-ended questions can help you convert the answers to close-ended ones.

Every Question Has a Goal

Make sure every question has a goal and is designed to solicit specific information. For example:

❑ determine true circulation by asking, "Do you regularly pass this newsletter along to someone else?"

❑ measure the effects of word-of-mouth by asking, "Do you regularly discuss items in the newsletter with friends or colleagues?"

To develop your newsletter content, ask readers which topics interest them. List possible subjects and ask respondents to check the ones they like. Although your content is influenced by your promotional goals, you can discover additional article themes through this kind of question.

By having respondents give you information, such as their job titles, you can match reader characteristics with the topics they say interest them. This will allow you to reach certain prospects with content that interests them. You may find that readers from smaller organizations have different interests than readers from larger ones, engineers have certain concerns that managers don't, and so on.

To determine which topics readers like, provide readers with a list of topics. You can have respondents check which ones they want, rank them in order of interest, or assign them A, B and C codes based on interest. You should always include some space where interested readers can add their own topic. For questions phrased as "how would you rate your interest in…" provide the respondents with a Likert scale. For example, "5" could be "very interesting" and "1" would be "not interesting at all."

Unmeasurable Benefits

At some point, you'll need to justify to yourself and others that your newsletter project is worth the money you've budgeted. However, like other marketing efforts, effects such as image, communication and feeling like part of the team are difficult to measure. They don't immediately appear on the bottom line. But you can measure readers' overall response to your newsletter and awareness of its content.

Rock Solid

A computer board manufacturer decided to launch a marketing campaign around its customers' reasons for buying its products. The marketing staff gathered in the conference room to decide why customers bought the products. The group finally settled on "ease of use."

Then someone in the group suggested surveying customers before the campaign was launched.

The company called 50 of its 1,000 customers. No one mentioned ease of use. In fact, the product was difficult to use. People bought the product because it was reliable.

After studying this feedback, future product articles in the newsletter focused on reliability, and the lifetime guarantee was mentioned in each newsletter.

Convert a Readership Survey to a Marketing Survey

A readership survey can be a powerful tool for discovering not only why someone is your client, but also why someone isn't. To find out why people support you, conduct a telephone survey. Call 10 or more of your customers and ask why they chose your services or why they continue to do business with you.

Find out the main benefit that your company offers customers. Ask them specific questions about what you should improve. From prospects, find out why they don't support you. Do they need your type of product or do they buy from a competitor? It is important not to give the impression that this is a sales call. Make sure your prospect knows that you are genuinely interested in knowing why they don't buy from you.

Many organizations already know their best prospects. Use your prospect list for your survey. You're targeting to precisely the people you want most. Ask them what type of information they need in order to support your organization. Use this information to promote to others as well.

The feedback from your surveys will help you create a newsletter consistent with the overall image you want your customers to have of you. Finding out why prospects don't do business with you can be equally as valuable. They may perceive you as being too small to fulfill their needs or too big to be responsive. They may not know you provide the services they need. Use your newsletter to overcome these objections. If the respondents find your organization too big, print a story about one of your smaller satisfied clients.

Determining the Promotional Level of Your Newsletter

Other questions can be used to determine your newsletter's success at each of the NEWS promotional levels—Name, Enticement, Writing and Sell. Choose questions from the following list to help determine a reader's interaction with your newsletter.

N?   Do you read the publication?
    [ ] entirely
    [ ] almost entirely
    [ ] about half
    [ ] at least one article
    [ ] read passages but seldom complete
    [ ] quick scan only
    [ ] don't read

N?   How much time do you spend reading each issue?
    _____ min.

N?   If you don't read the newsletter, why?
    [ ] no time
    [ ] intend to read it later
    [ ] not interested in content
    [ ] other _____

E?   When do you read the newsletter?
    [ ] immediately
    [ ] read by the end of the day
    [ ] read by the end of the weekend
    [ ] put in reading stack or save it to my desktop
    [ ] glance through to determine whether to read

W?   Do you pass along or forward the newsletter to others?
    [ ] yes; to how many? _____
    [ ] no

These answers will tell you how interesting readers find the newsletter.

W?   Do you discuss content with colleagues?
    [ ] yes
    [ ] no

Design With Elbow Room in Mind

If you use open-ended questions in your survey, make sure there is plenty of room for your respondents to answer. To give some leeway for your respondents in close-ended questions, leave an "other" category at the end, where they can add something. Leave ample room for these responses, too.

MTV & Internet Generations

Age can also affect your readership. If you are trying to attract younger people, for example, they're conditioned to the visual messages of television. They demand larger visuals and shorter blocks of text.

W?   How would you like to receive the newsletter?
[ ] by mail
[ ] by fax
[ ] on your Web site (with an e-mail reminder)
[ ] by e-mail
[ ] other _____

W?   Please rate from 1 to 5 your interest in the following features (where 1=not interested and 5=very interested): *(your list of features such as color, style, support)*

W?   Do you save the newsletter?
[ ] yes
[ ] no
[ ] some issues
This measures how interesting and helpful your newsletter is.

W?   What changes would you like to see?
[ ] more industry forecasts
[ ] more product information
[ ] more photographs
[ ] cartoons
[ ] shorter articles
[ ] leave it as is
[ ] other _____

S?   In the last year, have you (requested information/ attended an event/purchased a product or service/ volunteered/made a donation) as a result of something you read in the newsletter?
[ ] yes
[ ] no
[ ] don't recall

S?   Do you wish to continue receiving the newsletter?

[ ] yes

[ ] no

[ ] only issues specifically covering _____

Note those that only want specific information. Set up your database to code common interests and only mail to these readers when you've covered those subjects in your newsletter.

S?   Would anyone else in your organization like to receive this newsletter? If so, please add their names and titles below.

The Best Way to Survey

Your choices when deciding how to solicit information from readers are: mail-back questionnaires, e-mailed question, in-person surveys, surveys by phone, faxed surveys or online forms.

Mail-back surveys. Mail-back surveys are either included in the newsletter or sent as a separate mailing. Advantages and disadvantages exist for both.

When mailing a survey with the newsletter, you must separate out your sample names from the rest of your list. This can be a hassle, but you need to know which names you sent the questionnaire to for follow-up purposes. It's rare to get a high response after the first mailing.

If you send the survey along with the newsletter, readers immediately know what you're inquiring about. They don't have to remember the details of your publication. Response to the survey also benefits from the goodwill associated with coming in the same bundle as free information.

A possible drawback to including the survey with the newsletter is that readers plan to spend only a certain amount of time reading. By including the survey in the same mailing, you either harm your response to the survey or decrease the amount of time the reader spends with the rest of the newsletter.

It's All in the List

Remember that your mailing list may only include people who have supported you in the past. They are likely to purchase, join, donate or vote again. Expand your list of respondents beyond your newsletter list to gather responses to your marketing questions.

$1 for Your Thoughts

One commonly used incentive is a crisp $1 bill attached to the survey. This approach is likely to double your response, resulting in a rate between 35% and 50%.

See other postcard examples on pages 101 and 108.

You can combat this by sending along a sample of an old issue they've already seen. This helps them recall the publication, without taking away from the time people spend on the questionnaire. Another option for increasing recognition is to print the survey using the same size, colors and nameplate as your newsletter. You can use the first page for a cover letter about the survey, the two inside pages for the survey and the back of the newsletter for the reader to fold and return the survey to you.

Another problem with including the survey along with the newsletter is that those who don't read the newsletter won't see the survey. This is part of the reason why mailed surveys have the lowest response rates among all types of surveys.

If you're in the planning stages, you won't have a newsletter to show respondents. You may be able to find out more information and enjoy a higher response rate by talking to prospective readers in person or over the phone.

E-mail surveys. Select from the previous list of questions and send them out in the body of an e-mail. To increase your response rate, place an incentive in the subject line. Chances to win a large prize work well for e-mail surveys. Instruct recipients to copy the questions into an e-mail response and add their answers.

The one-minute survey. The easiest way to conduct a readership survey is to design it to fit on a return postcard. At least once a year, every newsletter publisher should do some type of investigating to confirm that the people on the list want the newsletter. Do this by attaching a postcard to every newsletter. Make it fast and painless to respond.

Please Take 2 Seconds to Answer this Question:

Do you wish to continue receiving this newsletter? ☐ yes ☐ no

Optional 5 seconds more:
How do you think we can improve it:

_____

_____

Please complete or tape business card.

Name:_____

Company: _____

Address:_____

City: _____ State:_____ Zip:_____

Telephone surveys. To generate a high response rate without much follow-up, conduct your survey by telephone. While mail surveys can take up to two months to complete (including follow-up), most phone surveys can be done in a few days.

When talking directly to your prospects, you can either use the same questions as a written survey, or you can have more of a general discussion. Regardless of the format, let your respondent know in the beginning how long the survey will take. Try your best to keep it as short as possible. Most people resent surveys lasting over five minutes. Also remember that respondents are doing you a favor. Make every effort to let them know you appreciate their kindness.

Focus groups. Focus groups are ideal if you're trying to get a general feel for your readers. These groups can be used if you have local readers or if your readers are already gathered in one location, such as a trade show. By conducting interviews with small groups of people, you can cover more points (frequency, usefulness, legibility, layout, story interest, etc.) in greater detail.

Other informal research can be accomplished using one-on-one interviews, or interviews with a few consumers or supporters simultaneously. Ask staff members for feedback during daily conversations. Have your representatives ask about the newsletter as part of taking an order, enlisting a new member or receiving a donation. Or you can randomly conduct spot checks by telephoning readers. Informal research can be as easy as mingling at a trade show or at your store, or answering the phone for a few days and talking to readers.

See more on fax strategies on pages 249-258.

Quick & Easy Surveys

One editor who took over a computer publication just wanted to get her feet wet. She first looked over data collected from user registration cards. The information included type of company, such as accounting firm or manufacturer, and the publications read.

She read through several months worth of back issues of the publication to get familiar with industry jargon. Two weeks later, she helped represent the company in its trade show booth. She asked people what type of information they had the most trouble keeping up with. Through her efforts, the editor now has an idea of what people want in the newsletter. She can use this in combination with the written goals of the newsletter.

Fax-back surveys. One of the fastest ways to do a paper survey is via fax. Design a one-page survey (two pages maximum) and fax it to your sample list. Provide an incentive to return the survey right away. Also, consider setting up a toll-free fax number for responses if you're surveying people from across the country.

Online surveys. The most valuable advantage of online newsletters over their printed counterparts is immediate, measurable feedback from readers.

Electronic newsletters let you easily collect feedback from readers. Readers like responding this way, because they don't have to go through any hassle. They simply select their choice and click "Okay" or "Send."

Automated surveys. Online surveying is easy but has its drawbacks. See online article by Debbie Weil on page 271.

In addition, depending on how your newsletter is set up, you can also track which articles people read—all without ever asking the reader. This data is automatically provided to the publisher on many Web sites. This interaction between publisher and reader will result in much improved content and design. For the first time in the history of publishing, editors know what people actually look at and how long they look at it.

Tips for Increasing Your Response Rate

Surveys often suffer from low response rates. Here are five ways to increase your response rate:

- ❑ keep the survey short and non-intrusive
- ❑ leave room for people to write and make sure the design of the survey is clean and professional-looking
- ❑ choose your questions carefully; avoid offending or demanding too much
- ❑ provide incentives to reply
- ❑ conduct a follow-up by phone, e-mail or mail to non-respondents

Keep the length to one page or two screens. State within the instructions how long it will take to complete the survey.

Begin the questionnaire with easy questions, such as title and company information. Write as many questions as possible with closed answers, and give the reader boxes to check or click on. This encourages respondents to continue, because they see how quickly they're moving through the questionnaire. Save open questions, such as, "Why are you a member of the professional association?" for the end of the survey.

Less is More

Generating a 100% response rate from a selected sample generates better and less biased results than a 5% response from the entire list.

Funny money. Instead of using the $1 technique to increase response, consider offering a discount on your own products.

Return Survey & Receive a Free Clip-on Flashlight!

Please complete survey on reverse side, fold, tape, and mail. For your convenience, postage has been pre-paid.

Your suggestions will be used to update future issues of this newsletter. Thank you for your input.

© WPP Co., Inc.

Give free stuff. A customer service consultant sent out a survey that qualified prospects and asked what they wanted to read in the newsletter. A free booklet, 10 Tips for Telephone Etiquette, was offered as an incentive. The booklet also showcased the consultant's snappy know-how.

Incentives also increase response rates. When each respondent wins something, the response will usually be higher than with promised incentives, such as prize drawings. Drawings are only effective if the prize is substantial and respondents feel they have a good chance of winning. In one survey, for example, the incentive was a drawing for a product worth $500. In a second example, each person who returned the survey received a mini-flashlight worth about $1 (see illustration on bottom of previous page). The first survey had an initial response rate of 3%, while the second enjoyed a 14% response.

Follow-up techniques can also help your response rate. About 10 days after the initial mailing, mail all non-respondents a reminder card that emphasizes the importance of the study and of a high response rate.

Keep track of those who have replied to the survey, and send a second copy of the survey to non-respondents. Usually, between 75% and 85% of the eventual return will be back within three weeks. From this, you can predict the final response rate from the first mailing.

To get a 100% response rate, call the remaining non-respondents and conduct the survey over the telephone.

Survey with a smile. This survey achieves four objectives— it repeats the store's services, it collects marketing information, it's a coupon and it reflects the fun-loving personality of the store owner.

15% OFF ANY PURCHASE WITH SURVEY - THANKS!

Why do you shop at Inkwood? ❑ location ❑ local independent ownership
❑ selection ❑ service ❑ staff recommendations ❑ author appearances
❑ children's storytimes ❑ candy jar ❑ other: _____

If you were ruler of Inkwood, would you ❑ expand hours ❑ add magazines
❑ start a frequent buyer discount ❑ carry more cards & blank books
❑ add book categories, such as_____ ❑ wear a tiara
❑ expand categories, such as _____ ❑ other: _____

If you recently purchased a book at another bookstore, was it because
❑ I was browsing, it was there ❑ they were open, Inkwood was closed
❑ Inkwood did not have the book ❑ it cost less ❑ I lost my head, I'm sorry
❑ other_____

What is the best book you read last year? _____

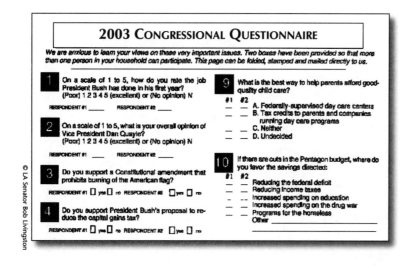

Survey built for two. Politicians and lobbying groups are always interested in the opinions of their prospects. The information can be used to help fine-tune campaign material, including the newsletter. Notice how this survey is designed so that two different members of a household can respond.

Using Results for Improved Promotions

For most editors, there's a great excitement in getting feedback from readers. Because many editors feel isolated from readers, returned surveys are a welcome change. But often, by the time all of the answers are in, editors are tired of the survey and never implement the new suggestions. This is especially true if the replies showed nothing drastic to change.

What will you do with your results? First, they can serve as a way to understand your readers better. If you get an overwhelmingly negative response, it's time to go back through the planning stages and evaluate your project, including your need for a newsletter.

Most results are supportive. However, with carefully scrutiny, you can find some good ideas to put to use. If your survey is an extensive data collection effort, you may want to involve a research firm or local college. Either one can computerize the data and generate statistically accurate results. Most surveys can be analyzed by simply noting the number of people who answered each question a certain way. Say you sampled 210 people and received a 100% response. The results show 150 people skim the newsletter, 50 read it cover to cover, and 10 never read it. You can say with reasonable confidence that 71% of all readers skim the newsletter, 24% read it entirely, and 5% never read it.

Develop your products along with the newsletter.
A vintage car parts manufacturer included a survey in its newsletter. The editor asked questions about types of ordering services, shipping, catalogs, brand names and product categories that customers and prospects wanted.

He asked why the readers were renovating their automobiles. The survey included questions like, "Are you more interested in maintaining your car's originality or in developing its performance?" The responses helped the company develop its product line and helped the editor choose the newsletter content.

CUSTOMER SURVEY

The Roadster Factory is putting alot of effort into building a new MGB spare parts service. We have spent seven months and thousands of work hours in writing an MGB parts catalogue; we are adding a seven-thousand-square-foot warehouse section to store the components, and we are financing an initial inventory valued at one-half million dollars. Before we go too much further, we would like to know our customers' opinions on certain subjects. We hope that you will take a little time to fill out the questionaire below. You can return it to us separately, or you can send it in with your next order. We will compile the results and let you know how they turned out later this year.

1. **Do you think that there is a need for another MGB spare parts service of the type that we describe in this publication?**
☐ Yes ☐ No

2. **The Roadster Factory offers a number of unique services. For instance, we have toll-free telephone lines answered by order takers who have no technical expertise, but we also have pay order lines on which you can talk to experienced professionals who can take your order and answer your technical questions. If you place an order on these full service lines, we give you a "telephone allowance" of up to $5.00 to pay for your call. We also accept orders by mail and by FAX machine, or you can come to our factory in person. How do you prefer to place orders?**
☐ Telephone—full service with telephone allowance
☐ Telephone—toll free ☐ Mail ☐ FAX
☐ Personal visit

3. **By offering allowances of up to $5.00 on orders placed on our full-service telephone lines and a 2% discount on orders placed by mail or by FAX, we at TRF have attempted to offer alternatives to the traditional "get-em-off-the-phone" toll-free ordering. Considering the benefits of dealing with a knowledgeable sales person on our full-service lines, do you consider these alternatives to be valid ones?**
☐ Yes ☐ No
Comments:

You may want to analyze more than one question at a time. In a survey prepared by an event planner, respondents were asked the number of special events they held each year. They were also asked to check their type of business. This information was combined using a cross-tabulation chart to see which types of businesses held the most special events. The event planner then used the data to target her most active prospects.

Present the results of your survey as quickly as possible. Include a note in the next newsletter issue thanking those who responded. In addition, respond directly to the suggestions. Promptness enhances your image as a responsive organization.

Regardless of the type of scouting you use, you're going to learn about your readers. Although it may be frightening at first, leaving the shelter of your office and reaching out to discover more about your readers is an enlightening experience. Readers give you ideas you would never think up on your own, and knowing them better makes producing a newsletter more fun.

With this knowledge and confidence in hand, you can produce a newsletter that brings revenue into your organization.

Professional association survey. A local Chamber of Commerce designed a survey to see if members wanted a newsletter. The survey was conducted through a written questionnaire completed as part of the yearly registration process. Members were asked if they wanted only a brief notice of upcoming meetings or a longer publication including business self-help articles. They found that members wanted more than just meeting notices. By asking members which subjects interested them, the Chamber gathered feedback that helped it plan its meeting programs and target prospective members.

Chapter 5:

Mailing List Magic

A sk anyone who's starting a newsletter what was their first step when creating it, and they'll say that they came up with a name and a design. Of course they did. That's the fun part. But it isn't the most crucial step.

The list you mail or e-mail to determines 40% of your success—with success defined as people reading and responding to your message. Distributing your newsletter to the right people involves setting up a good database. It also involves discovering who wants to receive your newsletter, whether or not they are potential buyers and recording this information in a way that's accurate and, for printed newsletters, takes advantage of postal discounts.

This chapter gives you ideas for who should be on your newsletter mailing list, how to automate your list, how to expand your distribution beyond the names you currently have and when to remove names from your list.

Creating Your "House" List

Your house list is the one you compile yourself. It includes current customers, members, supporters or prospects, along with suppliers and other people who can influence your sales. This list might be as few as 25, or as many as 25,000, or more.

The Right Way to Mail

Mailers set up to follow regulations for barcoding, tray labeling, banding and address certification pay the lowest rates and receive the speediest delivery service.

Use database software that can look up the zip+4 codes and add barcodes. Or use a mailing service that will take your list on disk and do this for you.

Customers. The most important names to get on your list are your current clients or supporters. Remember that the primary power of newsletters is marketing to current customers. If more than one person influences the decision to support your organization or purchase your services, include multiple names from the organization. Because your client base is a dynamic entity, your distribution list should be reviewed frequently, adding new clients, members and prospects, in addition to recoding inactive names.

Prospects. Remember to put only those prospects on the list whom you would want as customers or members. Along with other characteristics, determine the geographical area of your sales territory, and mail only within this area.

In addition to your clients and prospects, you should send your newsletter to several other groups.

Suppliers. Keep your suppliers informed of your progress. Send your newsletter to your accountants, attorneys, bankers and other subcontractors. They may be able to provide you with suggestions on your new products and services. In addition, your suppliers' salespeople are among your best sources for referrals.

Opting In. Collecting e-mail addresses from Web site visitors is much easier when you can offer a free e-mail. The challenge with e-mail databases is that you must also add the addresses of you best customers since you can't always be sure that they'll sign up on their own.

Remember to include the vendors who help you with the newsletter. Tell your printer, mailing house, or e-mail service you've added them to the list, asking them to evaluate the newsletter's condition when it arrives. They may spot problems with equipment or suggest changes that improve the newsletter's chances of making it through the mail or e-mail in good condition.

Employees. Make sure your newsletter is distributed to your employees, especially salespeople, prior to mailing. This avoids the embarrassment of a prospect inquiring about an item in the newsletter and the staff being unfamiliar with the topic. Stress to employees the importance of reading and understanding the articles in the newsletter.

Be sure to add your own name to the list so you know when the newsletter is delivered and in what condition. If you mail your newsletter nationwide, add a friend across the country to see how long it takes to make the trip.

The press. By sending your newsletter to the press, editors and reporters will know of your company and may remember it when writing articles related to your industry. Even if your market is local, having your company mentioned by local media helps your relationship with bankers and makes it easier to recruit top people.

Sent your news to influential people in your industry, such as trade journal editors; newsletter writers; and local radio, TV, and newspaper editors. When sending to large newspapers or magazines, make sure you research the name and address of a specific editor who reviews material in your field. If you send a printed newsletter, mail it first-class. The media relies on timely news.

When you send the first issue of your newsletter to the press, include a note telling why the individual has been added to your list. Ask if there are other names to be added to your list.

Non-competing organizations. Non-competing, complementary organizations are those who do well when you do well. Keeping these people informed is good for your business. For example, in the healthcare field, many doctors recommend other

Letter to the Editor

A manufacturer sent a cover letter, along with its newsletter, to a list of 50 editors. The letter included a reply card where other names could be added. Several of the publications responded with additional names and comments. One magazine called to request permission to reprint one of the newsletter articles. Thousands of dollars worth of publicity came from spending a few dollars a year to send one carefully targeted newsletter.

Stay Out of the Dumpster

Roughly 15% of all bulk business mail is trashed at the postal service, due to undeliverable addresses.

specialists. These two medical practices are complementary. Most organizations have complementary partners.

Ask vendors of complementary products if they want to trade lists, or offer to do a co-mailing. To entice others to give you their mailing list, create a special issue of your newsletter focusing on their organization and products, describing how they work with yours.

Community. Distribute your newsletter to community leaders, such as political representatives, professional associations and local market research firms. If applicable, send a copy to every library in your area on a regular basis.

Get other people to send it for you. Some companies are reluctant to release lists of their salespeople, dealers and distributors. However, they may agree to mail or forward your newsletter to these lists for you. Many organizations have been able to increase their distribution using this approach.

If you offer a service to businesses, consider sending multiple copies to consultants or others who may distribute them to their clients. One publisher sent several copies of an advertising agency newsletter to a management consultant. The consultant showed it to the clients he was working with. The agency acquired two stable, $25,000-per-year clients by printing an extra 15 newsletters.

Free lists. If you're a member of a trade association or Chamber of Commerce, you may be able to get the membership list for free, or you may already have it in a directory.

Newspaper or journal insert. If you find many of your customers in one area, consider inserting your newsletter into the local paper or business journal. Many service businesses, such as beauty salons, have successfully used this low-cost distribution method.

Links from other Web sites. Ask complementary companies if they will link to your newsletter archives from their Web site. Offer to trade a link back to them.

Dear Coca-Cola

One publisher was dumbfounded when his newsletter didn't generate any response, in spite of several aggressive marketing techniques. After further questioning, he admitted that his mailing list consisted only of company names and addresses; no individual names were on the list. He assumed the company owners would automatically get the newsletters, even without the name!

The e-mail equivalent would be to send a newsletter to the "info@" address listed on a company Web site.

Sidepage:

Cover Letters That Sell

Letters are proven persuaders in direct marketing. Letters are personal, one-to-one messages. Include an introductory sales letter on your Web site, as an intro message when signing up for a e-mail subscription or in your first newsletter mailing.

Write a headlines for your letter and open the body of the letter with a one-sentence paragraph. The headline, opening and postscript (P.S.) are the most read areas of any letter.

Sales letter writing is a unique art. The following sample outline, "Marlon Sanders' unique 11-step formula for writing sales letters that work," shares the secrets of a sales letter pro.

1. Write a headline that promises a specific benefit or result. The right headline can up overall response by up to 21 times.

2. Grab interest with an engaging first paragraph. Tell a story or elaborate on the promise from the headline.

3. Build value. People buy because what you're selling has more value than their money.

4. Sell your uniqueness. Explain how and why your products and services offer more value that those of others.

5. Summarize your benefits and give a price. The value you offer should seem virtually overwhelming when compared to the price.

6. Give a guarantee.

7. Give a free bonus for acting now.

8. Compare risk to reward.

9. Give testimonials.

10. Tell how to order.

11. Use the P.S. to reinforce your reason to act now.

Visit Marlon Sanders at www.higherresponse.com

Tips for Entering Addresses

According to the U.S. Postal Service, your address label should:

- be in all capital letters

- contain no punctuation (example: "AVE" instead of "AVE."), except the hyphen for the zip+4 digits

- include street information for universities and office buildings

- contain a 5- or 9-digit zip code

- be typed or hand-printed

Look at one of the address correction labels (the gold labels affixed by the post office) to see the postal standard in use.

Dazzling Databases for Printed Newsletters

When your customer list grows too large to keep track of on your fingers and toes, it's time to set up a database. Your software must allow you to add new fields (segments of information), combine lists and print directly onto labels. It must also be powerful enough to handle future growth.

When adding to your list, be sure to collect basic information, such as contact name, company name, address, city, state and zip code and to set each in a separate field. For example, if you set up city, state and zip code all in one field, you wouldn't be able to sort by zip code. If you plan to create personalized letters, set up the contact name with first name and last name in separate fields, along with a field for gender. This will allow you to address a letter to "Dear Ms. Smith."

Keep in mind that some larger organizations require mail stops—or the piece will be considered undeliverable and thrown away. Also, keep track of personnel changes, such as new titles and names. Using the correct name and title will please your prospects. It is cheaper to verify an address by phone or e-mail than to mail to an incorrect address for an entire year.

Even though this is a "mailing" list, you should also collect alternative ways to reach your customers, including phone and fax numbers and e-mail addresses. This way, you're set up when you want to send out a special edition or broadcast.

Develop codes for your customers. Perhaps you have a mix of dealers, distributors and end users (people who buy from you directly and use the product themselves). Or maybe your customers are from three or four general areas: government, educational institutions and Fortune 500 companies, for example. Coding customers allows you to select and mail to targeted groups.

If you sell a product, set up a field that tracks purchases. This will allow you to know who your "frequent buyers" are. Mail to these people often.

After you've collected basic information, record how the customer found out about your business. As you have contact with the customer, record other facts that come up in the conversation.

Assigning Codes to Prospects

Just as you code your customers, you should assign categories to prospects. Postage is too expensive to mail frequently to all of your prospects. A casual inquiry is less qualified than someone who's shopping around for additional suppliers. Coding the quality of the prospect and entering the source allows you to sort and mail more frequently to top prospects.

Leads who have recently inquired are usually more valuable than those several years old. Record the date of all inquiries in a way that allows you to sort them by year or month.

Request card. A distributor uses a reply card for readers to request catalogs. The names sent in are checked against those on the newsletter list. Those not on the list are added.

Calling names. Collect names and zip codes along with e-mail addresses for your newsletter. Then you can send personalized messages and let readers know when your company is in their area.

Why Coding Is Important

Your ability to use inserts depends on how specifically you can sort your list. You may code your list based on the types of products your customers buy, or by organization.

Another way to segment your readers is by the experience they have with your organization. For example, you could use a standard insert to welcome new customers and members. The insert might show pictures and descriptions of your staff, details on your policies or special background information.

Unless the prospective reader is a networking contact, a person should at least influence the decision to buy from or support your organization before being added to the list.

WRFM Sales Radio

Recency is the date of the customer's last purchase. This date tells you when customers are likely to buy again or need accessories for recent purchases. Combine knowledge of trends and habits with recency information to time your promotions.

Frequency tells you how often customers buy from you. If you're selling a consumable product, such as groceries or dry cleaning, and a customer isn't buying frequently, the customer is also giving business to your competitors. Survey these customers and find out how to get more of their business.

Monetary is the average amount of money or profitability from the customer's purchases or donations. It could be the number of volunteer hours someone has logged.

Finding Targeted Mailing Lists

In addition to your own list, you can rent the mailing lists of trade associations, industry journals, business directories, other organizations. Find an association or journal that caters to your targeted readers. Call the organization and ask if they rent their mailing lists. Some will refer you to a mailing list broker who handles the rental for them. When you talk with the broker, find out if they have lists of similar prospects from different sources.

Look for organizations promoting their services to the same prospects as you. Call them and ask if you can rent their mailing list. Some organizations, such as medical practices, must keep their list confidential. If you operate a medical practice, look for other ways to find new patients. People moving into a new area are good prospects. Look in the Yellow Pages under "mailing lists" to find a broker who handles the names of new residents. In some areas, these names are available free from utility companies.

Charities have the challenge of keeping mailings small and targeted. Mailing to every resident of a certain area is too expensive. Look at other organizations who have donors with similar interests. Members of an animal rights organization may also be interested in preserving the environment. Call other charities and see if they'll sell their list or exchange it for yours.

Mailing lists of periodicals usually have the most current and accurate names and addresses, since it's to the recipient's advantage to provide it. Many periodicals have additional information about their readers. This will allow you to create a more targeted list. Ask them to sort on size of company, products they use or sell, titles or whatever other categories they collect. If you know the characteristics of your best prospects—such as title, geographic location, company size—you can rent only the names that meet your criteria.

If you rent a mailing list for your newsletter, remember that the recipients are not as familiar with your organization as your customers, members and other prospects. To help avoid confusion and increase the effectiveness of the mailing, include a cover letter along with the first issue you send. Use it to introduce your organization and its products and services. This will save room in the newsletter and avoid boring the readers who are already familiar with you.

In addition to those from magazines, consumer and business lists are available. Consumer lists are compiled from sources such as census surveys, zip codes and automobile registrations. Business lists consist of names taken from the Yellow Pages, business and trade directories, trade show registrations and association rosters. A good source for both is available on CD-ROM from Pro-Phone.

Questions to Ask When Working With a Broker

List brokers keep abreast of the list marketplace and have information about how and where to buy the best lists for your needs. Some brokers even specialize in markets such as computers, medical or legal. The best way to locate a good broker is by referral. They can also be found in the Yellow Pages under "mailing lists" and in a directory published by the Standard Rate and Data Service called *Direct Mail List Rates and Data*.

When renting through a broker, find out when the list you're interested in was last updated. Sometimes, list owners and brokers will guarantee that a certain percentage are deliverable. For some markets, you can find response lists—lists that contain names of people who have made purchases by mail. Response lists typically have a higher response rate than other rented lists, because the people have already responded to direct mail. Response lists are also typically more expensive than compiled or subscription lists.

The cost of renting mailing lists varies greatly, depending on the source, type and size of the list you wish to rent. Costs are usually determined on a per-thousand name basis and can range from $20 to $180 per 1,000 names for a one-time use. Mailing lists provided on disk are usually less expensive than lists printed on labels.

You can find good mailing lists to rent. Having more well-qualified prospects on your list is more than worth the rental costs.

It's Great, But Who Are You?

One company learned this lesson firsthand when conducting a readers' survey. They had rented a list from a magazine and had been mailing to the names for almost a year when they conducted the survey. Many of those surveyed said they were unsure of what products the company produced, even though a product list appeared in each issue.

Share with a friend

Recycle to:

1._____

2._____

3._____

Reduce, reuse, recycle.
Appeal to your reader's environmental sensibilities and encourage sharing the newsletter with a friend.

Free Ways to Reach More People

Discover ways to reach your audience without renting mailing lists. Beyond mailing, there are a number of ways you can extend the distribution of your newsletter.

Encourage sharing. Exposure is increased when people save, display, pass along or forward your new to others. Add a "route to" box or a note to forward your news. You can also provide a coupon for those receiving the pass-along print copies or subscription information for your e-mail newsletter.

Piggyback. To save postage and increase exposure, you can enclose your newsletter with another promotional mailing or with monthly statements or invoices. You probably receive several newsletters this way from utility companies, investment firms and credit card issuers.

Package inserts. Makers of consumer products sometimes put their newsletter in their package or on the box or bag. This has been done for diet products, bread and cereal.

Make sharing fun. As an option to the "route to" box, Craftmasters assigns their readers the "mission" of passing along the newsletter.

MISSION POSSIBLE:
This newsletter will self-destruct if read only once. Be a pal! Pass it on or post it.
Mission accomplished!

© Craftmasters, Inc.

UPS route to. United Parcel Service puts a "route to" box next to the listing of articles. The box makes it easy for readers to pass along the newsletter to others. By putting the "route to" information in the same box as the contents, recipients can even note specific articles the other readers should look at.

In this Issue:	Route to:
Clearing Canada Customs	_____
Preparing Int'l. Shipments	_____
Document Shipping Tips	_____
UPS Drop-Off Boxes	_____
C.O.D. Service	_____

© United Parcel Service, Inc.

Press release. You can attract new subscribers by sending news releases about your newsletter to publications in your field. Some magazines will list it in their literature section. If a reporter is writing about your company, mention that readers can sign up for your newsletter at your Web site.

Press kits. Include your newsletter in your own press kits, along with your press releases on other products. Journalists will learn more about your company and may even get an idea for an article based on something in the newsletter.

Handouts. Newsletters can be handed out at trade shows and conventions or offered to seminar producers to include as giveaways. They can be used as leave-behinds by salespeople. Always have people from your company hand out copies when speaking at seminars, meetings and conventions. Keep a stack of newsletters in your lobby for new vendors, prospective employees and walk-in clients.

Unexpected requests. Always print and save extra copies of each of your publications. Put them in a secure place or archive your e-mail newsletter on your hard drive so that if someone needs a particular issue, it is readily available. This also serves as a good reference for subjects already covered. You may even find them a good training source for new employees.

Bulk Mailing

Depending on the timeliness of the content, promotional newsletters can be mailed bulk rate. The advantage is a savings of 33% over first-class. Nonprofit organizations can qualify for even greater discounts. The disadvantages are that the mail must be prepared according to specific post office rules (some left to local interpretation) and delivery can take a lot longer. By regulation, the post office has up to three weeks to deliver this mail.

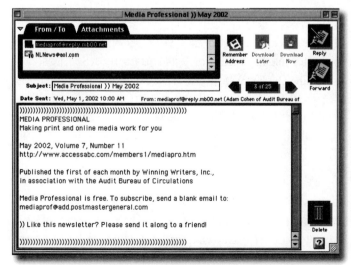

Forward to a friend. E-mail newsletters are easy for readers to forward on to their friends and colleagues. This broadcast of Media Professional reminds readers to pass it along right up at the top of the screen.

See fax news on pages 249-258 and Web site news on pages 267-272.

Finding the Right Database Software

The right software can ease a database marketer's job. If your business is growing and needs to keep up with thousands of customers, buy software with a high number of possible records.

Look for software that allows you to combine (merge) several lists together, remove duplicates, export the information, import other databases and add fields. For targeted mailings, you'll need software that lets you select names using multiple criteria. For example, you may want names in a certain zip code who have purchased from you in the past six months.

Reply cards. When renting a mailing list, using other people's lists, handing out newsletters to groups, or leaving stacks of newsletters for browsers, remember to include a sign-up card or Web site address for signing up so you can add interested readers to your list.

Fax to local numbers. Many companies and associations find local distribution via fax a faster and more effective than mailing or e-mailing. Local faxing is free and ensures immediate printed delivery.

Load into online libraries. If your newsletter is filled with helpful information, you can load it onto libraries of association or other complementary organization's Web sites.

Put it on your Web site. Convert your newsletter content into sample articles for your Web page. Offer the content from previous issues here, too.

Saving Money by Pruning Your List

The best way to avoid frequent pruning of your mailing list is to add only qualified names to begin with. Once that's done, periodically check to see if your prospect is still at the same address and still a valid prospect.

It's easy to get address corrections when you publish a pricey subscription newsletter. For free newsletters, this is a tougher job.

One out of five people moved last year. Keep addresses current by mailing to the list often, at least quarterly. (See postcard example on page 108.) When an address changes, the post office will forward first-class mail for 12 months. Place the line "address correction requested" on every mailing you send. The new address will come back to you, instead of the piece simply being forwarded until one day you receive the note "forwarding order expired."

When mailing via standard mail, the post office will discard undeliverable pieces and you'll never know it. However, you can pay extra to receive address updates. First-class mailings receive this service at no additional charge. You may also want to use address certification software.

The reply cards used in building a list are also helpful in pruning one. Up to 25% of the names or addresses on your list will become outdated each year. If you're going to publish an ongoing newsletter, you will have to update and prune your list at least once a year, preferably more often.

Higher postage costs are increasing the need for accurate lists. By ensuring that every newsletter reaches a targeted reader, you make more efficient use of your postage dollars.

Some direct marketers never remove a name from their mailing list except by specific request or when the piece is returned as undeliverable. Their statistics show that as long as a mailing is reaching someone, it may be read and produce results often enough to justify keeping all inactive names on the list. Obviously, this can work for mass appeal items like clothing and food, but most newsletters are written for targeted audiences.

At this point, we've looked at your organization's goals and abilities to produce a newsletter. We've also examined the characteristics of your best readers, their interests and the different ways to reach them. The next step is to combine this information to determine the best content for your newsletter.

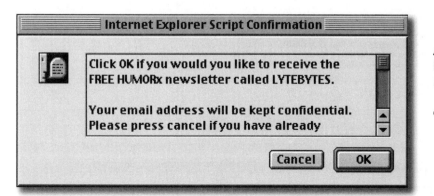

Automated signups.
Readers can subscribe to *LyteBytes*, shown on page 15, by clickicking on a link at www.humorx.com.

Sidepage:

Purge Your List With a Painless Postcard

How big a mailing list is too big? Most businesses build their mailing lists by collecting names from various sources. They add people they meet at trade shows or those who. have responded to ads or direct mailings.

As time goes by, many of these names become active customers, others so-so customers and still others remain in the prospect pile.

If you're like Bangs Laboratories, you may wake up one day and realize you're managing a list of over 11,000 names. Bangs publishes a promotional newsletter for its prospects and customers called Painless Particles. They wanted to keep anyone on the list who was reading the newsletter and remove those who weren't.

To purge their list, Bangs sent this bright yellow double postcard to names that were over three years old. The response rate was around 50% in favor of staying on the list. This allowed them to safely remove 2,100 inactive names from their list.

Your *free* subscription to "*Painless Particles*" is about to

We are cleaning up our mailing list ...
to save your time, our money, and the world's trees. According to our records, and we never make misteaks, we have not heard from you for over a year.

Do nothing and you'll be dropped...
from our mailing list. If you are not interested in our products, you probably won't mind. Simply throw away this card.

To continue to receive our quarterly newsletter ...
please check your address, refold this mailer with label inside, tape shut (no staples, please), and mail. If you are outside the US, please add proper postage.

Thank you!

Bangs Laboratories, Inc.
979 Keystone Way, Carmel, IN 46032
Tel: 317-844-7176 Fax: 317-575-8801

Chapter 6:

Six Types of Newsletter Content

Promotional newsletters walk a fine line between soft-sell and unbiased information. While you want the unique features of your products and services to appear in as many articles as possible, it's the useful information that keeps your readers coming back for more.

Walking the fine line between marketing copy and news copy is tricky. When you go too far to the promotional side, you end up with what readers consider company propaganda. When you go too far to the "news" side, you're confusing your marketing publication with an industry magazine or news broadcast.

This chapter helps you find the delicate balance between marketing and news. It shows you the difference between your newsletter and paid-subscription news. Readers don't expect newsletters to be helpful in passing idle time. One of my clients once asked if her newsletter should include a recipe. "Sure," I said, "as long as you offer consulting on nutrition."

If people are paying for a publication, they expect it to be packed with useful information. While you want to include helpful information in your newsletter, always make sure it's related to your product, organization or industry.

In this chapter:

- what to write about in your newsletter

- how to sell your products without compromising news value

- choosing customers to sell for you

- adding value with industry news and support tips

- content that makes readers call

- how all of the content comes together

Balance Promotion with News

Your newsletter's subject is the link back to your organization. When all the content follows the main subject, readers feel a clear sense of purpose. It also makes it easier to collect content for each issue.

Newsletter content can be broken down into six categories:

1. product
2. customer
3. support
4. organization
5. industry
6. response

The Key to Content

From the choice of interesting routes to take, fill your newsletter with only those leading to your final destination—your promotional goals.

Within each article, squeeze in reasons readers should buy from you. Adapt the text to attract prospects, too. There are basic assurances you need to give prospects. They want to know you can supply their needs and that you can deliver what you're promoting. Many prospects need to know that you won't abandon them after they buy, donate, vote or join.

At a glance. Remember that you have limited time to capture readers. If the main points of a topic can be handled more quickly by a table or graph, design one and use a caption to say what little still needs words. For example, a phone company showed readers the cost of its various calling plans in a table format. The editor promoted all of the company's services while also helping readers save money.

The Wrong Service Plan Could Be Costing You Money

Are you on the right service plan for the number of minutes you talk every month? Many of our customers outgrow their original plan without realizing that it would cost them *less* to switch programs. Check the chart below to see that your Cellular One phone is as cost efficient as possible.

Plan	Usage in Minutes								
	100	200	300	400	500	600	700	800	
Basic Service $35⁰⁰	65⁰⁰	95⁰⁰	125⁰⁰	155⁰⁰	185⁰⁰	215⁰⁰	245⁰⁰	275⁰⁰	No Free Minutes
Little Talk $29⁹⁵	58⁹⁵	87⁹⁵	116⁹⁵	145⁹⁵	174⁹⁵	203⁹⁵	232⁹⁵	261⁹⁵	No Free Minutes
Tiny Talk $39⁹⁵	39⁹⁵	78⁹⁵	117⁹⁵	156⁹⁵	195⁹⁵	234⁹⁵	273⁹⁵	312⁹⁵	100 Free minutes. Each additional minute 39¢
Occ. Talk $72⁹⁵	72⁹⁵	72⁹⁵	101⁹⁵	130⁹⁵	159⁹⁵	188⁹⁵	217⁹⁵	246⁹⁵	200 Free minutes. Each additional minute 29¢
Big Talk $99⁹⁵	99⁰⁰	99⁰⁰	99⁰⁰	119⁸¹	147⁸¹	175⁰¹	200⁰¹	225⁰¹	330 Free minutes. Free options, insurance, warranty, 331-400 29¢, 401-600 28¢, 600+ 25¢
Always Talk $199⁰⁰	199⁰⁰	199⁰⁰	199⁰⁰	199⁰⁰	199⁰⁰	199⁰⁰	199⁰⁰	199⁰⁰	800 Free minutes. 34¢ each additional minute. Free options, insurance, warranty

Are You Taking Advantage of the Feature Options Offered By Cellular One?

- Call Waiting
- No-Answer Call Transfer
- Call Forwarding
- Incoming Calls Only
- Outgoing Calls Only

- Local Calls Only
- Three-Party Conferencing
- Any Three Features
- Detailed Billing Option

Call Your Representative for Details

To win additional business from current customers, you need to provide different assurances. Persuade customers that it's not a risk to give one supplier all of their business. Assure customers that you offer more than one area of expertise. If you can save them time and money by providing more than one service or product, this may weigh in your favor. Also, the fact that the customer already knows you makes buying from you less of a risk.

To maintain the same level of business from existing clients, you must provide them with other decisive information. Restate that you appreciate their business. Convince them that your growth will bring them increased, not decreased, service. Give them insight into your future plans and show how you keep their needs in mind when making changes. Ask customers, voters, members and donors how you can serve their needs better.

Depending on the goals of your publication, you should include this type of assurance in each of the various types of articles. In addition to the assurances, keep your target promotional level in mind. Each of the six types of articles should operate within the four levels of marketing:

- ❑ **N**: **Name**: who you are
- ❑ **E**: **Enticement**: what you provide
- ❑ **W**: **Written Words**: how your service works
- ❑ **S**: **Sell**: what action to take

If one of your goals is to talk about the capabilities and virtues of your organization, the best way to demonstrate this is through your products and services. Within product articles, you can discuss the talents that went into designing them. On the other hand, if you talk only about your capabilities, without backing them up with concrete examples, the result is a "hot air" publication. Readers usually let these "brag rag" newsletters just blow on by. To keep reader interest, use product articles that show rather than tell about your organization.

What's News to You?

To choose the content for your newsletter, apply the knowledge you collected about your readers. For example, the publisher of a pharmaceutical publication found that physicians already stay abreast of changes in medicine. Instead of including general medical news, the newsletter concentrates exclusively on the applications of their new drugs.

The Weatherloy family of resins are designed for outdoor use by Washington Penn Plastic. The plastic compound is used by manufacturers for customers who want durable, reliable outdoor furniture that keeps its appearance and is easy to clean. Here's what goes in it and why.

Mineral Fillers:
Either talc, calcium carbonate, or a combination of both are used to give the furniture rigidity.

Polypropylene:
Both homopolymer and copolymer grades are used either together or separately to provide the furniture with impact resistance and "toughness."

UV Stabilizers:
UV additives improve polypropylene's resistance to sunlight, extending furniture's useful life.

Antistats:
Antistat additives make the furntiure easier to keep clean by lessening polypropylene's tendency to collect dust.

For more information, contact your sales representative or call Washington Penn Plastic at (412) 228-1260.

© WPP Co., Inc.

Plastic recipe. One manufacturer listed the main "ingredients" in one of its plastic formulations. The plastic was designed to withstand outdoor conditions. Following each technical name, the benefits of the additive were listed in nontechnical terms. The blurb included a photograph and an explanation of the equipment used to test exposure to sunlight.

Touting Your Products

"Specifics" fall under the category of articles on products, services, ideas and causes. Articles for manufacturers, professional services and healthcare providers should cover new additions or changes to existing products, services or equipment. For non-profit organizations, your articles should feature the services you provide to your members or community. Association newsletters usually offer specifics on events, such as meetings or seminars.

In every article, you should:

❑ tell readers your name

❑ list the name of your product, service or cause

❑ give readers specific information on how a product works

❑ interview people helped by the product or service

❑ tell prospects how to receive more information, give you their support, or make a purchase.

❑ explain your products and services with visuals (when possible)

To develop articles around existing products, consider:

❑ new uses

❑ tips for using

❑ new quantity discounts, pricing or terms

❑ samples or trial offers

❑ literature, packaging or displays

❑ co-op advertising

❑ demonstrations or workshops

❑ upgrades or trade-ins

❑ technical features

❑ benchmark comparisons

Products. Articles on products can be either information on new products or updates to existing ones. When structuring an article, remember the NEWS promotional levels.

- ❑ **N**: Within the text, repeat the name of your company and the name of your product line.
- ❑ **E**: Tell why the product is unique and what specific need it solves.
- ❑ **W**: Share your reasoning for developing the product. Tell how it came from requests from customers. List potential applications or users. If one is available, show a photograph of the product in use. All potential users will be interested in product details.
- ❑ **S**: Explain how to order or call for more details.

Since product articles are important to increase customer awareness and boost sales, show your products in as many issues or broadcasts of your newsletter as possible. Search for different angles to talk about the features of the same product.

Along with your current offerings, your existing customers need to know what new products you're developing. Providing readers with advance information ensures that your newsletter will be valued more by prospects. Selling additional products or services can be as easy as providing your prospects with this crucial information. Later, when the new invention is ready to ship, you can officially announce it in the newsletter.

Services. Service articles are structured similarly to product stories. Their purpose is to restate and explain the services you provide. Service articles give existing customers information about all the things you do. For example, a customer using your bookkeeping and tax services may not know that you also offer investment advice.

From a marketing perspective, it's important that your services have names. Names help clarify that your service is a "product." A business consultant, for instance, might offer a "5-Week Turnaround Program" for struggling companies. "Hit the Ground Running" would be a program for start-up ventures. Notice how the names give you a better feel for the consultant's services. They

One at a Time

Within your articles, feature one product at a time. According to research, ads featuring only one product sell better than those promoting an entire line.

See a product article on page 203.

Rotating Products

If your goal is to promote a variety of products to several markets, rotate the products you feature from issue to issue. You could also have different sections for each market. By segmenting topics within your newsletter or on your Web site, readers get used to finding the articles of interest to them. From a promotional standpoint, each section tells targeted readers how you can solve their unique problems.

explain and promote better than saying, "We provide consultation services to businesses of all sizes."

Along with the name of the service, tell readers whom the service is for and what benefits they'll receive by using it. If you have competition, explain how your service is unique. Because some of your articles may be previews, specify when each service will be available and how to buy or get more information.

For most organizations, your services are your products. Hospitals promote new tests and procedures. Banks explain various types of loans. Financial planners discuss investment opportunities. Associations offer advice and support.

Causes. Politicians, churches, charities and other community groups need articles on the causes they advocate. Remember that it's often difficult to get people to take action for the benefit of the community or the world. People usually respond best when the benefit is for themselves. Sometimes, to inspire the community activist latent in everyone, you have to take drastic steps. Other times, it's just a matter of educating people about a problem.

Articles on ideas and causes try to sway public opinion. You ask readers to change the way they vote or increase the money they contribute. Articles are structured to explain what you believe in, how your organization is making improvements and why readers' support is urgent. Timely articles are a must. Readers must take action immediately in order for you to maximize support.

Hard at work. A local politician promoted his administration by headlining all the legislation he had proposed. Most voters have to wait for election time to find out what their representative has done during the term. A regular update can pave the way for a politician's reelection campaign.

Public likes Missouri No Call Program

No Call Team vigilance makes law work

Attorneys general seek advice from Missouri

Let Your Customers Sell for You

Why should you have to do all of the hard work? The most effective way to promote your organization is to show examples of the people or causes you've helped. Much of the same information found in specifics articles can also be given through the testimonials of your supporters. Show your clients or supporters through case histories, profiles and customer news, and by welcoming new customers or members.

See how to get customers to say great things about you on pages 158-163.

Keep a list of the customer comments and ideas you hear as part of daily operations. Include news of customers through:

- ❑ customer quotes
- ❑ letters and e-mail from customers
- ❑ ideas on creative uses of your products and services
- ❑ customer reviews
- ❑ answers to customer surveys
- ❑ stories of how you solved specific customer problems with one of your products or services
- ❑ lists of customer suggestions

City of Baton Rouge Saves With Fuelman

Four years ago, Jim Thibodeaux, the vehicle equipment operations manager for the city of Baton Rouge, saw an inadequacy in the way his fleet operated. The city managed four fueling sites where all of the police and fire vehicles had to fill up. When officers were low on fuel, they would have to drive several miles away from their beat to a city station.

Fuelman automated the city's own stations, and the city now also uses Fuelman stations. As a result, they have six times the locations to choose from. "We pay the same price per gallon at the Fuelman stations as we pay for our own stations," says Jim. "Overall we save, though. We use less gallons since employees can refuel conveniently using their Fuelman cards."

City vehicles from the police department, fire department, the mayor's office, and the airport all use the Fuelman service.

The city has its own computer system to track vehicle performance and maintenance records. They are now interfacing their system with the Fuelman computer system to get their monthly reports sent electronically. The city uses the Fuelman reports to monitor vehicle performance and discourage fuel theft.

© Fuelman, Inc.

Fill 'er up. An automated fuel tracking system, Fuelman, woos fleet managers into giving them their business by showing how they have saved money for other fleets.

See another example of a case history on page 170.

Case histories. Case histories are your success stories. They explain how a client saved money, solved a problem or increased sales by using your product or services. The person in your case history essentially does the promoting for you.

A case history should describe the problem your client had and how you helped solve it. It's important to choose your case histories carefully. You should select either rare applications that challenge the limits of your product or common applications that apply to most of your readers. Rare occurrences are usually intriguing; common applications attract readers with similar problems. For a common application story, take your readers' most common need and then find a satisfied customer who is willing to be featured.

Donations to community groups increase when they highlight the individuals they are helping. People relate to pictures and stories about specific people better than to names of entire communities or countries.

Miracles, Hope Sustain Ugandan Family

"We live on miracles." The words are remarkable, having been spoken by a teenager. Though only 17, Daniel Wasswa possesses a muscular faith reminiscent of his Old Testament namesake.

Daniel's touching story is symbolic of many of the suffering people in Uganda. It all began with the heavy hand of Idi Amin in 1971.

Like many Ugandan people, 17-year-old Daniel Wassawa lives every day on the edge of disaster.

In that fateful year, Amin's military regime began to tear apart the country.

Daniel's family, despite their uncertain future, remained on their small farm until 1979. At that time, Milton Obote regained the Ugandan presidency, driving Amin into exile.

Unfortunately, the hope directed at the new leader was misplaced. He quickly proved himself to be even more brutal than the notorious Amin, especially in the area of the country in which Daniel lived.

Although the Wasswa family felt no loyalty toward Amin, they knew their lives were at risk if they remained. Obote's army conducted sweeping raids of the countryside, causing almost certain death to inhabitants.

In 1982, the family fled to Kampala, the capital of Uganda, preferring the prospects of homelessness and unemployment to the brutality of Obote's army. For two years, the Wasswa family lived on the grim edge of survival. Then in 1984, tragedy struck when Daniel's father became sick and died.

Since then, the family has had to live by faith—they have nothing else. They're not lazy, just caught in a vicious cycle of poverty, common to many Ugandans.

Faces in the cause. The newsletter of a charity, Food for the Hungry, uses case histories to explain the problems of hunger in the world and show how donations from readers are helping.

Client profile. A client profile includes some of the same information as a case history, but it has a different format. Profiles give more detail on the history and future plans of the person, group or company, along with their names, faces and, possibly, phone numbers to contact. The profile includes how and why they use your products or services.

See an example of a client profile on the bottom of page 307.

The sales power of profiles is weaker than that of case histories. However, they help build rapport with your customers, members or supporters. Including a profile in each issue lets your readers know you appreciate their business or involvement. Show photographs of your clients as part of the recognition. For example, include a photograph along with an article on your best customer being voted woman of the year.

One consultant used her local newsletter as a way to help her clients "network" with each other. She included information on clients' services, along with their phone numbers. Increasing business for your clients is a sure way to build customer loyalty.

Welcoming new clients. Organizations with expanding client bases may want to include a welcome message, along with a list of new clients or members. This not only recognizes the new customers, but tells existing clients that you are an active player in your industry.

Providing Support for Customers

Another way to demonstrate commitment to your readers is to give them technical information and support. Within this type of article, you can reiterate the features of your products or services. You allay one of the greatest fears of most customers: you assure them they won't be abandoned after their purchase or decision to support you.

Support inserts. Some manufacturers of complex products have so much technical information to provide customers that they choose to publish a special insert. The inserts can include special information, such as page after page of programming codes, that is of interest to some readers but too technical for others.

See another example of a case history on page 170.

Educational information can include:

- ❑ "how-to" lists
- ❑ ways to make better use of your products or services
- ❑ background information on an issue or current event
- ❑ educational material to help readers advance their careers
- ❑ worksheets to help readers save or budget money
- ❑ toll-free phone numbers for customers to call with questions
- ❑ e-mailed classes
- ❑ tips for dealers on how to promote your products

Often, the support articles you provide for your customers save you time or money as well. For example, answering common questions saves your customer support telephone and e-mail time.

A   **Offer from DataBack Systems!**

We invite you to participate in a **free** course. Using our Lessons On-Line service, we'll send you five (5) lessons over the next 5 days which describe how to compose great-looking email messages. Learn to use your email program better, and how to avoid formatting, line length, font, wordwrapping and other errors when composing email messages. Just submit your email address below - of course you can drop the class at any time if you choose not to complete it. Thanks for stopping by!

© Databack Systems, Inc.

Back to school. Databack Systems, a provider of Web hosting services and e-mail newsletter broadcasting, offers free classes sent by e-mail. Readers can sign up at www.databack.com.

If you're a manufacturer, you may be able to provide information that helps a customer prevent a problem. Support articles like these might include tips on installation, troubleshooting, maintenance or repair. You can also give assistance on product selection if you offer a broad product line.

You can easily include a standard support feature by gathering information about commonly asked questions from your technical support staff. You can also solicit questions from readers and answer their letters in the newsletter.

Including support information in your newsletter saves you time and encourages readers to save the publication. Most importantly, it assures readers that you take care of your customers and supporters after their purchase or donation.

Other helpful information to include: lists of events, book reviews and philosophical pieces offering helpful techniques on management or self-motivation. Although most of this information isn't promotional, make sure it has some relevance to your organization.

Future planning. Financial investment companies such as Oppenheimer help their customers plan for retirement with worksheets.

What You'll Need To Save

This worksheet will help you calculate the amount you may need to save to maintain your current standard of living. Two-income families can combine their benefits and expenses, but if they plan to retire at different times, separate worksheets may be more accurate.

The figures in the sample column are for a 45-year old man who plans to retire in 20 years and receive full retirement benefits. He has contributed the maximum amount to social security, but those benefits will only cover about one-third of his projected retirement income needs. Fortunately, he has a pension, has contributed to IRAs and invests in a variety of mutual funds with conservative portfolios.

Based on his worksheet, almost 12% of his annual salary is projected as the savings that would meet his goals. Now, see how much you may need to save!

		Sample	Your Retirement Needs
1	Current annual gross salary	$50,000	$
2	Annual income you would need if you retired today (80% of your current income)	$40,000	$
3	Assuming a 5% inflation rate, the annual income you will need to retire at a future date (line 2 times multiplier from Table A)	$108,000 ($40,000 × 2.7)	$ ◄
4	The annual amount your pension will provide. *Ask your employer's benefits office to project your pension, assuming inflation runs 5% annually between now and when you retire.*	$10,000	$
5	Annual social security income you will receive (use Table B for your annual benefit, then multiply by figure in Table A)	$40,727 ($15,084 × 2.7)	$
6	Total projected annual retirement income (add lines 4 and 5)	$50,727	$ ◄
7	Income shortfall that needs to be covered from another source of income (line 3 minus line 6)	$57,273	$
8	The savings you should have at retirement to provide enough income to make up shortfall (line 7 times multiplier from Table C) *Choose the multiplier that corresponds to your portfolio strategy.*	$962,186 ($57,273 × 16.8)	$ ◄
9	Value of your current investments. *These include those you have set aside for retirement, such as corporate savings plans, IRAs, Keoghs and the cash value of your life insurance policies.*	$150,000	$
10	What your current investments are likely to be worth when you retire (line 9 times multiplier from Table D). *Choose the multiplier that corresponds to your portfolio strategy.*	$585,000 ($150,000 × 3.9)	$ ◄
11	Additional capital you will need to provide sufficient investment income (line 8 minus line 10)	$377,186	$ ◄
12	Annual amount you should be saving to help reach your retirement goals (line 11 divided by divisor from Table E). *Choose the divisor that corresponds to your portfolio strategy.*	$5,794 ($377,186 ÷ 65.1)	$
13	Percentage of salary to be saved (divide line 12 by line 1)	11.6%	%

See an effective president's message in on page 168.

Including Your Organization's News

It's often a challenge to include your organization's news without appearing boastful. Along with articles detailing the specifics of your products or services, there are other ways to include your own news while keeping readers interested.

Remember that newsletters are "happy mail." Personalize your publication through your writing style and news of your staff and organization. Greet customers and help them get to know you on a first-name basis. Do this with:

- ❑ a "dear reader" section
- ❑ an executive editorial
- ❑ the history of your organization
- ❑ staff introductions

As with product articles, you have to show rather than tell. To show how your executives, members or doctors are capable administrators, list their industry activities. Include condensed versions of speeches, technical papers or seminars. Discuss upcoming trade shows and events that you support.

Articles by experts. Show that your president or other officers keep abreast with your industry by having them write regular columns on general trends in your industry or on technical subjects. For example, if your product or service fits in with a topic that's been hot in the news, assign one of your executives to write an editorial. Examples that come to mind include computer viruses, safe packaging, recycling, acid rain and controversial books or movies. Every industry has several hot topics to choose from at any given time, and these articles can also be forwarded to trade journals.

Clean thoughts. The owner of a pool and spa store used an editorial format to discuss methods of cleaning a pool. The article was written and presented as an opinion. Within the editorial, the author promoted the types of cleaning products his company carried.

Ozonators . . . For Sure, Safe Pool Care, The Easy Way

Bacquacil . . . Ionizers . . . Lectronators . . . the marketplace has been bombarded with alternative sanitizers these past few years. But many leading chemical engineers and industry specialists feel that the safest and best way to sanitize your pool or spa is a combination of ozone with chlorine or bromine. Henry Corradino of Atlantis agrees. His statement follows.

© Atlantis Pools

Provide a personalized, approachable image by including by-lines and photographs with all columns. Including photos will help regular columnists become familiar and ensure that people will recognize them at industry events.

Milestones. To demonstrate the stability of your organization, you should report on the milestones you've reached. Events such as the 100,000th unit shipped or your 25th anniversary are possibilities. Along with these milestones, you can include some background on your organization. Within milestone articles, recognize your customers or supporters for making the event possible. This shifts the focus of the article from your organization to your customers.

Employee & member profiles. To show the capabilities of new or existing staff, include profiles of employees or members. Print candid pictures next to these types of articles to attract attention.

Most customers want to see the people they're dealing with. Behind-the-scenes people can also make good profiles. Show how they help customers or contribute to the organization. For example, your customer may not be aware of the extremes your dispatch supervisor takes in finding trucking companies to deliver a shipment overnight. Because you always deliver on time, your customers assume it's easy. By focusing on a key employee, you give the employee recognition while showing customers how hard you work for them.

Unfortunately, some articles on employees aren't inherently interesting. Articles focusing on the personal accomplishments of your staff, such as number of years with the company, babies born and classes attended aren't appropriate for most promotional newsletters. Save them for your in-house publication.

Advertising. For organizations that want to include advertising in their publication, one option is to "report" it. Alert your customers or members to advertising or publicity appearing in trade journals. If an advertisement has been effective, include it in the newsletter. Add a commentary on why you feel it's doing well.

You can also announce when you have new literature by including a picture of the brochure or catalog. If you include an

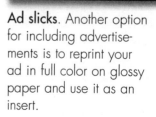

Ad slicks. Another option for including advertisements is to reprint your ad in full color on glossy paper and use it as an insert.

advertisement in your newsletter, separate it from the editorial material. Follow the guidelines of newspapers. Advertisements are clearly marked or boxed off. Any editorial material appearing on products or services is written in a news style.

Some companies report on any public relations exposure they've received. By listing the publication, date and page number or Web link of the articles written on your organization, you might inspire your newsletter readers to search the journals for more information about you. It also shows that you are making important enough progress to warrant industry-wide coverage.

Awards or achievements. Articles reporting on awards your organization has received are inherently dull. The only exception is when the award signifies a major achievement in the eyes of your readers.

See an effective example at the bottom of page 299.

Be cautious when reporting on awards received or given by your organization. Make sure they're really important, such as making the Inc. 500 list or something that's relevant to your customers' interest in your organization. They must be promotional to be worth reporting.

One last note here: if you include a photo of an award being received, avoid a "grip and grin" photo. (This is the photo with the person giving the award shaking hands with the person receiving it.) This style photo tells skimmers to skip the article.

Grab Readers With Industry Summaries

Industry information is the "news" part of your newsletter. It's often the feature that draws readers—especially prospects—to your publication. Your newsletter might include news items quoted from industry publications. Research findings, technology breakthroughs, pending legislation, opinions of prominent industry figures and information on other (noncompeting) products are all good news items. Write the reports in your own words (see Chapter 8 on Copyright) and list the publication and its date or the Web link so interested readers can find the complete article.

Every organization has industry news to report. An investment house can report on how changes in tax laws will affect people with retirement plans. Politicians can inform voters on pending legislation or new taxpayer rights.

Reporting on research reflects well on your organization and increases the value of your newsletter. Even if you didn't conduct the research yourself, readers credit you with the expertise.

The uniqueness of your publication lies not only in providing timely news, but in compiling information of interest to your readers. This saves them from having to gather the same information from several publications. These news blurbs usually fall under headlines like "industry news" or "news briefs."

People read news summaries. In reader surveys for two different publications, the news features received the highest percentage of readership—reaching 82% in one and 90% in the other. Because of high reader penetration, include a news blurb on your organization along with the others.

Longer industry articles report on trends, trade shows, technical meetings, seminars, assemblies, conventions, press tours, sales meetings and user groups. Summarize the important new things you learn by being active in your industry.

One method to cover a variety of clients or members at once is to report on an industry trend. Quote several different people and include their photographs. By doing your own interviews, you may end up with an angle not covered by trade publications. This will grab the attention not only of your readers, but also of the news editors on your distribution list. If you receive any interesting letters or e-mails as a result, publish them as letters to the editor (after first securing the author's permission).

IN THE NEWS

OEM Ties Push Unix to the Zenith

Demand for a standardized operating system, growing popularity of '386-based micros, the XENIX/UNIX merger and porting UNIX to the Apple Macintosh have combined to push AT&T's venerable operating system to the front in the PC marketplace.

As micro-based multi-user systems gained a stronghold in business, engineering and manufacturing applications, systems designers demanded more standardization, according to DigiBoard President John P. Schinas. Strategic alliances with OEMs such as Apple and IBM are also a sign that micro multi-user platforms will continue to grow in popularity, he added.

Pick Marketing PC Version

Pick Systems Inc. has set up a division to aggressively market the PC version of its Pick operating system through VARs and distributors, the company announced in early March.

Vice President of Sales and Marketing Frank Petyak said the company sold about 12,000 PC operating systems during the fiscal year ending February 29, and has set a goal to double sales of the operating system each year for the next three years.

IBM Gives Nod to UNIX

In what one industry analyst called a "ringing endorsement for the UNIX workstation market", IBM has announced a new version of its AIX operating system for the RT PC, as well as enhancements to the unreleased AIX system for the PS/2 Model 80.

IBM Vice President Andrew Heller said these enhancements will give the RT and Model 80 more connectivity options than anything currently available for competing UNIX systems.

AIX Version 2.2, available for the RT in June, will support new communications software including enhancements to the UNIX networking standard TCP/IP and Systems Network Architecture (SNA) services.

IBM Drops Gloves, Plans PS/2 Blitz

IBM officials in February disclosed an aggressive agenda calling for the release of as many as 11 new PS/2 models in 1988, also promising an extensive new line of support hardware including high-resolution graphics boards and high-capacity hard drives.

The company also said it will cut prices on existing PS/2s, with the '286-based Models 50 and 60 selling for approximately $1,350 by late 1988. A '386 machine at that price point was hinted at by the end of 1989.

Industry watchers call the price cuts a dramatic shift away from IBM's traditional high-margin marketing strategy.

© DigiBoard

Skimmable bites. In layout form, your newsbrief section looks not only useful but also "skimmable."

Reader Response Mechanisms

Without response mechanisms you cannot answer the question, "Is the newsletter working?" Here's how to get readers moving without endangering the high esteem they hold for your newsletter. "Enactment" tools include:

- ❑ reply cards
- ❑ order forms
- ❑ phone numbers
- ❑ your e-mail address
- ❑ unique Web site links only listed in the newsletter
- ❑ store hours
- ❑ directions to your company
- ❑ everyday discounts
- ❑ lists of products on sale
- ❑ coupons
- ❑ special discounts
- ❑ sale announcements
- ❑ shopping lists
- ❑ a "newsalog"—combination of newsletter with a catalog
- ❑ RSVPs for special events
- ❑ notice to pass along of forward the newsletter
- ❑ a notice to save the newsletter
- ❑ surveys
- ❑ suggestion forms
- ❑ contests and drawings
- ❑ a notice of what's in the next newsletter

You can also boost reader response by offering a free reprint of an interesting article, a free product sample or a premium. You can offer an annual index of articles, along with a form to request back issues (often appreciated by new readers). Some newsletters include contests, questions, trivia or other methods of attracting readers' interest.

Coupons also benefit readers by saving them money. Usually, lower ticket items are more appropriate for a coupon than more expensive ones. A coupon for a free item or money off the

TOO BUSY TO COME IN TO THE STORE to pick up a book you want? Just call the general book department at 8314 or 8315 and we'll get the book off the shelf (or order it for you), charge it to your credit card and mail it out to you right away. On-campus mailing is free, off-campus there is a small charge, depending on destination and weight of the book. And in the next newsletter look for information about ordering by email.

Give us a call. A bookstore gives readers a variety way to shop for books that are in the newsletter.

customer's next purchase outpulls coupons requiring an additional purchase. Always state the expiration date—sooner for low budget items, later for high-priced ones. Clearly indicate any restrictions. Inform your representatives of the coupon and make sure all your regular clients receive it.

To retain the integrity of your newsletter and keep it from looking like a sales piece, the offers included should be viewed as a service to readers. You can offer informative items such as free literature, buyer's guides, reprints of speeches or technical papers, videos or slide presentations.

See more examples of coupons on page 226.

By including helpful information, you encourage readers to save the publication. When readers save your newsletter, they might even read your promotional material a second time.

Free 4" Annual From
River Road Nursery's
Gift Area.

No purchase necessary.

River Road NURSERY

Limit one per customer

2625 River Rd.
*Between Ochsner
& Causeway*
837-7161

Expires Sept. 1, 1996

10% Off Non-Plant Items.

Including fertilizers, peat moss, soil, hardware, railroad ties, and more.

Sale merchandise excluded.

River Road NURSERY

Unlimited use

2625 River Rd.
*Between Ochsner
& Causeway*
837-7161

Expires Sept. 1, 1996

© River Road Nursery

Coupon clippers. A landscape supplier included coupons in his gardening publication. One of the goals of the newsletter was to increase traffic into the nursery. To entice readers, he included a coupon for a free plant. To help reduce inventory, he also included a coupon for 10% off non-plant items. The coupons do double duty—they catch those looking for plants as well as those who only want supplies.

Structure & Time Savings With Standing Columns

Some of these types of content will be used in every issue, in a standing column. Recurring columns help you:

- ❑ save time creating each issue
- ❑ give structure to a newsletter
- ❑ standardize design
- ❑ develop kickers and graphic icons
- ❑ make sure readers can easily find areas of interest

Note that while standing heads lend structure to your newsletter, you can have too many standing heads. Overuse will rob the newsletter of its freshness and newsworthiness.

Required Reading

Listing of tabloids, magazines and books which cover a variety of direct mail marketing subjects.

This column showcases various titles for you to consider on the subjects of creative copy and design, direct mail marketing, telemarketing . . . and more!

Encyclopedia of Mailing List Terminology and Techniques: A Practical Guide for Marketers

Nat Bodian provides a resource for all those needing to increase their knowledge of the mailing list industry. Includes almost everything you need to know—from A-Z concerning list management. Includes techniques, list security, segmentation and compilation.

A Manual Of Comparative Typography

Bauermeister wrote this book for direct mail art directors and designers. This guide highlights full alphabets for 200-plus typefaces. Provides names and suppliers, different variations and similar fonts.

Business-To-Business Direct Marketing

How does business-to-business direct marketing differ from consumer? This 400-page compilation by Tracy Emerick and Bernie Goldberg provides answers to those managers needing to know. Its instruction-manual format delves into direct mail planning, promotion, data base marketing, cataloging and much, much more.

Who's Who In Direct Marketing Creative Services, 1988

Over 200 writers and designers are profiled in a book which provides you with the information you need to know concerning the top direct marketing pros. Synopsis provides names, addresses, specialties, fees and phone numbers.

Start-up Telemarketing: How To Launch A Profitable Sales Operation

Stan Fidel provides tips, techniques and checklists for those companies wanting to put a telemarketing operation into effect at their company—and do it quickly. Recordkeeping forms, telemarketing scripts, even a start-up checklist is included to help the newcomer to telemarketing understand the process and implement it.

Maximarketing

Much-discussed book by Stan Rapp and Thomas Collins uncovers the new ways in which products and services are being brought to the awareness of various target markets. This 278-page book goes into depth on various topics including: the launch of new products; the discovery of new distribution channels; the advantages of cross-selling; plus, how to find your best prospects and how to keep your current customers happy.

Breakthrough Advertising

236-page book by Eugene M. Schwartz profiles the seven basic techniques of breakthrough advertising.

To cut production costs, experiment with less expensive grades of paper.

Coming To Terms

Direct mail jargon defined into a working vocabulary for you.

Becoming familiar with the terminology used in the direct mail industry is a basic step to becoming comfortable with this unique sales tool. Here is a listing of some words which can be used as a foundation for future direct mail communication.

ACTIVE SUBSCRIBER: A person who has committed for regular delivery of magazines, books or other goods or services for a time period still in effect.

CARD DECK: Collection of 3x5" stand-alone sales and response cards gathered in a wrap, bound together and/or placed in an envelope. Cards offer to sell or provide info about a product or service. Each participant pays a fixed fee for each card in the deck.

CHESHIRE LABEL: Specially prepared paper used to reproduce names and addresses to be mechanically affixed, one at a time, to a mailing piece.

DEADBEAT: A person who has ordered a product and or service and has yet to pay for it.

DECOY: A name inserted into a mailing list for verification of list usage.

DUPE ELIMINATION: The identification and subsequent removal of duplicate names and addresses. Process also uncovers misspellings, scrambled addresses, miskeyed zip codes and phonetically misspelled names.

LIST MANAGERS: Companies acting as agents for list owners. They are responsible for use by others of a specific mailing list or lists. Job duties include list maintenance, clearance, record keeping, billing, accounting, promotion and marketing.

LIST COMPILERS: Companies which develop lists of names and addresses from various directories, trade show registrations, warranty cards, newspapers, public records, sales slips, etc.

MEDIA: Vehicles used to transmit an advertising message, (direct mail, radio, television, telephone, match book covers, catalogs, package inserts, magazines, newspapers, among others).

PERSONALIZATION: The printing of letters or other promotional pieces with the use of names, addresses, special phrases and other information based on data appearing in one or more computer records.

PRESSURE SENSITIVE LABEL: A label that can be removed from a sheet and repasted on an order form of a carrier.

RETURN ENVELOPES: Self-addressed envelopes, either stamped or unstamped.

ZIP CODE SEQUENCE: Arranging names and addresses in a list according to the numerical progression of the zip code in each record.

Never assume a mailing will meet postal requirements. Always check with the post office before printing any unique component.

Reaching Wide

Many organizations have the challenge of balancing technical and nontechnical articles to reach a wider range of readership. For example, associations have to serve both seasoned professionals and newcomers. Many industrial and high tech companies sell to technical audiences as well as to those in administration or management. Let your audience mix tell you how to balance the information for both types of readers.

Graphically pleasing. The standing columns and accompanying artwork in this newsletter from Lakewood Publications create an easy-to-read publication.

Theme Issues

Other publishers concentrate on one specific subject per issue. These are called theme issues. For example, an association's theme issue might center around its annual membership drive. The issue could include event calendars, a message from national headquarters, and a page with member testimonials accompanied by photographs.

Use theme issues:

❑ to achieve one specific goal (fund drive, special sale)

❑ when all the content for an issue covers one subject

❑ when a subject is so broad is needs the entire space of the newsletter

❑ to thoroughly cover each segment of your market

❑ to better attract attention

❑ when your audience likes in-depth reporting, versus lots of news tidbits

If you're announcing a new product or service, you can mention it several times in your newsletter. Include an announcement in the industry news section. Devote an entire article to the new product or service on a different page. Insert a reprint of the ad you're running in industry publications.

Theme inserts. If your organization serves more than one specific market, consider special inserts for each segment. For example, a computer dealer inserts the "Notes from the Desktop" in the newsletters of its desktop publishing clients. Its other clients (healthcare, construction and legal) receive separate inserts.

Themes with a catchy tune. Many professional associations hold annual seminars and events. The main event for one association is a half-day workshop, followed by an afternoon of golf. The group strives to get 80% of its membership to sign up. The event is the group's top fund raiser. Although the workshop topics change from year to year, the event is usually remembered by the competitive game of golf that follows. To make sure no one would forget, the association president published reminders of the event in the six newsletters leading up to the outing. Each reminder used the same graphic of a golf club. In the issue just prior to the event, the golf club was used on the cover, on the schedule and on the seminar description. The constant reminder, plus the use of a consistent graphic, increased attendance to over 90%.

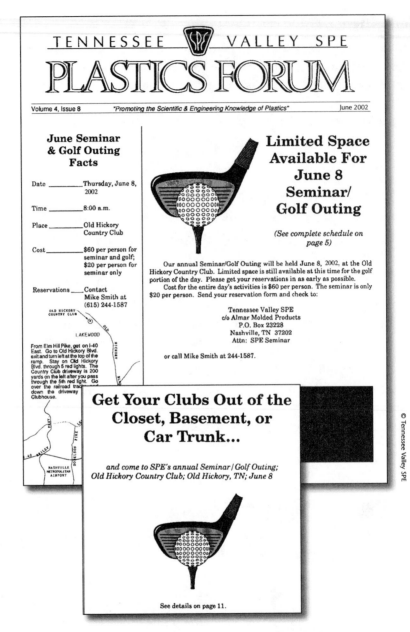

Do You Need Multiple Newsletters?

The mixture of content discussed so far assumes you can reach all of your readers with the same newsletter. For some types of organizations, this is not possible. To be more effective, some editors produce more than one version of their newsletter.

If your organization has more than one area of expertise, consider doing more than one newsletter or producing several versions of the same one. This allows you to target the various markets you serve.

Organizations such as banks and hospitals find their clients have specialized needs depending on their age. Young adults are having babies and buying new homes. Middle-aged people are trying to stay healthy, send their children to college and plan for retirement. People who are older may live on a fixed budget and often need specialized care. Savvy marketers of banks and hospitals target each of these age groups with different messages.

If you sell both to consumers and dealers and distributors, you may want to create separate publications for each of these segments. You can also design a publication for your dealers to mail to their own clients. (Leave space on the newsletter for the dealer to customize it with a photo, address, ad, logo or article.)

Face-to-face visit. An industrial controls distributor used this approach for eight representatives throughout the Southeast. They printed postcard newsletters with the sales representative's photograph on the front and return address on the back. This further enhanced the readers' feelings of being called on personally by their representative.

How It All Comes Together

Most newsletters contain a mixture of the six types of articles. Mix and match the various types depending on your promotional needs. Coupons are useful for increasing traffic into your business. Case histories reassure first-time buyers or supporters. Employee profiles make your staff more approachable.

To give you a feel for what the mixture might look like, study the newsletter published by a music store. The store wanted to increase sales by announcing new products. To convince readers of the expertise of the store's sales staff, the newsletter includes employee profiles showing that each person is a musical expert. Support articles, a brief list of hard-to-find items and announcements of upcoming seminars give the newsletter added value. Each of these articles works to increase business.

New product *Special event* *Client profile* *"How to"* *Technical support*

New product *Special event* *Masthead* *Employee profile*

It's easy to fall into the trap of scrambling to write your newsletter just to get it in the mail. But don't lose sight of your promotional goals. Take the time to choose the content of your newsletter carefully. It's critical to the promotional aspect of your newsletter.

Response   *Education*   *News*   *People*

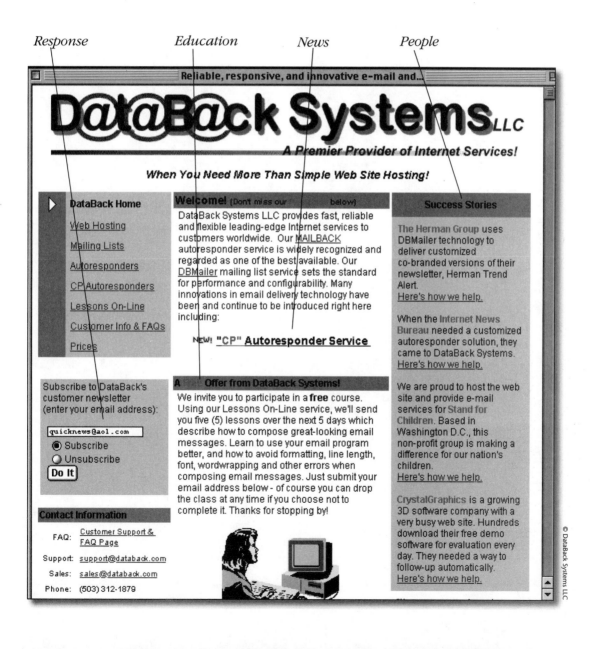

Chapter 7:

Naming Your Newsletter

O nce you've chosen a newsletter subject, you need to clearly tell your readers what it is—right in the name and tagline of your newsletter. This chapter covers the name game and helps you carefully consider the name you give your "baby."

Noteworthy Names

Your newsletter's name should tell readers what kind of information it contains, to whom it's addressed, and what your product, service or purpose is. The name should also include a tagline, or subtitle. Some names are creative and clever while others are more simple. Both get the job done.

Here are some tips:

- ❑ try to work in a benefit to your name
- ❑ if you don't have a benefit in the name, include it in the tagline
- ❑ put the newsletter's subject in the name
- ❑ put the intended reader in the name or the tagline
- ❑ use words in the name and tagline that say "timely news"

In this chapter:

- start selling right away with your newsletter's name

- what's a tag-line and why to include it

- example of note-worthy names

- powerful selling words to choose from

- do's and don'ts of naming contests

For example, the name of a manufacturer's newsletter, *Retail Success*, explains why retailers should read the publication. The tagline is "The latest product news and sales ideas for retailers of home furnishings."

news, reviews, no recipes for stews   from Wild Rumpus books for young readers

© Wild Rumpus Books

Leaping taglines. From the cartwheeling frogs to the playful typeface, Wild Rumpus bookstore starts off its newsletter with a chuckle. The tagline for each issue changes. Other taglines include, "news, reviews, we'll tie your shoes," "news, reviews, no singing the blues" and "news, reviews, let sleeping dogs snooze."

Tips for Taglines

Not all newsletter names can include benefits. If you can't get a benefit into the name, put the subject in the name and the benefit and targeted reader in the tagline. A tagline is a promotional opportunity you should never pass up.

Items to include in the tagline:

- ❑ your organization's name (if not part of the newsletter name)
- ❑ the intended readers (friends, customers, prospects)
- ❑ the newsletter's content or speciality (news, reviews)
- ❑ the benefit offered by reading

If the name of your newsletter is the subject, then the tagline should contain the benefit and the reader. For example, *Underground Storage Tank Update* has the tagline "The only news source that helps fuel distributors comply with EPA regulations."

Examples of Great Names & Taglines

The following are several examples of newsletter names, along with their taglines. Some are straightforward, others are more clever. Notice how the taglines clarify the name of the publication. Also, notice how some of the taglines promote with words like "exclusive" and "opportunities."

See how to design name-plates on pages 192-196.

❑ *News Splash*

"Tips for painless pool maintenance for homeowners"
Pools & Spas Unlimited

❑ *Managing Growth*

"Management ideas & techniques to help companies grow"
Ernst & Associates

❑ *The Franklin Investor*

"Insights & opportunities for investors of the Franklin Group of Funds"
The Franklin Group of Funds

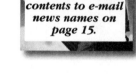

See how to add contents to e-mail news names on page 15.

❑ *RoundUPS*

"Published quarterly for customers & friends of United Parcel Service"
United Parcel Service

❑ *Legal Ease*

"Legal information for everyone from JG&W"
Jordan, Gfroerer & Weddleton Attorneys at Law

See Quick and Easy Newsletters for hundreds of more words.

Newsworthy Words

Some newsletters have a word in the name that instantly tells the reader that the contents of the publication are newsworthy. Most of the words in the following list were borrowed from newspaper names and feature headlines. Consider them when naming your publication.

> Advocate, Announcer, Briefings, Broadcast, Bulletin, Comment, Communicator, Communiqué, Courier, Clips, Dateline, Dispatch, Examiner, Facts, Flash, Focus, Forum, Highlights, Hotline, In Brief, Inside, Keynotes, Letter, Line, Link, Message, Messenger, Monthly, News, Newsbrief, Newsline, Notes, Observer, Perspective, Profile, Relay, Release, Report, Reporter, Review, Scene, Scope, Spotlight, Talk, Transmit, Update, View, Vision, Voice, Wire, Word

Powerful Sales Words

In addition to news words, look for words that tell the reader there is a benefit to reading. Here are some powerful marketing words for business newsletters:

> Profit, Money, Growth, Success, Wealth, Thrive, Save, Free, Results, Easy, Fast

Here are some words that help promote to volunteers and donors:

> Improve, Change, Influence, Impact, Make a Difference, Breakthroughs, Forward, Inspire, Brighten, Make a Mark, Affect

Keep these words in mind for headlines, features and articles, as well as for your name and tagline.

The Danger of Ignoring This Chapter

Not all newsletters effectively identify their intentions in the name. Think about how long it would take a new reader to figure out the scope of the publication without it.

For example, years ago, I picked up a newsletter called *Power Bar News* in a bicycle shop and couldn't figure out what a "Power Bar" was. Because the newsletter was in a cycling store, I first assumed they were talking about customized handlebars. Then I saw an article in the publication about how Billy Idol used them for training and assumed it was a weight lifting system. I scanned the nameplate and the masthead, I looked for a small ad, anything, but I couldn't find a clue. Then, buried in one of the articles, the writer talked about eating them. Aha! Candy bars. This must have taken 15 minutes.

I went through this exercise out of my curiosity for newsletters. No other new reader would have done it. The publisher could have avoided this problem by adding a tagline like this one to Power Bar News: "How athletes can achieve maximum performance with Power Bar high-energy snacks."

Before

What a difference a name makes. This makeover from the St. Louis Public Library illustrates the power of an active name.

After

Chapter 8:

Copyright Overview for Publishers

Copyright law confuses many newsletter editors. Heck, it boggles many lawyers, so don't feel like you're alone. Let's bravely forge ahead and learn to swim the muddy copyright waters. (We'll rinse off at the end.)

This chapter covers what copyright law is, what you can and can't copy without permission and how to receive copyright releases on commonly reprinted items in newsletters such as cartoons, photographs and articles.

What Copyright Law Is

Copyright law protects the combinations of words or graphic images as the property of their creator. While it protects the means used to express an idea, it does not guard the idea itself. This means that you are freed from copyright violation if you cull information from magazines and summarize it in your own words ("reporting" on them). Industry ethics say that you must credit the source, especially when using the information for promotion.

Quoting directly from an article is permissible up to an ambiguous point. Then, it becomes copyright infringement. A few sentences from a long article is safe. Beyond that, it gets muddy.

In this chapter:

- the basics of copyright

- how much is safe to quote

- finding owners of copyrights

- copyrighting your own publication

- avoiding libel and other dangerous content

Fair Usage Laws—How Much Is Safe?

Fair use exceptions state that you may quote briefly from a copyrighted work without asking permission for purposes of criticism, comment, news reporting, teaching, scholarship or research. The amount you can quote without permission is difficult to establish. The law states that the portion quoted can't be a substantial portion of the copyrighted work. It also can't significantly affect the market value of the work.

These two criteria are not clear-cut. The interpretation of your newsletter's purpose and what constitutes a "substantial portion" is left up to a judge to decide. You may consider your use news reporting. A judge may consider it advertising. "Protection under fair use is so limited that you shouldn't take solace that you'll be protected by it," says lawyer Brian Smith of Brian L. Smith & Associates, Nashville, TN.

If you decide to quote a copyrighted work, cite the title, publisher and publication date. Do not copy and paste an article from the Web and just list the source information and assume that you'll be okay.

The © Symbol

A work doesn't have to be accompanied by the "©" symbol to be protected.

What Is Public Domain?

Material that is not copyrighted is referred to as public domain. Some material is in the public domain because copyrights have expired or were never secured. Works created by the U.S. Government do not carry copyright protection. You may, without permission, reproduce materials in the public domain. Most everything else is copyrighted.

How to Track Down Copyright Owners

Here are some items commonly reprinted in newsletters along with tips on how to track down the copyright owners.

Clip art. The publishers of clip art collections grant buyers a license to reprint the art, but these rights vary dramatically by collection. Some licenses specify use only in free publications or those under a certain circulation. Read the rights carefully. As long as your use falls within your rights, you do not need to request reprint permission. Many clip art collections require that you list their copyright information in a specific way.

Cartoons. If you wish to reprint a cartoon, write for permission. Most owners charge a fee. If your newsletter is a free publication, state this in your letter of request as it may lower or remove the fee. To reprint any cartoon found in a newspaper, look at the small print within the frame for the company who syndicates the strip. Once you have the name, use one of the online search engines (see page 151) to find the contact information.

Poems & lyrics. Poems and lyrics are probably the most frequently infringed items. It's hard to track down the author of unsigned poems. The rights on lyrics are held by the music publisher. Contact BMI for information on music publishers. (See Resources Section at the back of this book.)

News articles. To be on the safe side, you must get permission to quote even a brief sentence or two from a short article. You don't need permission if you paraphrase the material. When clipping news articles, form the habit of noting the publication and date on the clipping. This way, if you want to reprint, you know where it came from.

Letters & e-mail. If a message is addressed to the editor, there's an implied permission to reprint it. However, all letters and e-mails are copyrighted. Most editors call the author for verbal approval. You also want to call to verify that the person sent the letter (that someone else didn't use that person's name as a prank).

Custom photographs & illustrations. Write for permission to reprint or scan. Also, obtain a model release from any person appearing in the photographs. Though photographers own the copyrights to the photos they create, people appearing in the photos have legal rights to privacy and must also sign releases.

Stock photographs & illustrations. "Stock" denotes that the work comes from a pre-made collection. When you buy from these collections you are usually buying one-time use. If the stock is from a CD collection, you are usually buying multiple uses. Check the fine print to make sure.

Always Cite Sources

The same publications that you are culling from may be on your PR list. They will see your use of their work. Make sure you cite the source. Don't endanger the PR goodwill generated by your newsletter by violating industry ethics.

Many collections limit where you can reprint the work. For example, using an image on a T-shirt or poster is often prohibited but the same images can be used on newsletter pages.

Quotations. Quotations are covered under copyright protection. However, few, if any, publications write for permission to reprint.

Subcontracted work. It shocks most editors to find that work you pay writers and designers $50 to $150 per hour to create is actually owned by the subcontractor. In the absence of an agreement stating otherwise, you have one-time usage rights. For com-

Subcontractors Own the Rights

In the absence of an agreement stating otherwise, you only have one-time usage rights to work that you pay subcontractors to design and write.

Works For Hire Agreement

your name & address here

Artist/Writer: _____

Address: _____

_____

Phone #:_____

Publication Name: _____

I hereby assign to the company listed above ("the Company") and/or its clients any and all copyright and/or other intellectual property rights I may have in the material listed below and submitted to the Company.

To the extent permitted by copyright laws, the work submitted is a work for hire. In the event that this work is not a work for hire, any and all copyright rights are assigned to the Company.

I warrant that the work(s) assigned is unpublished, original works of authorship authored and owned solely by myself and does not violate any other person or entity's copyright, trademark, rights of publicity, right of privacy, and/or any other such right.

Title of Work(s): _____

Payment:_____

Date: _____

Artist's/Writer's signature:

_____

plete rights, you need a copyright release which spells this out. The work of employees of a company belongs to the company as a "work for hire" under U.S. Copyright law.

Requesting Reprint Permission

To use copyrighted information in a way not covered by fair usage law, request a written release from the owner. To determine who holds the copyright, look in the masthead (in a magazine or newsletter) or on the page after the title page in a book. Photographs will usually carry a stamp at the bottom or on the back.

Send a form along with a copy of your newsletter and a photocopy of the material you want to use. Most people will grant permission free of charge. In some instances, though, you may have to pay for it. Unless otherwise specified, the fee is for one-time use only.

If you see an article you'd like to use that's written about a specific organization, call the featured company directly. Chances are that the article came from one of their news releases. Request a copy of the release. Contact the person listed on the release to get the rest of the story—more details or maybe a "story behind the story." The result will be a piece far more interesting and significant than the original release.

Many organizations and companies will send you photographs, catalogs, drawings and other useful items, including complete press kits. The implication is that you are free to use them in your newsletter. However, few of those who send you that material also send you written permission. Be safe. Send them a release form like the one on page 144.

Use the form on page 144 to solicit written releases for everything else you use in your newsletter (letters from customers, for example). If you reprint a letter that wasn't intended as a letter to the editor, you must obtain permission. The author of the letter owns the copyright.

The Copyright Clearance Center

Publishers can register their publications with the Copyright Clearance Center. The center grants rights and collects fees on behalf of the publishers. You can either register your newsletter here or contact this service when you want to reprint something. Over 1.5 million publications from more than 8,000 publishers are registered with CCC. Publishers establish a per-page, per issue or per-article cost for their materials.

The Copyright Clearance Center, Danvers, MA; (978-750-8400; www.copyright.com

See more on reprinting articles on page 152.

Copyright Assignment

Name of publication: _____

Please complete and return promptly to:

> *your name & address here*

Name: _____

Address: _____

I am licensing to _____

☐ One-Time Use: I hereby grant the rights for one-time use (the copying, distributing, displaying, performing, and derivating) of the work(s) in the above -listed publication for:

_____

☐ First-Time Use: I hereby grant the rights for one-time use (the copying, distributing, displaying, performing, and derivating) of the work(s) in the above -listed publication for:

_____

☐ Exclusive License: I hereby grant the exclusive right(s) to use the work(s) for:

_____

☐ Nonexclusive: I hereby grant nonexclusive license to copy, distribute, display publicly, perform publicly, and derivate the work(s) for: _____

I warrant that the material submitted is an original work of authorship authored and owned solely by myself and does not violate any other person or entity's copyright, trademark, rights of publicity, right of privacy, and/or any other such right.

I agree that any submitted material is subject to editing and that publication cannot be guaranteed. I acknowledge the ownership of copyright rights in any edited version belongs to the publisher as original creations of derivative works. If I sell the submitted material for use in any other magazine or other medium, I acknowledge that I do not have the right to use the edited version. Further, I am licensing nonexclusive rights for the use of the produced work(s), at no additional compensation, in any of the publisher's promotional material.

Title of work(s): _____ Payment: _____

Executed this ___ day of _____ , 19___

_____   _____
Author/Artist Signature   Publication Signature

Cartoons and poems are often the most tempting to use without permission. Other people's writing isn't as tempting because you can always rewrite it and often want to anyway. Read on to see why you shouldn't use your favorite cartoon without permission.

Asking for Forgiveness Rather Than Permission

Realistically speaking, many newsletter editors will quote a line of a song or reprint a cartoon from time to time without asking for permission. If you do this you must realize that the deeper the pockets of your organization and the larger the newsletter circulation, the greater the risk you take. A disgruntled employee may sue you for not getting a model release on a photograph. Or your newsletter may be placed into a press kit and sent to the author of the article you reprinted without permission.

In copyrightland, asking for forgiveness rather than permission is expensive. Under current laws, statutory damages of at least $250 per copy have been set. This means that if 2,000 copies of your newsletter are printed, the copyright owner will be entitled to a minimum of $250 x 2,000 or $500,000, plus legal fees.

Copyrighting Your Own Publication

You can copyright your newsletter by including the statement , "Copyright or © + year + name of individual and/or organization." This doesn't register your copyright with the Copyright Office of the Library of Congress. If someone plagiarizes your material and you wish to take legal action, as part of filing suit you must register the copyright by using a form available from the Copyright Office, Library of Congress, Washington, DC 20559.

Most publishers of free newsletters see no particular value in barring others from borrowing their information. In fact, it often results in free publicity. Some organizations copyright the publication and print a notice in the masthead advising readers they are free to copy and republish anything in the newsletter, as long as they credit the source.

While you can copyright the content of your newsletter, you can't copyright its name. The closest you can come is by trademarking the name's graphic design as it appears in your nameplate.

If you start receiving requests from other publishers to reprint information from your newsletter, develop a release form similar to the form on page 144 to save time. Keep copies of the blank forms on file.

Watch Those Downloads

Content you pull down from The Web and other online sources is copyrighted. Do not simply dump the text into your newsletter without realizing that you are violating the author's copyrights.

ISSN Numbers & the Internet

Along with registering your own copyright, considering registering for an ISSN (International Standard Serial Number). These numbers will be increasingly important as librarians use them to classify newsletters into databases that are available over the World Wide Web. Interested readers could find your company based on the subject you cover.

To get an ISSN assigned to your publication, complete the Serial Data Sheet for Publishers and send it to the National Serials Data Program. The form is available from The Library of Congress, National Serials Data Program, Washington, DC 20540; www.loc.gov.

Once you are assigned an ISSN, it is with your newsletter forever. If your newsletter changes names, a new number is issued and the previous number retired. There is no cost.

Libel & Other Dangerous Content

Whether you generate all of the content yourself, or utilize a news service, you are legally responsible for what is printed in your newsletter. To conclude the discussion on content, heed a few warnings.

Whenever you publish a news piece, you are opening yourself up to a certain degree of liability. If you let this bother you too much, you'll publish a stilted, boring newsletter. Caution is necessary, however, to assure your publication promotes rather than harms client relations. For this reason, let's discuss some of the potential problems with newsletter content.

Libel. If you publish an article, statement or piece of art that injures a person's reputation and is not provably true, you can be sued for libel. If you have to print this type of material, verify all names and facts, and if you are unsure about an item, consult a lawyer or do not print it.

In a promotional newsletter, stick to more positive information. Avoid printing any potentially defamatory information. This doesn't mean you can't include controversial stories; just be sure you represent the facts in a fair, unbiased and accurate manner free from personal attacks.

Disclaimers & Compliance. If you are carrying professional advice in your newsletter, consult your lawyer. Request an appropriate disclaimer to place in each issue. Such a disclaimer might read, "Information provided in this newsletter is general in nature and should not be relied upon to solve any particular situation." If you offer stock tips or financial advice, consult your trade association or parent company for information on compliance.

See compliance information on a masthead on page 221.

While you want your newsletter to be helpful, you don't want your readers to rely solely on the information contained in the newsletter. Try, wherever possible, to encourage readers to call for complete information such as to request a prospectus.

Letting the Competition Know. There's a problem with keeping your prospects well informed of your activities and new products. You run the risk of your competition seeing the publication and finding out, too. That's especially true if you have an online sign-up form where it's easy for competitors to sign up to receive your news.

Your job of making the newsletter content newsworthy and attention-getting becomes quite challenging when faced with the decision of whether or not your newsletter is dangerous in the hands of your competition. The benefits of spreading your organization's news far outweigh these drawbacks. The exposure and increased sales gained by educating readers outweigh any losses occurred from competitors seeing your products.

If your news will truly hurt your company, consider including intriguing information that keeps interest and alerts dealers and customers that you have something coming but doesn't divulge enough information to get you in trouble.

Telling Too Much. An interesting psychological phenomenon occurs when you tell your customers and prospects exactly how you do what you do: they want you to do it. Publishing a newsletter is a lot like teaching. When you teach others, you always learn more about the subject in the process. Instead of having your "students" catch up with you, you advance even further.

Chapter 9:

Where to Find Great Content Fast

S ome fact-finding shortcuts can greatly decrease the time it takes you to research and pull together the content for your newsletters.

You don't have to generate all original material for each issue. In fact, a lot of great newsletter content is sitting within a stone's throw of your desk. This chapter tells you how to find content from newspapers and magazines, online, in people's memories or in other materials that your organization has already created.

Draw a Research Map

Research requires more time to complete than writing. When you first break ground on a new issue, draw a research map. Think about who would know or care about your particular subject. More importantly, think about who would benefit by helping you get the information in print. Thinking this through is important, because a research map will lead you to the best treasures as quickly as possible.

Start with sources close to home. Search out experts in your own camp. Talk to members, doctors, salespeople, engineers, fund raisers and so on. Your beat could also include other organizations or industry experts. Request information, and ask if they've seen a similar article in a recent publication or online.

In this chapter:

- a bit of planning saves a bunch of time

- researching the world right from your desk

- ethically using materials from magazines

- finding pre-written newsletters

- encouraging readers to send in news

- interviewing secrets from the pros

- creativity on demand

Sources for Expertise

You can also check these directories for experts to interview:

- ❑ National Speakers Association
- ❑ Encyclopedia of Associations
- ❑ Editor & Publisher International Yearbook

Simplify, Simplify

If overwhelmed, simplify. If you find too much information while researching an article topic, narrow the subject.

If you're writing about a service or product, collect any marketing materials already written. Web sites, brochures and fliers are helpful, because they already include benefits and reasons for buying.

Keep in mind other sources for specialists. Look for people who have something to gain by helping you—customers who'd enjoy the publicity, consultants, suppliers and associations.

QUICK and EASY NEWSLETTERS

*This form is **map.pdf** on the CD.*

Research Map

Newsletter: _____

Issue/Date: _____

Reporter Name: _____

Phone #: _____

Story Idea or Title: _____
_____

What already exists that I can reprint/modify (articles, brochures, catalogs, press releases): _____

What's within my office: _____

What's within the building: _____

What's in the city (at the library, through a trade association, etc.): _____

Who can I call for ideas or leads of people to interview: _____

Who can I call for interviews: _____

Who has the most to gain by helping me with this article (example: managers, employee, customer, consultant, association, supplier, publication): _____

Other people to contact: _____

From **Quick & Easy Newsletters**, by Elaine Floyd. www.newsletterinfo.com and www.paperdirect.com

When writing about a broader subject, you'll need to dig deeper. If you have time, hike over to the library. .

Most periodical listings are available on research databases. Enter the subject name you're researching, and see how many magazine sources you find. For newsletters, magazine articles are usually more current than books. In addition, the information has already been condensed, since there's limited space in most periodicals.

Researching Online

If you've done much Web surfing in the past, you know that you can find out about almost anything online. Chances are that you also know that some of the information isn't accurate or verified and you have to wade through a lot of junk to get to the gems.

A good search engine combined with some searching tips can save you time and get you the results you want. Keywords are the key to fast finds. In the search box of your favorite search engine, type in at least two keywords. Place the keywords in quotes and separate them by the word "and."

Start Your Engines

Here are the names and addresses of some popular search engines (all begin with http://www.).

Yahoo:
yahoo.com

Google:
google.com

Dog Pile:
dogpile.com

Searching for marble. A restoration consultant wanted to write about restoring old marble. She went to google.com and found two perfect sources using the search shown below.

See more on reprinting articles on page 143.

Using Magazines, Newspapers & Journals

Be sure to read your industry publications and clip all of the articles related to your particular service or product. Then sift and summarize the news for your readers, noting trends and writing them up in brief articles. While you can't quote directly from others' copyrighted publications, you can use the information by rewriting it in your own words.

The short news items you uncover can be grouped together under headings such as "Newsbriefs," "In the News," and so on. Try to condense related material under one heading to reduce repetition. Weed out unnecessary words, to give skimmers a feeling of "compartmentalization." List the magazines, Web sites and other sources you use to create the newsbriefs. This will keep you clear from copyright violation and helps readers who want more information on the subject.

Reprinting Articles From Other Sources

Sometimes you want to reprint a news article exactly as it appears. In this case, you should ask for reprint permission. Although some writers charge a fee for using their material, many people—industry experts and even professional writers—contribute material for free. Their motives are varied. Some want publicity; some enjoy seeing their names and thoughts in print. Others are sincerely eager to make a contribution to their field.

Request to Reprint Material

The following material has caught our attention and we'd like to reprint it in our newsletter. Please sign this form and return it using the enclosed envelope.

We look forward to receiving your permission and giving your material greater exposure. Please indicate the acknowledgement you wish to appear along with your work in the newsletter.

Material to be Reprinted:

Title: _____

Author: _____

Copyright Date & Holder: _____

Permission Granted by: _____ Date: _____

Acknowledgement to read: _____

Publication Your Material is to be Reprinted in:

Newsletter Name: _____

Publisher: _____

Address: _____
_____

Phone #: _____

Contact: _____

Thank you for your prompt response.

Reprint form. You can design a form that's strictly for reprinting articles. A form like this may be less intimidating than the copyright release form (shown on page 144).

Syndicated Newsletters Save Time & Money

You may not need to generate all original content. A syndicated newsletter or syndicated content may be available for your industry.

Syndicated (or franchised) newsletters are mass-produced for specific markets. Common users are doctors, banks, chiropractors and accountants. These organizations buy newsletters pre-written by someone else. The same newsletter is sold to other organizations in other areas of the country.

Most syndicated newsletter companies offer their clients exclusivity within zip code areas, in order to eliminate the possibility of competitors sending the same publication to identical prospects. Many of these services also make customization possible by leaving space on the front or back cover for clients to print their names and their pictures.

You may have already received promotional material from a syndicated newsletter supplier. If not, check with the national headquarters of your professional association. The research department should have names of syndicated newsletters for your industry. Many professional associations have entered the syndicated newsletter field. For example, the American Academy of Ophthalmology offers members a publication called *Your Vision*. Magazine publishers have jumped on the bandwagon, too. For instance, Practical Accountant magazine offers *Client's Monthly Alert*.

Motorcycle Madness

Say you're writing an article for a travel agency newsletter about touring by motorcycle. You've noticed more older people on motorcycles and wonder if it's a trend. Call the public relations department of Harley-Davidson or Honda to see if they have statistics on their buyers. You might also call Cycle magazine to see if they have information or visit a local motorcycle dealer.

Pros and Cons of Syndicated Newsletters

There are several advantages to using a syndicated newsletter service. First, you can produce a quality product without having any editorial and design experience. Second, it saves you the time you would have had to spend researching, writing, editing and producing a newsletter. The overall cost is usually lower, because syndicated newsletters benefit from the economy of larger print runs. They can also spread out editorial and production costs.

On the other hand, there are some important advantages to producing the newsletter yourself. Your own publication has more of a personal touch. You have complete control of the content and can better match the newsletter to your current marketing goals and your client profile. By self-publishing, you can also set your own schedule and change the size, length or graphic design to fit your needs.

An alternative is to combine the benefits of syndicated newsletters with those of self-publishing. You can use a syndicated newsletter but personalize it by enclosing a note. You might include an insert page of news unique to your organization and clients. When you do this, try to match the graphic "feel," so the publication appears to come from a single source.

Often, syndicated news services will customize a version of their standard newsletter for you. They can include an article submitted by you targeting your specific readers. Or they may let you purchase the articles alone and use them in your own newsletter.

Franchising Your Own Newsletter

If you decide to publish your own newsletter, you may want to consider franchising it; you can sell it to businesses similar to yours in other areas. This is how many syndicated newsletters get started. Since you're already going through the steps of publishing your own newsletter, your organization may want to turn it into a profit-generating venture.

A bookstore owner has done this with her newsletter. Now, in addition to her store, she operates Book News Publications. She publishes four issues per year of *BookNews* and *Kids' Line*. Over 70 other bookstores buy her publications.

Front page customized for T&W Corporation.

Front page customized for Vinyard Construction.

Standard inside spread filled with business and construction related news along with humorous tidbits.

Subcontract your newsletter construction. The Construction Break, a syndicated newsletter offered to contractors by David Wood, contains a customized front and back page and a stock inside spread. This way, the contractors get to show their work while benefiting from two pages of pre-written material, lower printing prices and higher paper and design quality.

Resource: David Wood, Weare, NH; (800) HEY-WOODY; woody@wordsfromwoody.com

Readers Send in the Content

See more on finding volunteer contributors on page 58.

Solicit articles from vendors, customers, members and industry experts. Just make sure they're of strong interest to your readers and that they satisfy the goals of your publication.

To generate interest, publish open invitations for contributors in your newsletter or news broadcast. Write an explanation of how to submit an article, and place it in the masthead or elsewhere in the newsletter. Something like "Contributions welcome" will do.

The only potential problem with accepting contributions is that you often encounter bad writers. And it's often the case that writers without much experience or skill are the most sensitive when their article is rewritten, cut or rejected. (It's no accident that good writers are interested in how you changed or improved their writing.) Avoid offending contributors by calling them and discussing your policy of editing articles to fit the tone of your publication and the space available.

If you regularly include articles on clients and members, solicit information in advance. Send out letters to all of your readers requesting information on their organizations. This gives everyone an equal opportunity to appear in the newsletter. It also provides you with a response to any charges of favoritism.

Soliciting information accelerates you into the sifting stage. Sort through the information you receive, and choose the most interesting items. Contact the organizations to collect further data and set up interviews.

We need Alumni Personals!

Use this handy form to send us news about you and yours ! The item(s) will be printed in the next issue of the Newsletter. We Promise!

To Susan Mullin Toutant
10200 Statia Lynn Court
Louisville, Ky 40223

Here's a news item about _____
_____
_____
Class of _____
_____
_____
_____
_____
_____
_____
_____
Interested in becoming a Class Represenative? _____

© Speed Scientific School, Univ. of Louisville

Contribution form. You can design a standard contribution form for each newsletter. An alumni publication uses this to gather information from members.

QUICK and EASY NEWSLETTERS

*This form is **reporter.pdf** on the CD.*

Reporter Form

Newsletter: _____

Issue/Date: _____

Reporter Name: _____

Phone #: _____

Story Idea or Title: _____

_____

Who is involved/invited: _____

What is the event: _____

When did it (will it) happen: _____

Where: _____

Why did it (will it) happen: _____

How did it happen: _____

Other details: _____

Other people to contact: _____

From **Quick & Easy Newsletters**, by Elaine Floyd. www.newsletterinfo.com and www.paperdirect.com

Roving reporters. The best method for encouraging contributions is to make it as painless as possible (i.e. no writing involved) with a reporter form.

While it's important to use the news of others, don't forget to use your own organization's press releases. If public relations is handled in a department different from your own, ask to be added to the media list. This not only saves writing time, it adds continuity to your marketing and public relations efforts.

Show Your Stuff to Contributors

When soliciting information from other people, send along a copy of your newsletter (or a sample sketch if it doesn't yet exist). This gives the writer a better understanding of what you're looking for. Provide a maximum word count so their material will fit the allocated space.

Automation Tip

Ask for all submissions via e-mail or on disk. This makes editing go much faster.

The Idea File Saves Back-Tracking

As you're thinking about each newsletter (or even between issues), you'll uncover information for future issues. Other times, you may have "spillover" information that didn't fit into the current publication.

Safely store backlog information, along with all necessary reference notes, in an "idea file." Set up an "idea directory" on your computer for e-mails and Web sites. Create a paper file or binder for printed pieces that cross your desk. Binders are particularly helpful for noting and tracking thoughts that surface in editorial board meetings.

Your stash of ideas is not only helpful for the next issue, it can also save you during disasters. In case an article isn't ready at deadline, something in your idea file can fill the gap. Try to keep an up-to-date, safety net article on hand.

Government Property & Other Information

The government is actively involved in gathering a variety of information. Before you embark on a long research project, see if the information is already available from a government office. Call, write or visit the Web site of the Government Printing Office in Washington, D.C. for more information.

You can also swap information with other newsletter publishers. Although this is more common among nonprofit organizations, you may find a willing editor in your industry.

Secrets to Successful Interviews

Undoubtedly, the best source for unique and timely information is interviews. Use interviews:

- ❑ for a place to start
- ❑ for one quote
- ❑ to write an industry roundup
- ❑ to write a customer feature
- ❑ for quotes for a new product announcement

Fresh Ideas

Having current information in your idea file is often a challenge. Some industries, such as medical, computer and insurance, change rapidly. If an article is more than six months old, it's out-of-date.

Tip: Verify Spellings

Remember, even Smith has variations. Misprinted names and titles are embarrassing.

Interviews add credibility and "newsworthiness" to the information in your newsletter articles. They keep your newsletter fresh by injecting other people's voices into your writing. Sometimes this other voice can be used to inject blatant sales pitches that would otherwise reduce the credibility of your article. For example, you can quote your sales manager as saying a product is the "best" or "fastest," but you shouldn't write these superlatives as regular news copy.

Interviews also give a spark of humanity to your story. They can transform a story about anything—a building, a product, a system—into a story about *people*. Most readers find it more interesting to read about people than things.

Good interviews don't just happen. They require work before, during and after the actual conversation.

Before: Preparing for the Interview

Preparation is the best insurance policy you can have for a successful interview. If you only have a quick question to ask, just pick up the phone and call or send a quick e-mail. If you're writing an entire article about someone, arrange an interview.

To prepare for an interview:

- ❑ Arrange an appointment, even if the interview is held over the phone. Let the person know the focus of your article and how much time it will take.

- ❑ Do your homework before the interview. Request background materials, such as brochures or press kits. Visit the company's Web site. Reflect this knowledge in the questions you create.

- ❑ If you want to bring a camera to the interview, ask first. The interviewee may want to dress for the occasion or may need to request permission from a supervisor.

- ❑ Ask yourself, "What is the focus?" "What do readers want to know?" "How and where in the article will quotes be used?"

- ❑ Draft a list of questions. Strive for precise, lively questions. These will solicit the best responses.

Slammed for Not Doing Homework

"I was interviewing the national marketing director of a Fortune 500 company. The interview never got off the ground. I used the same format as I had for smaller companies. I asked the easiest questions first, trying to put him at ease. He became progressively angry. He finally told me to contact the PR department for this basic information. He didn't have time. He said not to call back until I'd done my homework."

—An Anonymous Editor

During: Listen, Listen, Listen

The first few minutes are the most critical. It's your job to set the person at ease. Smile—even if you're on the phone. People can "hear" a smile through your conversational tone of voice. If interviewing in person, don't take out your notebook right away. Once the person begins to smile or laugh, the interview will flow more easily.

Before you start, ask if the person has any questions about your article or publication. Some people need the reassurance that they'll be able to see a copy of the article before it is printed.

Start with easy questions to establish a rapport and get the person to relax. The exception to this is when you're interviewing someone who's extremely busy. In that case, cut right to the important questions, and get the more basic information from their assistants.

Once you've dispensed with the chitchat and moved on to the meatier questions, listen carefully to what is being said. The only way to uncover the human element for your story is to be genuinely interested. You never know what you're going to learn... and that's the thrill of the hunt. Let a response lead you into new territory. Also, if something comes up that you don't understand, ask, "Can you help me find the words and terms our readers would understand?"

Some people are quite reticent and will require some sparring—approaching the same subject from several different angles—before you get the information you need. Be pleasant, yet persistent. Come back to the important questions several times.

Probe for human interest items. Search for tension, drama and opposing forces. Conflicts and resolutions or problems and solutions make an article come alive.

At the conclusion of the interview, keep your ears open. Key information often emerges once you've shut off the tape recorder or put away the note pad. Write any final quotes down quickly once you're back in your car or in the elevator.

Interview Questions to Consider

1. Who are your heroes?

2. If you could have lunch with anyone (from the present or past) who would it be?

3. What would you be doing if I weren't here?

4. What is your typical day like?

5. What is the one question you've never been asked that you'd like to be asked?

6. What is the one thing that irritates you most?

7. What motivates you?

8. If you were me, what would you ask?

9. What kind of books do you like to read?

10. What was the last book you read?

After: Work While It's Fresh

After the interview is over, fill in your notes immediately. It's easy to forget many of the interview's details once a few days go by. For telephone interviews, either type or handwrite your notes. Develop your own system of abbreviations, especially for terms common to your industry.

If you're concerned about catching all of the person's quotes, find out if it's okay to tape the interview. If you do use a tape recorder, take notes as well; this will give you a place to write down a follow-up question while the person continues to talk.

Also, be sure to set the counter on the recorder to "0" before-hand. When the person says something you know you'll use, jot down where on the tape the quote occurs. This saves you from listening to the entire tape. Assure the person being taped that no one will hear the tape but you.

When you start to write the article, you'll often think of additional questions. If this happens, make a quick call or send a quick e-mail.

Once the article is written, send a copy for approval to the interviewee or his or her company. Usually, people won't make extensive changes, but they invariably find would-be-embarrassing mistakes, such as misspelled names or incorrect phone numbers.

To assure future cooperation, follow up with a thank-you note and extra copies of the newsletter. If a company is profiled in a newsletter, they will often want extra copies for promotional purposes.

Remember that even Barbara Walters has bad interviews. Regardless of how well prepared or friendly you are, you'll eventually experience an interview that just doesn't work. Take heart. Interviewing is like writing—the more you practice, the better you'll become.

Top 5 Interviewing Etiquette No-Nos

❑ discussing your own opinions

❑ lack of homework

❑ imposing on someone else's space

❑ overextending your stay

❑ failure to follow up with copies of publication

❑ not sending a thank-you note

Sifting With a Promotional Screen

Uncover all the information you have time to find, which is usually two to three times the information you actually need. Then you're ready to sift. The article you ultimately write should be packed with information aimed at your specific audience. In order to pack your article tightly, you need to extract the essence. And in order to customize it to your audience, you need a promotional filter.

The way you achieve this conciseness is independent of writing style. Before you sit down to write, pull out all the facts and quotes from the information you've gathered. List them all on one sheet of paper; then rank the items on the list in order of interest to your reader. Since not all your gems will fit, be prepared to leave some behind.

Study the top items and see how your promotional material relates to it. Choose the focus of the article based on your promotional objectives. How do you want your readers to react after reading the article? Do you want to inspire them to request more information, volunteer, donate or buy? Or do you simply want to leave them knowing more about your products and services than they did before?

If the organization of the article immediately takes shape and you catch yourself starting to write, go ahead. Otherwise, take care to transcribe all of your notes into legible form and (assuming you have a bit of time) set them aside for a day or two.

Let Your Subconscious Do the Writing

With a bit of time, you can clear your thoughts and put your facts in order—and clear thinking becomes clear writing. Often, ideas will come to you when you're not working on the article. Many writers get their "ah-ha" moments in the shower, while driving or during a jog.

It's important to identify the difference between giving an article some time and procrastinating. If you're under a tight deadline and you're waiting, then, yes, it's procrastinating. But if you have time, letting an article rest usually results in a better article with less writing time.

Sidepage:

Pros & Cons of Recorders

Some reporters swear by tape recorders, while others swear at them and prefer note-taking. Others use a combination of both. Here are some pros and cons of recorders.

Pros:

- ❑ less distracting than note-taking
- ❑ lets you maintain eye contact
- ❑ keeps up with the conversation
- ❑ everything is recorded
- ❑ you can use it at night, in a car, while walking, etc.
- ❑ you're free to jot down notes for follow-up questions

Cons:

- ❑ can malfunction
- ❑ makes some people uneasy
- ❑ requires more time to compose notes

Tips for recorders:

- ❑ avoid 120 minute tapes—they are too thin
- ❑ make sure sprockets are turning
- ❑ carry spare batteries
- ❑ bring a backup recorder
- ❑ remove the tape immediately and label it
- ❑ check for background noise (computers, voices)
- ❑ ask for spelling of names

Save Follow-up Time

If you interview several people per issue, keep their names and addresses together on a separate sheet of paper. Once your newsletter is printed, you'll have this to refer to, rather than having to dig through your notes.

As your deadline approaches, sit down in a quiet room at your computer or with a sharpened pencil and start writing your news. Good writing comes from uncovering interesting information and truly being excited about sharing it with other people.

Creativity Warm-Up

Newsletter editors must strike a balance between strict organization and creativity. The following tips are especially helpful when you're on a very tight schedule.

- ❑ Start with a clean slate—remove any bias or pre-existing ideas of what you should do.
- ❑ Pretend you have all the time in the world.
- ❑ Think in terms of solutions, not problems.
- ❑ Have fun.
- ❑ Develop actions or images of things from key words.
- ❑ Dream up as many ideas as you can.
- ❑ Doodle.
- ❑ Think of features and benefits of your products that appeal to sight, smell, taste, sound, touch.
- ❑ Take a break and come back later.
- ❑ Think about the project last thing at night.
- ❑ Write down several ideas early in the morning.
- ❑ Bounce ideas off of other people.
- ❑ Role-play, with one person playing your prospect.

POE'S COUSIN, MOE

Once upon a midnight dreary,
While I pondered weak and...
sorry... merry... furry... ferry... weedy...
weenie... wheezy... really... reeky...
wacky... tacky... sake... sappy...

Chapter 10:

Writing Newsletter Copy That Sings

Every word in your newsletter should be designed to capture and keep your reader's attention. As a writer, your challenge is to minimize the distance between you and your readers until you're acting as their personal guide.

When writing, you must work backwards in this order:

❑ decide what action you want readers to take as a result of reading the article

❑ list the benefits that readers will receive by reading your news item

❑ give readers the specific information they need to make a purchasing decision

❑ catch the skimmers by relaying your promotional points through the headline, link name, leading sentence, photograph captions, pull quotes, kickers and subheads

❑ write the body of the article in news style

❑ carefully word your contents box or front/back page teasers to convince readers to open the publication

This chapter is dedicated to promotional writing that achieves all four levels of NEWS—name, enticement, written words and sell.

No Free Lunch

If you're providing free information to readers, try to solicit at least one piece of information back from them that you can use to understand your prospects better.

The Most Important Writing You Do

The seven key writing areas in marketing-style newsletters are:

1. headlines
2. the first sentence
3. kickers
4. contents boxes
5. subheads
6. photo captions
7. names for Web site links

Look for attention-getting benefits when deciding what to place in these areas. When your newsletter is finished, test it for "marketing through skimming." Do the key areas include the most promotional messages of the newsletter? Do the key areas contain the most important items?

Ideas for Free Offers

❑ special reports or white papers
❑ T-shirts, mugs, pens or other premiums
❑ consultations
❑ critiques or evaluations
❑ special pricing or discounts
❑ money-saving coupons
❑ samples
❑ seminars
❑ demonstrations

Start With the Desired Response

When organizing any article for your newsletter, think first about what you want readers to do or know after reading. Then carefully consider what you'll need to tell readers in order to initiate this response. Try some of the following selling techniques:

❑ give the benefits of purchasing or participating
❑ summarize the offer
❑ reduce risk with guarantees or warranties
❑ discuss options for payment plans
❑ explain your after-the-sale technical support
❑ show why the product is a good value
❑ show how your products solve problems
❑ show your product in use
❑ support claims with quotes from customers
❑ compare your products to competing ones
❑ suggest cost-saving replacements
❑ show or link to the technical features and capabilities
❑ give information on how to choose the right product
❑ give deadlines to offers and other incentives
❑ include phone numbers, contact names, reply cards

Ask yourself, "What do I hope readers will do after reading this article?" Include your desired response in the article and in the skimmers' spots. The conclusion of your articles should repeat what to do—order today, write your legislator, come to the meeting.

Remember that few people read newsletters from cover to cover. Most people pick them up and "skim." Skimmers read the headlines, subheads, captions and first sentences, looking to see if they want to take the time to read the article.

These skimmer areas should contain the bulk of your sales message. They should also entice the reader into the article by summarizing the main ideas, concepts or feelings presented in the article.

Headlines Bring Your News to Life

Good headlines give your newsletter an edge over competing publications. In fact, more than five times as many people read headlines as read the articles. So, make sure to write each line for maximum impact.

All headlines should focus on your readers—telling them the article has some benefit to them. You can even use a direct mail trick and offer a benefit in the headline: "17 Ways to Improve Your Business," or "Save 50% by Using New Packaging."

A headline can contain a benefit, an unusual statement or twisted cliché, set up a problem/solution format or call out to only one segment of your readers. A feature's headline can also be a quote from one of the interviewees.

The following checklist is helpful when writing headlines.

Headlines need verbs. Verbless headlines are called *standing heads, label heads* or, my favorite, *deadheads*. These are fine for use as kickers but headlines need more.

Activate your voice. The dynamic active voice saves words. *Acme Helps Customer* versus *Customer is Helped by Acme.*

Ad Headlines

Here are advertising great John Caples' rules for writing great ad headlines.

1. Work reader's self-interest into the headline whenever possible. Suggest that the article contains something the reader wants.

2. Work any announcement of news into the headline with key words like "new," "announcing."

3. Avoid cute or clever headlines. Curiosity alone isn't enough to create a winning headline.

4. Avoid negative presentation of the headline. Use positive points.

5. Tell how your article shows an easy path for achieving its promise.

Resource: Tested Advertising Methods by John Caples. Prentice-Hall, Englewood Cliffs, NJ.

Write in the present. Write *Acme Announces* rather than *Acme Announced*.

Use short, pithy words. Use short synonyms for long words. *Panel* or *group* will fit better into a headline than *committee*.

Try numbers. *The One Minute Manager* is the title of a book that was remarkably successful.

Include benefits. *Quick Tips to Reduce Your Chances of Cancer* includes the benefit words *quick* and *tips*. These words tell readers they'll get fast, condensed information.

Avoid "to be" verbs. Headline writers delete helping verbs such as is and are. This omission saves space and punches up the headline. *Physicians Asked to Staff Clinic* omits the verb *are*.

Avoid confusing line divisions. Don't divide hyphenated words or words that go together from one line to the next.

Omit articles. Generally, the articles *a, an* and *the* are omitted to improve action and to save space.

Avoid exclamation points! Replace exclamation points with strong, accurate verbs.

Limit punctuation. Avoid periods (they bring the eye to a stop). Use commas sparingly, although you can use commas in place of the word *and*.

Watch for overuse of your name. If every headline begins with your company or product name, the headline won't tell readers that you offer benefits to reading the article. Instead, they say, "These articles are written from our point of view." That's not the message you want to convey in your promotional newsletter.

Kickers Jump Start Headlines

A kicker is a line run in smaller type above the headline. It helps keep the headline shorter. A kicker is often used for regular features, such as editorials, technical support tips, newsbriefs or updates. Kickers give the writer the freedom to write a new

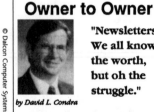

Owner to Owner

"How do we get the numbers we need?"

by David L. Condra

© Dalcon Computer Systems

Owner to Owner

"Newsletters. We all know the worth, but oh the struggle."

by David L. Condra

© Dalcon Computer Systems

Avoiding the dreaded "President's Message." The president of a computer dealership wrote an article for each of the company's newsletters. Every issue, he would choose a subject he thought was of interest to other business owners. The headlines are above in quotation marks.

headline for standing columns in each issue, rather than using the same headline every time.

In e-mail newsletters, kickers are used for readers to find articles when scrolling from a contents box to the actual article.

Kickers can also be used to target your readers. For example, an article's headline might be *Save On All Pet Supplies* with a kicker that reads "Cat owners."

Decks as Headline Extenders

To avoid long headlines in print and Web site newsletters, consider a deck—a few lines of description placed underneath the headline. Decks can be used to give the reader more information about the article or to attract attention. An effective deck guides readers into the rest of the article before they know it.

Use decks to:

- ❑ give people more information about the article
- ❑ set a scene
- ❑ warm up readers for a launch right into the article

LETTER FROM THE PRESIDENT

Before

EXECUTIVE UPDATE

New Marketing Strategy Ready for Launch

Changing industry calls for changing companies. Here are some of the changes you'll be seeing...

After

Skimming through the headlines. Notice how much more information you learn by skimming the second kicker/headline/deck combination than the first "deadhead."

Subheads Net in Skimmers

After you write the headline, look at the other promotional points in your article and use them as subheads. Subheads are used to divide lengthy articles into logical breaks. They may indicate to the reader a change of topic or a link of content, or simply break up a mass of type.

Place subheads about every four paragraphs, to allow readers to skip sections of the article without losing their train of thought. Subheads are especially important in Web site articles. Reading on the screen is much harder on the eyes. Subheads provide a welcome relief.

Most importantly, subheads include your top promotional points. By skimming the headline, lead and subheads, your readers can understand your main sales points in a few seconds.

Reading can be a good experience. The white space that subheads and short paragraphs create makes reading easier.

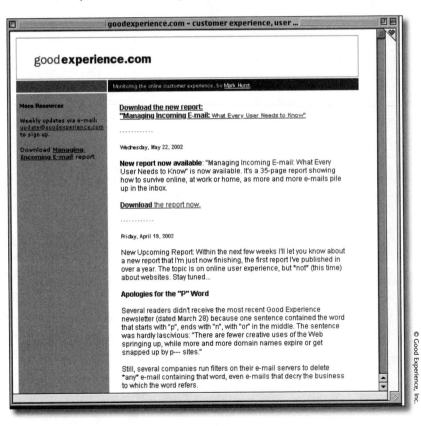

Sidepage:

Headlines That Sell

If you're still a bit skeptical on just how much a good head-line influences readership, look at how a mail order company increased sales of its books by finding the right title.

Fleece of Gold	6,000
The Quest for a Blonde Mistress	50,000
Honey and Gall	0
Studies in Mystic Materialism	15,000
Cupbearers of Wine and Hellbore	0
A Book of Intellectual Rowdies	11,000
Art of Controversy	0
How to Argue Logically	30,000
Casanova and His Loves	8,000
Casanova, History's Greatest Lover	28,000
Markheim	0
Markheim's Murder	7,000
The Man Who Apes Nobility	0
The Show-Off	10,000
The Sonnets of a Portrait Painter	0
The Love Sonnets of an Artist	6,000

Source: The First 100 Million by E. Haldeman-Julius; Simon and Schuster (1928).

Captions Draw from Photo Appeal

Captions (also called *cutlines*) are the descriptive text placed under, over, or next to a photo in a print newsletter. Because most people first glance at the illustrations on a page, captions are a promotional opportunity you should never pass up.

Include information that makes people want to read the accompanying article. Try these tips:

- ❑ include information that entices readers
- ❑ include promotional information if you can work it in
- ❑ leave out obvious information that the photograph includes
- ❑ identify people and settings

© Atlantis Pools

Atlantis Pools offers both pre-designed pools and spas as well as unique designs for you and your yard. The pool above was designed using Arkansas stone for the deck, walk-up steps and waterfall.

Capturing captions. While a photograph can capture the attention of your reader, the caption sells your idea. A pool installation company shows one of its pool designs in each issue. Every photo includes a caption describing the design along with its benefits.

© Roadster Factory

"Do you want to trust the safety of your friends and family to a brake part that is a dollar cheaper?"

Drive-by information. This pull quote from an auto parts Web site newsletter contains the most promotional point of the article in a way that's also interesting to readers.

Magnetize the Eyes With Pull Quotes

Pull quotes (also called *callouts*, *lift-out quotes* or *outquotes*) are sentences taken from the article. They add life to a page or screen, while providing a juicy excerpt from the article that pulls readers in. Pull quotes are also used as a layout device to break up type and add white space.

Choose a sentence or phrase that:

- ❑ stands alone
- ❑ holds its meaning out of context
- ❑ is an interesting point
- ❑ is the most promotional point

Teasing Readers to Open Your Newsletter

Once all of your articles are written, return to the subjects and motivating words you chose to promote specifics. Use these words for the teasers and contents box that readers see first when looking at the mailing area of a print newsletter, the top of the screen of an e-mail newsletter or the main page of a Web site newsletter.

The contents box should encourage readers to open the publication or continue reading or scrolling. Use teasers to:

❑ Attract attention or capture the readers you desire. If you want tax clients, write, "Important Tax Information Enclosed." If you're promoting to retailers, exclaim, "Important News For Retailers." Of course, you must make sure you have covered these subjects inside.

❑ Describe your feature articles by telling readers the benefits of reading them.

❑ Give the headlines of your newsletter articles. This makes it easier for readers to find the articles they want.

Guiding Readers to the Reply Card

Refer readers to a reply card or reply screen or form if it's one of your desired responses. Reply cards and forms give readers an opportunity to tell you they're interested by requesting more information, a demonstration, a phone call, a sales visit.

When writing the copy for the card or form:

❑ Make your offer something of value, something that people want or think is really interesting. Convince readers to send it in or submit it. Place this offer in a benefit-oriented headline and refer to the reply form within the editorial of the newsletter. "Yes! I want to learn more about planning for a comfortable retirement. Send information about your retirement fund."

❑ Give the offer a deadline. Because you don't want to be sending out your freebie for years to come or having to print more when you run out, print a deadline on the offer or state, "while quantities last."

Fund Raising Reply Cards

For donations, the reply card should repeat again why the donation is important. "I agree that my support is necessary to help the individuals who need hope in order to become self-sufficient."

See reply card examples on pages 24 and 223-225.

Most Popular Sections in Newsletters

Industry news—write solid, condensed summaries of the happenings in your industry. Collect information from a variety of magazines and Web sites and distill only the best, most interesting into newsbriefs.

Inside information—include privileged insider tips on what's happening either in the company, to the technology or around the industry.

Honest, hard-hitting editorials—avoid weak "letters from the president." Good editorials are interpretations of what's happening in the industry.

Cartoons, humor or inspiration—give your readers a good laugh or tips for success.

People—include news of respected and interesting people in the industry.

❑ Urge readers to respond immediately. "Take advantage of this special offer. Mail today!" For more action, call it a response card instead of a reply card.

❑ Solicit some information that allows you to qualify leads. Ask readers if they want to stay on the list. Ask them how they intend to use your product, when they plan to buy or what products they are currently using.

❑ Include your telephone number, in case the reader wants take immediate action.

❑ Include your fax number and encourage readers to fax back the card.

Subjects That Attract Attention

It's important to match the right article subject to the desired reader action. Some subjects always attract readers; for example, surveys. "We recently *surveyed* customers and asked questions about their future plans. This is what they said..." Readers' ears will immediately perk up. Giving the answers to common questions will generate a similar response.

How to save money is another universal desire. For example, almost everyone would be interested in "How to Save Money on Car Insurance."

Studies show that the 16 most promotional words are:

❑ you/your
❑ love
❑ free
❑ fun
❑ money
❑ save
❑ results
❑ new

❑ health
❑ easy
❑ proven
❑ safe
❑ guarantee
❑ benefit
❑ how to
❑ now

Without becoming excessive, you should work these words into your article headlines and e-mail subject lines.

Writing in Lean, Mean Newsletter Style

Brevity is paramount in news writing—in both a physical and a psychological sense. Newsletters are physically shorter than most publications. The brevity of newsletters leaves readers feeling that they have gained maximum information in a minimum amount of time. Busy people like this pace.

However, just because your publication looks like a newsletter doesn't automatically ensure you'll achieve this brevity. You have to work at it.

Here are several writing methods used to pack an article full of information:

- ❑ include as much of the story as possible in the headline, and don't repeat it in the first paragraph
- ❑ use a short paragraph to begin the story
- ❑ plunge right into the subject in the lead sentence
- ❑ use short paragraphs throughout your articles to add white space to the page or screen and make it look inviting

> ### Appeal to Emotions
>
> If you're trying to tell potential donors about the plight of the homeless, show people's discomfort to generate donations. Show the urgency for donor's help by appealing to their emotions.

Part of an article's fast pace will come from the sifting you do before writing. Then, after the first draft is completed, go back and tighten the writing even further.

Cut extraneous words and shorten sentences.

- ❑ **Use pronouns and abbreviations**. In a second reference, "personal computer" shortens to "PC," "Wallingford B. Smith" becomes "he," and the "University of California at Irvine" reduces to "UCI," "the university" or "it."
- ❑ **Look for single words to replace phrases**. Use "now" in place of "at the present time." Replace "in order to" with "to."
- ❑ **Don't repeat quoted information**. If you have quotes in your articles, check to see if information is repeated or summarized outside the quote. If it is, cut the information outside the quote.

Technology That Speeds Up Writing

Use your computer for all steps of production.

When writing:

❑ take notes and transcribe interviews directly into the computer

❑ use grammar and spell checkers as a preliminary check

❑ use optical character readers to input articles that are in print only

❑ ask contributors to submit articles via e-mail

❑ **Separate out details into a sidebar**. To keep the pace of your article from becoming bogged down, separate detailed facts from the body of the article by putting them into ruled boxes called *sidebars*. The Web site and e-mail equivalent of a sidebar is a linked page.

❑ **Condense information**. Pack articles full of details. If there is not enough information on a topic, either try to find additional sources, or hold the story for another issue while information is being collected.

News style is used in the three main writing formats for marketing newsletters—straight news reporting, feature and editorial.

Straight News Reporting

The news format is used for announcements, for reporting on trends, and for new product and service introductions. There is a set format for news writing that's taught in journalism school. For promotional newsletters, you must modify this formula to assure that you write in an interesting way. Here's why.

News articles are usually written using an inverted pyramid format. The inverted pyramid is a method of organization used by newspapers in which the answers to the questions who, what, where, when, why and how are given first. It has its roots in the American Civil War when reporters filing stories by telegraph knew that the lines might be cut at any point during the transmission.

A true news story starts with the climax, with details following in diminishing order of importance until all the elaborating facts have been given. The story finally ends with the least significant information in the last paragraph. Thus, an article may be shortened from the end without losing much.

What's wrong with this?

First, if you answer questions in the order of who, what, where, when, why, and how, you're probably going to start with who. Most likely this will be your organization. Right away you're writing from your interest, not your readers'.

Here's what happens when you do this:

Before: **Northern Announces New Phone System**

Northern Telecom is currently offering a professional time-tracking package for the Meridian Norstar Key Telephone System. The time-management software is designed for attorneys, architects and advertising agencies. Professionals who bill their time can productively manage and record their client activities—right from their office phone.

This first paragraph includes who, when, what, why and how. The article ends with a detailed list of features. But it would have been better to use the news format as a guideline only. For example, in a new product introduction, first tell for whom the product was designed and why it is used. Try to use a catchy lead to do this. Think of your customers.

After: **Money in the Bank as Close as Your Phone**

Professionals guard their time like banks guard their vaults. Successful consultants, attorneys, architects and advertising agencies know that productive use of time is money in the bank.

Northern Telecom knows it, too. That's why the time-tracking package for the Meridian Norstar Key Telephone System is being offered to professional customers. Using time-management software, people who bill their time can productively manage and record their client activities—right from their office phone.

Even in news articles, storytelling is important. For example, you can add a human element to the strictest of news formats by quoting someone, such as your president or a user of the product. The example above could include a quote from an attorney who's tried the product. "The first month I used the system, I billed 10 additional hours that I would have forgotten. The software more than paid for itself right then."

Writing Up Interviews

When writing features that center around an interview, follow a few guidelines:

❑ select the best quotes

❑ paraphrase and condense other thoughts within the text of the article

❑ present the opinions and thoughts of the interviewee accurately

❑ rearrange the order of quotes only if they don't change in meaning by doing so

❑ avoid writing up interviews in question and answer style

❑ mix quotes with narration and background details

Quotes are also important when you report on industry trends. One organization discovered this in the third year of producing its newsletter. The biggest response it had ever received was from an article that was comprised of interviews about an industry trend. Interviewing different sources for your articles allows you to "report" on a general consensus.

Write in traditional news style to announce new products and other timely events. Include who, what, why, where, when and how, but modify this to:

❑ start with the most important information
❑ give detail in order of diminishing importance
❑ make sure the "who" is your customer first, and you second
❑ organize from your customer's point of view
❑ include a good lead before launching into the facts
❑ work in lively quotes
❑ tell "why" early on

Features Show Your Products & Services in Action

Once new products and services have been announced, they lose their "newsworthiness." Feature articles allow you to reiterate your product and services by having other people talk about you. They can also include news of everyday (or unusual) applications of your products.

Write in a feature style for articles on clients, case histories, unusual applications for products, educational information and inspirational stories of people. The feature style:

❑ captures and holds readers' attention
❑ contains a good lead
❑ weaves interesting facts throughout the article
❑ develops and supports themes
❑ ends with a strong, memorable conclusion
❑ includes quotes from interviews
❑ often concludes with a quote

The style of features encourages promotional writing. In well-written features, there is an initial point of contact that is sharp, quick and obvious. A light opening follows to grab the reader's interest. This could be an incident, an anecdote or a conversation. Finally the bulk of the story includes a description and facts. The last paragraph usually concludes the article by repeating the theme. This style is the opposite of the inverted pyramid news style, in which the facts are presented first and there is no need for a summary.

When you write features, think of a strawberry packer. Tell the story with sustained interest. Place a layer of good berries on the top, but save the best berries for readers to see when they turn the basket upside down. Give almost as much importance to your last sentence as your lead. Words like "in summary," signal to your reader that you are bored or the article has gone on too long and you don't know how to stop it. Quotes work well for endings. Find one that has a sense of finality, is funny or adds a last surprise.

The hardest part of writing a feature is coming up with a theme and writing the conclusion. By remembering the strawberry packer, you'll know to save an interesting tidbit for last. You'll also use that tidbit to develop the theme for the article. Pack up your berries and come on down to the ranch to see how.

Top Berries:

With a name like RBR Computer Ranch, you'd expect to find this dealer in the outskirts of Dallas or Houston, or at least somewhere west of the Rockies. Well, venture into the "cement ranch" of New York's Manhattan and you'll find RBR nestled on the 4th floor at Fifth Avenue and 20th Street.

Why "Computer Ranch"? "You have to be different," says Jose Ristorucci, president of RBR. "Look at Egghead Software; you remember their name before you'd remember Alpha Omega Software. We thought of Computer Zoo, but that was already taken."

Breaking Habits

One newsletter writer used to joke about her standard "Have you ever wondered?" opening.

She would catch herself starting every article with, "Have you ever looked into your closet and wondered how fabric companies keep track of all the different designs?" or, "Have you ever wondered where all the old movies are kept?"

Since she was aware of her habit, she could go back and modify the formula to give each article a fresh opening.

Bottom Berries:

The technical knowledge and personal approach found at RBR sets them apart from the rest of the herd. "Every customer has a different need," Ristorucci says. "They can come here or we will go to them. Some days we have five or six people in here being trained or looking at software packages."

Ah, life is good down on the ranch.

It's easier to find themes for some articles than others. For an article on a company that uses a computer product to design a flood control system, finding a theme was easy.

Top Berries:

Reliability—Lives Depend On It

Sierra Misco is in the business of telling people that water runs downhill. The trick is to figure out how much water and when it's going to get there. When you're talking about the raging waters of China's Yangtze and Yellow Rivers, that's no small trick.

Bottom Berries:

The systems have to be reliable—people's lives depend on the performance of the equipment.

It's important in an ongoing publication to avoid formula writing. For example, you wouldn't want to start every customer feature with a question. Instead, look for ways to write feature stories in unusual ways. You'll find that some subjects give you the opportunity to write truly unique pieces.

Writing Lively Editorials

Editorials are used to promote your image. They establish the people in your organization as experts. Editorials include letters from the president and opinions on industry trends. They are usually written in first person and are designed to share ideas, opinions and forecasts.

For more information on newsletter writing, see newsletterinfo.com

Signature lines. Sometimes the desired response is placed in what's called a signature line. In most publications, signature lines identify the author of an article. In promotional newsletters, they may also contain information about where to call for more information or where to send orders or donations.

Before you start to yawn, remember that editorials don't have to be boring. One company president adamantly believed layoffs could be avoided and wanted to share his ideas with readers. His editorial on avoiding layoffs began:

> "It was the hardest thing I've ever done. When I looked around at the faces of the nine people I had just called into the conference room, I felt a sharp pain in the pit of my stomach. My voice quavered as I tried to explain why I had to lay them off, but it didn't matter. After my first few strained words, they stopped listening. As far as they were concerned, it was over."

I'm willing to bet you're not yawning, nor will your readers be, if you choose writers who are passionate about specific issues and willing to spend the time necessary to write an interesting editorial.

Good editorials:

- ❑ are written in first person
- ❑ share ideas, opinions and forecasts
- ❑ cover subjects close to the writer's heart

How to Write Elevating Leads

Regardless of the writing format you choose, the first sentence is the most important one in your article. Its job is to pull your readers into the second sentence and beyond.

The opening line of the article is called the *lead*. From your collection of facts, use the most unique, most important or most unusual item you have. Is there a colorful word or dramatic story you can work in? Most articles should include your readers or their immediate interests in the lead. Don't make readers have to work to find the subject.

The lead should be a short paragraph. It can even be as short as one word. Then follow it with a few paragraphs and quickly hit them with a subhead. This gives your story a fast pace.

Write It for Them

Often, you can interview a member of your organization and write an editorial for them. Your job is to encourage them to talk openly to you—not the way they think an editorial should sound. Spend 30 minutes talking to the person. Then take his or her opinions and thoughts and write them in an editorial format. You'll save the person lots of time, and you'll get the editorial you need, written the way you want.

Here are five types of leads:

1. **The benefit lead**—answers the reader's question, "What's in it for me?" "Cut your air conditioning bills in half. No, not with scissors. With the right landscaping."

2. **Direct address**—Sift out your best prospects by speaking directly to them. "Retirement! It's a time of life we all look forward to. Bask in the sun, play golf, attack those projects you've always wanted to."

3. **Problem/solution lead**—Set up the format for a problem/solution article. "Have you ever found yourself at a 'gala' event staring at a piece of boiled chicken, a hard potato and a spoonful of peas while a monotone speaker drones on and on?"

4. **The unusual lead**—Write something odd or unusual to nudge readers to continue out of curiosity. "Although not widely publicized, Mumps has been spreading rapidly in the medical computing community." The article goes on to describe a new software program called *Mumps*.

5. **Narrative**—Set your article in action by describing an event. "When Monica Ball arrived to work Monday morning, she was greeted by the smell of smoke."

Why is the lead so important? The following article from a marketing consultant demonstrates the answer to this question.

The 15-Second Buzzer

Basketball uses the shot clock. In the pros, the offensive team has 24 seconds to take a shot at the basket or face a penalty of turning the ball over to the competition.

In marketing your product or service, a similar clock resides in the minds of prospects. It's the time available for you, the marketer, to attract the prospect's attention and motivate that person to invest more in reviewing your benefits. How much time? It could be as little as 10 to 15 seconds before their mental buzzer sounds, and you lose the prospect.

Can you express your company's advantages to a prospect in 15 seconds? Work with others in your company on your

15-second strategy. The results can point the way to inexpensive adjustments you can make to score higher with new business opportunities.

Keep in mind your 15-second shot clock when writing leads. Use a benefit lead to attract as many readers as possible to your articles. Benefit leads answer the reader's question, "What's in it for me?" and can even be used when writing straight news style articles.

Look at the following examples. The first one is written from the publisher's perspective. The second one is rewritten to include readers during the first few seconds.

> *Before:* **House Prepares to Consider Catastrophic Health Care Plan**
>
> The House of Representatives will soon consider legislation aimed at protecting the nation's elderly from catastrophic health care costs. There are more than 28 million elderly and three million disabled people in the U.S.

> *After:* **Protecting the Nation's Elderly From Catastrophic Care Costs**
>
> Over 28 million elderly people and three million disabled people could be helped by upcoming legislation considered by the House of Representatives.

Not all newsletter articles are written alike. To keep your newsletter fresh, you'll want to include a variety of lead styles.

Check for "You" Versus "We"

Keep in mind that your newsletter is promotional. When appropriate, you should write sentences from the reader's point of view.

A good test to make sure your articles are on target is to check for the use of "you" rather than "we." Using "you" not only gets the reader involved, it also gets you thinking in terms of the reader. Avoid using "we at..." "We at First Financial are proud to announce that…" sounds stuffy. Instead say, "First Financial now provides you with…"

As with headlines, don't begin every article with your company name. Begin them with your readers.

Writing is the Launchpad to Design

As we get ready to launch into design in the next chapter, realize that all of the elements you've learned to write in this chapter are design elements, too. Visualize how they will look in the design and plan for them as you're writing.

Your page designs are affected by:

- ❑ **Paragraph length**. Long paragraphs make pages look uninviting and hard to read. Shorter paragraphs breathe air into a layout. So, when in doubt, hit the return key.
- ❑ **Short lead**. A short lead gives readers a quick piece of information to bite into. A long lead, at a glance, looks like too much work.
- ❑ **Short articles**. The definition of a newsletter is a publication with three or more articles per page. E-mail newsletters should have at least two articles per screenful. Short articles invite readers in by offering the choice of several topics on each page.
- ❑ **Headline capitalization**. Avoid all capital letters in printed newsletters. Use either upper and lower case or downstyle (only the first word is capitalized). On the other hand, all capital letters work well in e-mail newsletters to differentiate the headline from the text.
- ❑ **Kickers and decks**. Keep an all-text page from looking intimidating by providing short snippets with the headline.
- ❑ **Text style**. Use bold and italics in moderation. Avoid underlining.
- ❑ **Sidebars**. Make one article look like two. Statistics, testimonials, research and survey results are good items for sidebars.

Legibility & Readability Affected by Writing

This includes the:

- ❑ amount of type on the page or screen
- ❑ organization of information
- ❑ ease of language
- ❑ average word length

- ❑ **Subheads**. When writing longer articles, provide a pause from the reading marathon with a subhead every three to four paragraphs.

- ❑ **Indent amount**. Use the width of three or four characters. The default in some programs of 1/2" is too deep.

- ❑ **Punctuation**. Use curly quotes (or smart quotes). Space only once after periods. The two spaces is a carryover from typewriter days and isn't needed in typesetting.

Now that you know how to guide your readers through your newsletter using words, let's attract even more readers with graphics, such as photographs, charts, cartoons and illustrations. These are covered in the next chapter.

An online guide. As readers scroll over each of the sections of kidnews.com, the text in the center of the circle changes to describe what the section contains.

Sidepage:

Make a List, Check It Twice

Lists make good news. Look at the ones appearing in the general media: *People* magazine's best and worst dressers, David Letterman's list of top 10, *The New York Times* best-seller list.

These lists are not only publicized in the media that created them, they are picked up by other publications. My local paper's sports section regularly reprints the David Letterman list, for example.

Why They Work So Well

When you glance at a publication and see a list, what does it tell you? Lists say, "organized, summarized, condensed news." They give you knowledge at a glance, time-saving summaries, and funny or interesting information.

Use lists within a newsletter article as a sidebar or as a stand-alone article. Convert instructions listed in paragraph form to lists. List things to do, checklists, packing or content lists.

How to Set Up Your Own

Design them with care. Use tabs that align the type under the words, not the number. To add interest, use boxes (with or without a check mark), numbers, bullets or dingbats (like ☞, ◆ or ❑) that are found on your keyboard under the typefaces Zapf Dingbats or Microsoft Wingdings.

Consider making a list a standard part of your newsletter (just as David Letterman, *People* and *The New York Times* do). Readers will look for it the minute the newsletter lands on their desks. Your list may even get picked up by other publications.

Chapter 11:

The Sales Job of Each Design Element

Your newsletter is comprised of several different design elements. These components direct readers through the publication, making them stop, take a detour or move in a certain direction. Most design elements are produced only once, whether they appear in every issue or only when needed. For example, the nameplate appears on every newsletter. Sidebars and photographs are included only when available or needed.

This chapter shows you how to design each promotional element in your newsletter to have a friendly, approachable image that warms up prospects and supporters and helps you achieve your desired goals. How these elements are combined is covered in the next chapter.

Design for Rapid Recognition

Because readers move through the recognition level at top speed, graphics are important to prompt reader recognition and interest.

This chapter covers printed newsletters. Skip to page 259 for e-mail and 267 for Web.

In this chapter:

- encourage readers to take your news-letter into their hands

- making a good first impression through paper, color and front-page design

- catching skimmers with good graph-ics

- choosing reader-friendly typefaces and formats

- how to graphically encourage readers to respond

- increasing your distribution reach

Most readers see your newsletter as they sort the day's stack of mail, so you must make your newsletter pop out, drawing readers into the publication immediately. Readership declines if the newsletter isn't opened or read right away.

You can also prompt recognition with your organization's logo. Consider using it as part of the design in the following areas. (Note that it may be overkill if you use it in all items on the list.) Use your logo as part of:

❑ the nameplate
❑ the mailing panel
❑ an end mark
❑ the folio
❑ the masthead
❑ a watermark on part of the page
❑ a special imprint (slug) in the postage mark of your meter

A good location, visible signage and accessible parking are important to most businesses. Newsletters have their own prime locations. The following areas are particularly important to the "recognition" level of marketing:

❑ the size
❑ the mailing panel
❑ the front page
❑ the back page

Masthead

Sales Success is published by Newsletter & Co., 222 W. Main St., Newtown, PA 09200. www.nlco.com.

Free subscriptions are available by calling or e-mailing Tim Hunter, (800) 555-1212 or timh@nlco.com

Editor: Jane Jones
Designer: John Smith
Circulation: Tim Hunter

The whatchamacallit. The nameplate is often mistakenly called a "masthead." A masthead is the box of information concerning the publishing, copyright and circulation of the publication.

Thank you for joining! Your membership is good through 8/04.

Pat Cline
123 W. Main St.
Beanstalk, MT 79112

Label design. Remember that people look at their name first. Print your labels with interesting fonts and special messages.

Size—Muscling Through the Mail Stack

Does your newsletter get stacked in with the magazines, fliers, letters, or somewhere in between? Your newsletter's page size and number of folds will determine where it lands in the stack.

The standard page size of most newsletters is 8 1/2 x 11 inches. Standard sizes have the advantages of lower cost, matching standard envelopes and their ability to fit in binders if readers want to save them (and many do).

If you mail a standard size newsletter flat, it falls with the magazines. If you fold it down to 5 1/2 x 8 1/2 inches, it's between the magazines and the letters. And if you fold it like a letter and mail it with or without an envelope, it appears with the letters. Because magazines are set aside for later reading, you should stay away from this size by folding your newsletter for mailing.

Build anticipation.
George Allen stamped the envelope of his newsletter with the message above. After the envelope was sealed, this stamp was printed over the "V" on the flap.

The most attention-getting location of the mail stack is on top with the letters. People pay special attention to this section. They look here for personalized correspondence and checks. Fold your newsletter in thirds to land here.

If your readers enjoy newsletters and look for them in their stack, fold you newsletter the newsletter in half, versus in thirds. You'll have more room on the mailing panel for teasers and other information about the newsletter.

Newsletters are sometimes mailed in envelopes. Some publishers feel it's well worth the expense. Newsletters mailed in envelopes arrive in better condition and look more like official correspondence. In addition, you can add fliers, letters, reply cards and other promotions to the envelope.

Unusual stamps.
Newsletter design trainer Polly Pattison added seasonal appeal to her holiday newsletter with a Santa stamp.

Postcard newsletters have special mail stack advantages. They arrive "pre-opened" and look easy to read. People don't feel like they're reading other people's mail when they read postcards. You can print your news on an oversized postcard with lots of room for your news or enjoy special postcard mailing rates when keeping its size to 4 1/4 x 6 inches.

Directory assistance.
This mailing area from Narrative Strategies includes phone number, a "route to" box and information on the company's editorial services.

Please Don't Staple

When mailing your newsletter, you may be tempted to staple it shut. Don't. Staples irritate your readers, who must find a staple remover, tear up their nails or rip open the newsletter. The post office does not require fastening of loose sheets. In fact, staples scratch postal workers and jam the machines. Often, your newsletters get mangled in the process and end up in a plastic bag.

After all of your hard work, why ruin your promotional punch with a tattered letter? If you need to use a closure to hold in inserts, stickers, wafer seals or tape allow the reader to open the piece without ripping it.

Mailing Areas That Say "Read Me"

Once your newsletter jumps out of the mail stack, the reader glances at the return address and mailing area. They may need another nudge to read it now with a slogan or teaser.

Cancel all meetings!
Newsletter writer David Wood includes this starburst on every envelope containing his Words from Woody. The return address with his caricature sets the mood for this fun-loving newsletter. Note the type size and boldness of the name on the mailing label. This gives readers special recognition.

With few exceptions, every mailing panel should include your:

- ❑ company name and logo
- ❑ return address
- ❑ phone number
- ❑ e-mail address
- ❑ Web site

You should also include one or more of the following sales elements:

- ❑ the newsletter nameplate or logo
- ❑ slogan or specialty
- ❑ fax number
- ❑ masthead
- ❑ "inside this issue" box
- ❑ teasers
- ❑ a short article or newsbrief
- ❑ location map
- ❑ hours of operation (if retail)

Of course, all of this won't fit on the mailing panel if you want to retain a simple, professional-looking design. Choose the elements that are most important for your organization's promotion.

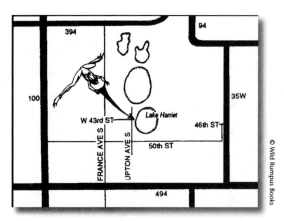

© Wild Rumpus Books

A map to your doorstep. Location maps are important for retailers in highly competitive markets. In fact, the convenience of your location can help make the sale. Wild Rumpus Books prints this map (including its frog mascot) on its newsletter mailing panel.

Enclosed: Your copy of DESKTOP MARKETER, the FREE newsletter for users of MarketPlace Business. **You'll find:**

- Useful tips and shortcuts
- Information about new features
- Stories about innovative MarketPlace users
- And much more...

In this issue: MarketPlace lowers data price!

© MarketPlace Information Corp.

List incentives. These teasers are printed on the mailing panel of Desktop Marketer from D&B Marketplace. They give readers information and incentives to read on.

Nameplate—The Foundation of Your Newsletter's Design

When readers open your newsletter, the first graphic element they see is the nameplate. The nameplate is the stylized representation of your newsletter name, along with other information.

The nameplate is the cornerstone for the design of your newsletter. It's impossible to have a well-designed newsletter without a good nameplate. Conversely, with a good nameplate, the rest of your newsletter design can be simple, and the piece will still look professional. Design your own nameplate only if you have a qualified designer on staff. Otherwise, subcontract this one-time, worthwhile expense.

Readers notice and remember unique nameplate designs. The nameplate is the "you are here" sign. It identifies the publication, your organization, and its products, services or purpose. For readers who are unfamiliar with your organization, the nameplate communicates its purpose or market niche. This is achieved through the name and tagline you choose.

All nameplates include the newsletter's:

- ❑ name
- ❑ tagline
- ❑ dateline

They may also include:

- ❑ illustrations
- ❑ logos
- ❑ volume and number
- ❑ color
- ❑ lines and screens
- ❑ a "route to" box
- ❑ an "inside this issue" listing
- ❑ famous quotes
- ❑ illustrations of highlighted products or articles

Straight to the top. Dalcon Computer Systems uses a mountain in its logo and in some of its marketing. One of its campaigns emphasizes the importance of choosing a mountain-climbing partner you can trust and communicate with. In the newsletter nameplate, a mountain, along with the word "summit," reinforces the ongoing campaign.

Nameplate Design Tips

Do:

- ❑ set the name of newsletter in strong typography
- ❑ enlarge the name until it's the dominant element
- ❑ test to see if you can read the nameplate from 10 feet away (often, the passing along of newsletters is initiated when someone sees the newsletter on someone else's desk)
- ❑ make full use of the horizontal space
- ❑ include black, white and shades of gray
- ❑ place your tagline below the name near the dateline
- ❑ use bold type for the tagline; consider italics, too

Attract attention with:

- ❑ attention-getting colors
- ❑ dynamic shapes
- ❑ dominant sizes
- ❑ tall, dark typography
- ❑ tilted text, lines or visuals
- ❑ drop shadows

Watch for:

- ❑ wimpy typography in the newsletter name
- ❑ poor use of white space
- ❑ more than two pieces of artwork the same size

Design tip: Whatever the final design of your nameplate, a bleed will make it look larger. A bleed is created by printing all the way to the edge of the given space. In the nameplate, that would mean running the color all of the way to the top and right and left sides of the page. Depending on how your printer sets up your newsletter on the press, it may not cost extra to bleed the nameplate.

No Name News

The nameplate usually does not contain:

- ❑ the editor's name
- ❑ the company address and phone number (the exception is retail newsletters)

Nameplate Safety

Store your newsletter layout as a template on a separate disk to avoid unintentional changes. Put your design style sheet in writing in case your system crashes.

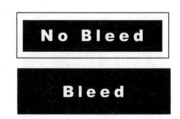

For readers familiar with your organization, one way to prompt recognition is to design your newsletter using your logo and company colors. That way, your newsletter will complement your other publicity pieces, such as Web sites, press kits, promotional packets, catalogs and trade show displays. This adds consistency to all your promotions.

Use of logo. The following promotional nameplates contain the logo of the publisher. Notice how the organizations' logos accent, rather than overpower, the name of the newsletter.

Animal attraction. Consultants can add a bit of spunk by personalizing their newsletters. In addition to Woody's caricature on the nameplate, he also affixes a color sticker of himself and his "staff" on the cover of each newsletter. When he follows up with prospects and describes himself as the guy who sends the newsletter with his dogs' picture on it, everyone says "Oh, yeah."
Resource: Photo Label, Lombard, IL 60148; (800) 323-0776.

Along with identifying the publication and the publisher, the nameplate can be used to communicate your publication schedule. This is done by listing the date in a certain way. Date a monthly "January," a bi-monthly "January/February" and a quarterly "1st Quarter" (or according to the four seasons).

Some newsletters follow a system used by subscription publications and print volumes and numbers along with the date. Volumes and numbers are used primarily by libraries to aid in cataloging publications. They can also indicate to your readers the length of time your publication has been produced. For example, "Volume 3 Number 4" indicates the third year of publishing and the fourth newsletter of that particular year. Use them only if stability and longevity are important to your prospects. If so, add them after your first year of publishing. Since space is at a premium on most nameplate designs, consider putting the volume and number in the masthead.

Once the readers get past the nameplate and into the first article in the newsletter, other design elements start to work. These elements guide readers through the rest of the newsletter.

Nameplate vertigo. The nameplate is usually placed horizontally at the top of the first page. Some organizations, however, place it vertically for an attractive design, as above. If you use a vertical nameplate, make sure it doesn't interfere with the front-page articles.

Bold and beautiful. Effective nameplates are simple and contain only a few elements. The largest of the elements is the type containing the name of the publication. Strong, bold typography is often enough to create an attractive nameplate.

Dash of spice. Sometimes a graphic or photograph is added as an accent to the nameplate. Like logos, graphics should not overpower the type containing the newsletter's name.

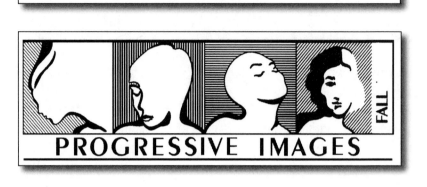

See tips for newsletter names on pages 133-138.

Break out. Unify the nameplate with the rest of the page by placing one graphic element that "breaks out" of the box.

Image: Quick Communication Continues

The 15 to 20 seconds you have to attract your reader is the total amount of time you have for both recognition and image. The graphic tools used for recognition are designed to encourage your prospect to open the publication and start skimming.

Several design elements work together to draw the reader:

- ❑ paper determines how the graphics, extra color and type appear on the page
- ❑ color highlights important items by drawing readers' eyes to a headline or message
- ❑ graphics and photographs also capture readers' eyes

Obviously, everything on your newsletter page can't be fighting for attention. When you combine these elements to form the layout, you should highlight only the most important promotional items.

Paper—The Right Touch

From the crisp reproduction of photographs to showing your ecological concerns, paper sets the image of your newsletter. It is the one element of your newsletter design that appeals to four of our five senses. We see its color, feel its texture, hear its crisp rustle and even smell its fibers and ink. (I suppose each type of paper even has its own taste, but if your readers are going this far you're in trouble.)

The weight, texture and finish of your newsletter's paper determine how it feels in readers' hands. Because heavy paper conveys a solid, stable image, most organizations print on paper weights of 70# text and higher. Aside from its stable image, thicker paper also eliminates bleed-through of printing on the reverse side.

An added texture, such as a linen finish, can also boost the "thickness" of the paper. However, one of the main drawbacks to using textured paper is that photographs don't reproduce as well as on a smooth surface.

Ten Steps to a High-Class Image

If image is your most important sales step, newsletter design trainer Polly Pattison advises you to consider concentrating on the following ten uses of your budget:

1. quality paper
2. an extra ink color
3. four-color reproduction
4. professional photographs
5. high-resolution output
6. quality graphics and illustrations
7. quality printing
8. quality nameplate design
9. quality page design
10. quality mailing area design

Watch Printer Resolution

When using matte- and dull-coated papers, keep in mind the resolution of your printer or final output. Printing 300 dpi output onto a coated paper is unattractive, because you'll be able to see every imperfection in the type.

For economic reasons, uncoated papers with a vellum, or smooth, finish are commonly used for newsletters. Uncoated papers are resilient for mailing and work well for newsletters without photographs. If you regularly include photographs, investigate using coated paper. There are three kinds of coated papers used for publications: gloss, matte-coated and dull coat.

Photo Finish

On glossy paper, photographs appear crisper and colors brighter than on uncoated paper. But it is also the type of paper used for most brochures. A newsletter that looks too slick may have the psychological drawback of appearing like a sales promotion, rather than useful news. Also, glossy paper can be hard to read because of light reflections.

One possible compromise is matte-finished paper—a coated sheet without a glossy finish. Matte-finished paper reproduces photographs and colors well and diffuses light better. Dull coat also reproduces extremely well but can be more expensive than a matte-coated stock.

If you want to give your readers the feeling of receiving late breaking news, consider printing on newsprint. Although the paper is thin, it tends to hold ink well and it can be jazzed up with an extra color.

One last thought on paper. Many readers are sensitive to the need to recycle. You can show your support by printing on recycled paper. Both coated and uncoated grades are available. If you choose a recycled paper, inform readers. Print the recycle logo and the line, "This newsletter is printed on recycled paper," somewhere in the newsletter.

Off With Flying Colors

Colors set the mood of your publication—from friendly to formal. Readership increases threefold if a publication is illustrated with a second ink color. But to preserve legibility, use color judiciously. For example, print your text in black ink on white paper. Use the second ink color, known as "spot color," for headlines, bars, captions, and other elements of the layout.

To keep the design of your marketing pieces consistent, consider using your organization's color as the spot color. Some editors change the second color of the newsletter from issue to issue. This helps readers recognize each issue as a new one. You may even have the printing budget for three colors.

For best legibility, keep the color of the paper as light as possible and the color of the ink as dark as possible. Black ink on white paper is always the easiest on the eyes. Dark blue, dark green, brown or charcoal ink are nearly as legible. Another method of making a newsletter colorful is to print it on colored paper. However, most designers recommend using white paper with two ink colors instead.

Change colors with the seasons. An event planner changed the colors of the confetti and the headlines on each issue of her newsletter to get people into the mood for the coming holidays. Her Christmas issue was red, spring was purple, summer was yellow, and fall was orange. The color created a festive appeal and told prospects the events she produces are full of pizzazz.

Change top to bottom. An attractive effect for nameplates and sidebar boxes is a graduated screen. Subtle shifts in halftone screening give the box dimension and light without interrupting readability.

Colors arouse emotion. Dark blue and dark green are colors of stability. If you're promoting a bank or an investment firm, this may be important to your image. Gray also gives a dignified image and is pleasing to the eye, but can be depressing. With this in mind, avoid printing on gray paper.

Brighter colors are more friendly—bright blue, teal, purple or melon. The most attention-grabbing colors are red, orange and yellow. But if you want to suggest stability, avoid bright red. Bright red should also be avoided by hospitals and other health professionals, because of its association with blood. The same goes for banks, accountants and financial institutions. Customers want to be "in the black," not "in the red." Burgundy is a suitable substitute for bright red.

Creating other colors. Tints and screen give one- and two-color publications the effect of having many colors. A tint creates the illusion of another color by breaking the color into dots. The side-bars in this book are created using screens.

Screens are used to highlight or separate areas of your newsletter, such as short articles, sidebars, contents boxes and tables. When screened, some ink colors create a highlight that draws your eye to that area. Yellow, orange, purple, and other bright colors create attention-getting screens.

Color trick. Get the look of a two-color publication while saving money by designing your newsletter with a second color on the front and back (for a 4-pager) only. This attracts the skimmers to the highly visible spots.

Red

Shells. One way to save money when printing more than one color is to preprint a large quantity of shells. Shells are pages of your newsletter preprinted with colors you won't be using for text. If you want to use shells, design the publication so that the second color areas are in fixed places from issue to issue. Then preprint the second color onto your newsletter's paper. For each issue, the printer adds the text and photos in your main color, usually black.

For promotional newsletters, shells have a few drawbacks. Preprinted shells may keep you from using color to draw attention to a special promotional item. One option is to find a printer who frequently runs the highlight color you've chosen—maybe the printing company has a large client using a similar color. Or perhaps you can strike a deal to get the second color free if you print on a certain day. Many quick printers have days when certain second colors are free.

Using shells is also not advisable for rapidly changing organizations or for the first few issues of your newsletter. You're bound to want to make changes.

Create "Points of Entry" With Color

Designing with color is more than just using spot color. The paper you print on and the ink you use for text can also create colors, from white space with no text to the "gray" formed by words on a page.

Add some Southern hospitality to your newsletter. Beckon readers to your publication by defining points of entry with white space, headlines, kickers and initial caps. These elements signal readers where to start. The more articles you have on a page, the more points of entry you've created.

Just as walking into a crowded room of strangers is intimidating, so is a page filled only with text. Many publishers are tempted to cram every last bit of news onto a page. After all, blank space is a lost opportunity to promote. While this is true, some extra white space can actually help hold your readers' attention.

Briefs, before and after. If you can design your publication with promotional highlights in fixed places, print up some shells.

White space is created with page margins, subheads, pull quotes, headlines and captions. These elements break up what would otherwise be a mass of gray. Large blocks of type are called "blocks of gray," because that's the way the page looks if you hold it at a distance.

Leaving extra white space at the top of pages gives your design visual relief. It helps the reader move more quickly through the publication. Subheads and pull quotes are also used to break up the gray of long articles. They separate columns of text into smaller, less intimidating blocks.

Photographs Provide Instant Communication

The best way to break up blocks of type on a page is to use graphics, such as photographs, illustrations, charts and cartoons. Approximately twice as many people will read your articles if they are illustrated. However, you must carefully choose graphics that enforce and enhance your promotional message. Readers retain visual images longer than they retain words.

Photographs play an important role in providing condensed information. Rather than taking several sentences to describe a product or person, use a photo. Photographs of people provide an element of emotion by showing smiling, concentrating or concerned faces.

Many people are afraid of technology. If you show a photograph of equipment, prospects may be intimidated rather than inspired to call you. Use a photograph to help ease their fears. Show people and results, rather than the equipment. Show people interacting with your products in a happy, human way.

It's important to make your photographs of people approachable. If someone is looking straight at the camera, make sure they are smiling (even if it's only slightly). Avoid having barriers in front of executive photos.

Nice guys finish first. Someone sitting in a suit and tie at a desk isn't nearly as approachable as a freestanding person smiling in shirt-sleeves.

The quality of photographs will greatly affect the overall quality of your publication. Even though you may not be in the position to hire a professional to take each picture, remember that using in-focus, candid, interesting photographs will improve the look of your pages.

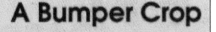

Coordinate headlines and photos. Clearly communicate to skimmers the subject of the article. A lot of promotion— maybe even enough to win a customer—can be achieved in these two areas.

A Bumper Crop

Washington Penn has discovered that its TPO is especially well-suited for bumper applications. Since this discovery, product engineers have studied TPO in an effort to shorten cycle times, improve paintability, and increase impact strength and high temperature stiffness. As a result, WPP is winning worldwide approval for its TPO.

these new paint testing ca very important. "We see a toward companies wanting mend paint systems for use molded from our material,

Record-Breaking Cycle
Although TPOs man Washington Penn compar several wa peting bra significan between Penn's TP is exceller Washing material c cycle time peratures a full sho was dram onstrated test last n "At a re trial in Ja given 90 our trial," explains Dom asked the operator to lowe temperature he looked stu even more shocked when quality parts from the fir cycle times were exceller ished in 50 minutes." Because some bumpe require parts of up to 15 p

New Equipment Aids Development
To help produce materials of the highest quality available, Washington Penn Plastic has purchased a paint system test machine and a condensing humidity test tank. This state-of-the-art testing equipment will enable engineers to evaluate the capability of their TPO products with current automotive paint

© WPP Co., Inc.

The following are some resources for professional-quality photographs.

Keeping Photo Files. For an on-going publication, keep all of the photographs you receive on file. Photographs you've already used may be run again in a follow-up article. Once run, it's a good idea to file photos by issue for easy retrieval. Those not chosen for a particular issue may be needed for a different article.

The Yearbook Effect

If you're using several presentation pictures showing recipients of awards, photograph the group together with their plaques after the ceremony. This avoids the dreaded "yearbook" effect of having rows of photographs in your newsletter. It also avoids having your executives appear in the photos as often as your clients or members—they're not the ones being recognized.

Too Small

A manufacturer had to reprint an entire issue of a newsletter and remove a picture of one of the company's sites. The president felt that the photo made his company look too small.

Photo Makeovers

Barbara Fanson, editor of *Newsletter Trends*, says that the photos that will make your newsletter look old-fashioned are:

❑ "grip and grin" (photos of someone receiving a check, handshake or certificate)

❑ executive behind desk—it's not only unfriendly, it's too clichéd

❑ executive on phone—the person usually looks uncomfortable

Use shots with some life—with people that are relaxed. These types of photos also work well when silhouetted.

Photo compositions in newsletters are changing, with people in photos looking more natural, more "human." Executives are shown in shirtsleeves instead of ties (or the female equivalent—the silk scarf).

If you are going to highlight employees or members or have internally written columns, have pictures to accompany the article. Save time and increase quality by having everyone's picture taken at once.

When including photographs of employees, make sure they look friendly and approachable. If your first attempt results in an unflattering or unfriendly photograph, publish the article without it and try again.

Give the photograph as much "texture" as possible. A wool jacket looks friendlier than slick pinstripe; a sweater is more approachable than a suit and tie.

Sources of good photographs. Sometimes you won't have the luxury of taking photographs yourself. If you're reporting on someone else's products or people and they're hundreds of miles away, call or e-mail their public relations or advertising department and find out if a photograph is available.

If you regularly ask your subjects to take photographs themselves, design a photograph requirements list. Include specifications for photograph resolution and sizes. Request that your product appear in the picture along with your customer.

Hiring a professional will ensure you get top quality photographs. For out-of-town shots, find a photographer in that area to take the picture for you.

You can rent photographs of common sites, such as the Grand Canyon or the moon. These are called stock photographs. The fee you pay is for a one-time use. Look online under the keywords "stock photograph services", as well as "photos on CD."

When not to show photographs. Many smaller organizations choose not to show pictures of their building or group pictures of their departments. These publishers are maximizing one of the major benefits of newsletters—positioning an organization as a leader and industry expert. Because many people associate leadership and expertise with size, you may not want to draw attention to size if your organization is small.

Soft Line Drawings

An alternative to serious business photos is line drawings. Many publications are following the lead of *The Wall Street Journal* and replacing photographs with pen-and-ink sketches, especially for regular columnists. This is an especially good option if your newsletter is faxed.

Keep in mind that this method works only if you use very high quality drawings. A bad line drawing is worse than a bad photo. However, quality line drawings become an important part of the look and feel of your newsletter, much more so than regular photographs.

Quentin Crisp & Eileen Myles by James Breeden

James Broughton, writer, poet, filmmaker, and visionary, lived among avant-garde circles and created experimental films in San Francisco during the 1950's.

THE NEWSLETTER OF A **DIFFERENT** LIGHT BOOKSTORE
489 CASTRO STREET SAN FRANCISCO CA 94114
phone: 415 431 0891 fax: 415 431 0892 BBS: 415 431 6660

Herein the past and future meet. Though this issue is primarily devoted to the elders within our community—with a view of gay San Francisco in the 1950's, and an interview with mystery writer Joseph Hansen--take note of our bulletin board number in the lower right hand corner of the masthead. A Different Light Online is now in service. We also talk about the small but growing number of meta-books in CD-ROM filling our shelves. In addition, there are stories from our second literary conference, and you'll discover the first fiction to grace these pages. Also: a review of Mabel Maney's latest girl-detective thriller, a look at queer punk music--and a video buyer's lament. Enjoy.

Illustrations by James Breeden

Jewelle Gomez, writer, activist, vampire lore aficionado. She spoke at **Readers & Writers II** *on the panel* Do Our Political Struggles Make Good Art?

A different design. James Breeden creates pen-and-ink sketches that are an integral part of his publication's design.

Sum Up Numbers With Charts & Graphs

Charts, graphs and diagrams help present numbers in a quickly digestible form. Your organization may want to show how your products are used, what type of members you have or how donations are appropriated. Instead of listing the percentages or numbers of each, construct a pie chart or bar graph.

Charts and diagrams keep your article from getting bogged down with numerical data. People would rather look at a graph of sales or production data than read the numbers. Graphic methods also help readers remember the information.

You don't have to be a graphic artist to create a unique and successful graphic. The trick is to keep it as simple as possible. For example, donations can be shown in a bar graph with the bars made from canned goods or stacks of coins. Add a caption underneath your charts and graphs to explain the data.

Paper and paperboard—38%

Food and yard waste—25%

Metals—8%

Plastics—8%

Glass—7%

Wood—6%

Other—8%

Throw numbers around. Waste Management of Baton Rouge shows readers the composition of American garbage by placing text over clip art of a garbage can.

"Oxygen masks. When a meeting gets so boring as to be life-threatening, they automatically drop down!"

Cartoon opener. Direct mail experts say that cartoons get envelopes opened. (Cartoonists Brad Veley, whose cartoon is above, and Dan Rosandich, whose work is to the right, are listed in the Resources Section.)

"NO CAN DO... THAT PARTICULAR CORPORATION HAS ENOUGH DINOSAURS ALREADY."

Cartoons Show the Lighter Side

People like to laugh. Salespeople frequently tell their prospects funny stories and jokes. Laughter is an important part of making your prospects look forward to your visits. (Creativity expert Doug Hall says that "ha-ha" leads to "aha.") Regularly including cartoons can create the same effect for your newsletter. Even if readers are opening it only to look at the cartoon, you've elevated them to the image level.

People used to think that cartoons destroyed an organization's dignity. However, this trend is reversing. It's now recognized that cartoons lend an approachable image to an organization.

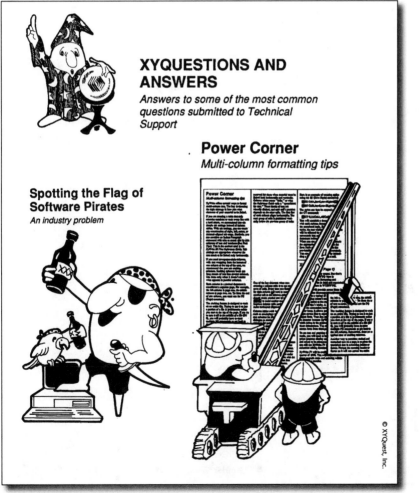

Part of design. If possible, use the same cartoonist or illustration artist throughout your newsletter. The caricatures to the left give life to XYWrite's newsletter, *XYI*.

Quality clip art. Image Club has a huge collection of clip art and clip photos, as well as typefaces.

Cartoons included in your newsletter offer several benefits. They help explain abstract ideas, draw attention to a related article, and add a human element. Unlike photographs, they have the power to exaggerate the truth while making it real and understandable.

Cartoons in promotional publications highlight the humor in your special area. Check the Resources Section for clip art and cartoon services. Some are available online. Or look in your industry magazines for cartoons appropriate for your newsletter. Write for permission to reprint them. Most cartoonists charge a nominal fee.

To avoid seeking reprint permission, convert your own ideas into cartoons by contracting a cartoonist or artist. Decide on the most important promotional point of an article and have a cartoon drawn to emphasize it—speedy delivery, quality control, friendly service, whatever.

Clip Art & Custom Illustrations

Custom illustrations and clip art can also emphasize the main point of your article. Often, illustrations are used when you can't find a photograph to accompany the article. Even when a photograph is available, custom drawings or clip art may more accurately communicate your promotional point.

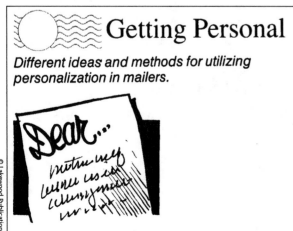

Getting Personal

Different ideas and methods for utilizing personalization in mailers.

Graphic kicker. You can use graphics along with kickers for standard features. Readers will become accustomed to looking for the graphic that covers their interest.

Clip art can be purchased in collections on CDs and is usually organized by subject. You can also buy individual images online. Quality varies from one supplier to another. Before buying a large collection, get samples of the work and read the copyright provisions. Some clip art is limited to use in a publication of noncommercial purposes.

Most clip art collections contain a wide choice of full-color, gray-scale or line-drawn clip art. If your newsletter is printed in four-color, colorful artwork can be a great addition to color photographs. If you're printing in one or two colors and printing your master pages on film or high-resolution laser printers (1200 dpi or more), an illustration's shades of gray can add depth to a two-dimensional page. If your newsletter is printed from 300 or 600 dots-per-inch laser master pages or if it is distributed by fax, use the line art images.

Make Reading a Breeze

Create designs that make reading easy. The less work readers' eyes have to do, the more energy readers have to think about your messages.

Ease of reading is affected by all of the following:

- ❑ typeface (font) you use
- ❑ size it appears in
- ❑ leading or space between lines of text
- ❑ justification of the paragraphs
- ❑ number of columns
- ❑ width of columns (number of words on each line)
- ❑ length of the paragraphs
- ❑ amount of indenting
- ❑ spacing between paragraphs

Retain in Black & White

Since research has shown that people retain a message longer if it's printed in black and white, use your second color only for highlight and print the main text in a dark color. Alternately, highlight the text area by framing in the entire page with the second color.

Font

1Stone Serif
25 Helvetica UltraLight
2Stone Sans
35 Helvetica Thin
3Stone Informal
45 Helvetica Light
55 Helvetica Roman
65 Helvetica Medium
95 Helvetica Black

Silicon Valley overrides Gutenberg. All desktop publishing and word processing programs list typefaces or type families under a menu called "Fonts." However, a font is a specific typeface in a specific style in a specific size—10 point Times italic, for example. Typesetters used to own sets of fonts in large cases and would set the type by hand using the fonts.

Sample Body Copy Typefaces:

Garamond

Times Roman

Galliard

Palatino

Goudy

Optima

Helvetica

Type—Increase Your Readers' Endurance

Ease the burden of reading by choosing a common typeface (or font). Certain fonts are "known" to our minds, such as those used in newspapers. Since most people read word by word—not letter by letter—it's important to have the words in your newsletter look the way people are used to reading them.

When selecting the typography for your newsletter, you may be choosing from hundreds of faces available from a typesetter, or you may be choosing from those you have on your desktop publishing system. Before we get into the specifics, keep in mind your primary goal is to make your newsletter easy to read.

The most common point sizes for newsletters are 10 and 11. Use 11 point for the quickest scanning and easiest reading.

The typography, unlike other design elements, should not be immediately noticed by the reader. If it is, you've chosen typefaces that readers have never seen before.

The benefit of having a basic desktop publishing system is that you probably have some form of the most common typefaces, like Times Roman and Helvetica. Most readers can easily distinguish words in these typefaces. They may have trouble, however, if you set large chunks of body copy in bold, italic or all capital letters. Any of these styles will make the body copy harder to read.

Be forewarned that some designers emphasize design over ease of reading. It's your job to look out for your reader. To assure easy reading, have the designer set several paragraphs in his or her chosen style. Test this sample for easy reading before you approve the type.

If your designer suggests a typeface you think is hard to read, choose some others and show them to the artist or test them on potential readers. To find good examples of typefaces, look in magazines and newspapers. Consider a more unusual style for headlines.

Image of Type

Because some typefaces are more formal than others, you can use type to create a mood in your newsletter. It may be either formal or informal. The typography can also communicate a feeling of being a direct communication, like a letter.

Typefaces can be broadly classified into serif and sans-serif (*sans* is the French word for *without*). Serifs are the finishing strokes at the ends of letters. In general, sans-serif typefaces are considered more informal and are good for headlines and small amounts of body copy. Serif faces are more formal and are generally considered to be easier to read in longer blocks of copy.

But these distinctions only begin to describe the character of a typeface. One of the most important features of a typeface's design is its x-height, which is the height of a letter like a, o, and, yes, x, as compared to an h, l, or f. The part of the letter that extends below the line is called the descender (g, j, p and q). The part that extends above the "body" or x-height, is the ascender. Modern (informal) typefaces have taller x-heights than classic (formal) typefaces.

Selecting Headline Typefaces

The headline is often the first element noticed on your newsletter page. The headline attracts attention through its appearance (the typeface used, its size, the type style and the spacing around and within it). Some headlines are set in all capital letters and stretch the full width of the article. Others are set smaller with white space around them. The kerning (spacing between letters) and tracking (the spacing between words) of most headlines usually need to be manually adjusted to give them a professional, powerful look.

The typeface you choose should depend on the mood you're trying to create. Many headlines are set in sans-serif type for a clean, easy-to-read look. Editorial-style headlines are often set in serif type for a news-style look.

The x-height of the typeface you choose will also affect the image of the headline. Remember that a tall x-height typeface, whether

---

The Squint Test

Hold the page at arm's length and squint. If you have trouble reading the text and headline, modify the type.

Contrasting combinations. Here are some sample combinations.

Futura Bold/Palatino:

Create grays with black & white

If you're producing a one-color newsletter, you can create interesting-looking pages in black, white and the many shades of gray in between.

Stone Sans Bold/Optima:

Create grays with black & white

If you're producing a one-color newsletter, you can create interesting-looking pages in black, white and the many shades of gray in between.

See how to place headlines in the layout on page 237.

Stay With the Standards

Stick with standard fonts available for most laser printers. This will allow you to switch desktop publishing systems or printers and get your newsletter produced easily, regardless of your location.

serif or sans-serif, will make the headline look informal, while a short x-height face always looks more formal.

Choose tall, bold typefaces that will attract attention and take up less space horizontally, allowing you to leave some white space to attract attention.

The appearance of your headlines will be affected by:

- ❑ boldness
- ❑ capitalization
- ❑ leading
- ❑ condensing
- ❑ kerning

Boldness. The typeface you select for your headlines should appear much bolder than the body copy on the page. This lends good "color" to the page and makes the headlines stand out.

Capitalization. When deciding whether to use uppercase, lowercase or a combination of both, remember that people skim headlines by looking at the upper halves of the letters. It's difficult to distinguish letters set in all capitals. It is somewhat easier when they're set in initial capitals (uppercase/lowercase). The easiest of all to skim is the "downstyle" headline—in downstyle, only the first letter of the first word in the headline is capitalized.

Line spacing. You will probably want to override the automatic line spacing (or leading) setting in your software program when you create your headlines. The default setting often adds too much space between lines of a headline. Most headlines can be set "solid" (leading equals type size). For example, an 18-point headline would be set with 18-point leading. The amount of leading your headline requires also depends on the typeface you use and the height of the descenders and ascenders of the lowercase letters.

Condensing headlines. This technique allows you to pack more information into a small space. It creates a modern look without sacrificing legibility. How much condensing is too much? Let common sense and the squint test be your judge.

Sidepage:

Create Color in Black & White

Who says a one-color newsletter is dull? It's 29 colors. If you're producing a one-color newsletter, you can create interesting-looking pages in black, white and the many shades of gray in between. One printer estimates that with black ink, up to 27 different shades of gray are possible. Counting the black and white, that's a 29-color newsletter!

The key lies in how you select typography, photographs and illustrations. Train your eye to see many shades of gray.

The Color of Type

Each typeface has its own color. In addition, the color can be lightened or darkened through changes in line spacing (leading), type size, kerning and scaling (condensing/expanding).

One characteristic that affects a typeface's color is its stroke. A light face, such as Eras Light or the Garamond you're reading, has a finer stroke than a bold face, such as Futura Extra Bold.

The x-height (the height of the letters x, e, o, m, etc.) and the counter (the amount of space inside letters like o and e) also affect how dark the typeface looks on the page.

Colorful Contrasts

Once you get a feel for the color of the typefaces you have available, choose faces that complement and contrast. Use a light face for body copy (but not too light) and a darker one for headlines, subheads and pull quotes.

Good choice for body copy include typefaces like Janson, Century, Garamond and Caslon. Stone Sans and Stone Serif make a great headline/body copy combination.

Use Templates

Most word processing and desktop programs include news-letter templates (see Page Wizards in MS-Word and MS-Publisher). Look in the back of your software manual under "templates" to find them.

Two-column format.

Three-column format

Number of Columns Determines Reading Pace

Another design element affecting the readability of the type is the number of columns in your layout. Column width, like typography, can greatly affect your prospect's reading endurance. The proper column width, along with the right size and style of type, will promote fast, easy reading. This increases comprehension by decreasing eye fatigue.

The number of columns in most newsletters varies from one to five. Advantages and disadvantages exist for all. For most newsletters, a line length of 35 to 45 characters has been found to be the most comfortable to the eye. People have difficulty reading extremely long or short lines.

One-column formats. The longest lines appear in the one-column format. This format preserves the feel of a "letter" and is the way many typed newsletters look.

Finding ways to reduce line length will increase the readability of a one-column format. One of the best ways is to use a deep left margin, called a "scholar's margin." Placing or extending headlines, subheads, sketches and photographs into the scholar's margin decreases the line length and improves readability. Readers can also use the margin for notes or comments.

Two-column formats. For larger type sizes, newsletters with two equal columns provide a comfortable line length. However, a two-column format is rigid from a design viewpoint. Each page is split in half, making it difficult to create pages with visual appeal. Visual appeal is often caused by imbalance, rather than the perfect balance found in two-column formats. A more flexible format is three columns.

Three-column formats. The three-column format gives the feel of a newspaper or magazine and has become the most common design for newsletters. The popularity of a three-column format is due to the flexibility it provides for the layout, while keeping the average number of words per line at a level that's easy to read. Photographs, text and headlines can be placed in one of the three columns or stretched across two.

Sidepage:

The "Retro" Look

An alternative to desktop publishing your newsletter is to use your standard word processor. Some people feel that newsletters that look like a letter are more personal and have the image of containing the "inside scoop." Many subscription newsletters, such as *The Kiplinger Washington Letter*, are produced this way and do contain the inside scoop.

If you are a consultant—a one-person law practice, a financial planner, an accountant—consider this format. It gives prospects the impression of having a one-on-one talk with you. This way, you are perceived as a "person" and not an "organization." Even for larger firms, a client letter carries the image of being a service, rather than a promotion.

You should also consider a letter-style newsletter if you're trying to stretch your budget. But keep in mind that desktop published composition lets you pack as much as 50% more content into the available space.

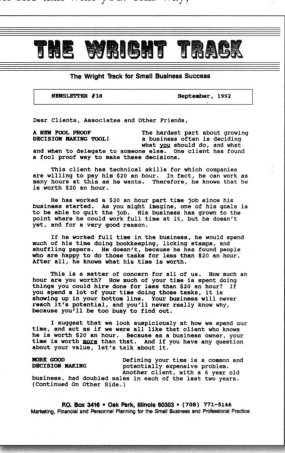

Four-column format

Grid Versus Speed
The fancier your grid, the longer it will take to lay out your pages.

Four-column formats. A four-column format also provides flexibility for illustrations and headlines. For newsletters that have short stories and several photographs, using four columns causes your articles to take up more depth than using three columns. However, the shorter line lengths can disturb the reader's eye rhythms. The line length is even more awkward if you use long words.

Flexible grids. Complex page grids, a design technique formerly used by only the top-level designers, have now become mainstream. Today, five- and seven-column grids are being created with ease by desktop publishers. Five-column grids are flexible, allowing you to create designs with pull quotes, photographs, sidebars or newsbriefs placed in narrow margins.

Changing grid structures have influenced photo placement on the page. The narrow left and right margins (and sometimes even the middle column) are often used to place tightly cropped, vertically oriented photos.

Benefactors. The left-hand column of this five-column grid is used to place photographs and sidebars.

Jury's Out on Justification

Another decision when setting up columns is whether to set the type with justified or unjustified margins. A justified margin is one in which every line ends at the same place. You can lay a ruler along the edge of a column of justified type and each line will meet it. An unjustified or ragged-right margin means that some lines will be a few units shorter than others.

The decision to use ragged-right over justified text is usually based on desired image and personal taste. Most designers agree that justified text has a more formal look than ragged-right. Some readability studies say that justification has no effect on ease of reading, while others say that ragged-right is easier to read.

The main pitfall of any readability study is that it doesn't consider the software that you are using. For example, justifying columns often creates gaping spaces between words that are very distracting to the eye. When running copy ragged-right, you must be able to control what's called the "hyphenation zone" in order to avoid having a right margin that's too ragged.

Make your choice based on the image you'd like to portray, along with the capabilities of your software. However, if you are using a four-column format use ragged-right alignment. Because of the shorter line length, spacing between words would be too awkward if the text was justified.

Image created by shape. The advantage of fully justified copy is that the text blocks form a rectangle. Text set ragged-right creates an irregular shape. That's why fully justified type is considered more formal than ragged-right.

Pulling It Together in the Page Design

Your newsletter's page design includes some of the design elements we've already discussed—paper, ink colors and grids. It also includes:

- ❑ folios to continue your design theme
- ❑ standing column headers
- ❑ drop caps to signal article beginnings
- ❑ end marks to signal article ends

It's important for these design elements to work together so they help portray your image and tell your story.

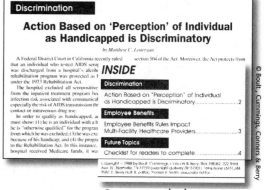

Contents to kickers. Use your contents box along with kickers to guide readers inside.

Design Folios for Pass-Along Readership

Chances are, your newsletter has an "underground" distribution that you can reach through folios. When readers find a newsletter helpful, they pass it along to an average of three other people. Often only one page is removed or photocopied. When individual pages are separated from the body of the newsletter, a good folio design makes the difference between prospects being able to contact you or being lost forever.

Surprisingly, few marketing newsletters have folio designs that "sell." Most copy the folio styles used in magazines and include the page number, the name of the publication and the date. A good marketing folio lists the page number, the name of the newsletter, the name of the publisher and your contact information.

Depending on your newsletter's page grid, the folio may be placed at the top, bottom or in the scholar's margin. Try to coordinate the folio design with the nameplate while keeping it simple enough that it doesn't fight headlines for attention.

Use light type that is legible without overshadowing the headline type. Light sans-serif typefaces, such as Helvetica Light or Futura Light, work well in small sizes.

Initial cap as part of design. The floral style of the script is consistent with the ambiance of the newsletter.

Drop Caps or Initial Caps

Initial caps and drop caps were discovered by hard-working monks as a way to decorate hand-drawn pages in the Middle Ages. They must have known something because, according to advertising guru David Ogilvy, initial caps increase ad readership by 13%.

A drop cap signals to your reader the starting point of your article. The size of the initial letter is usually as tall as three lines of the text. You can use the same font as you use for the body copy or use the headline typeface. Some clip art collections contain illustrative drop caps.

A few cautions on drop caps. Use no more than three per page. Check to make sure they don't spell an undesirable word if strung together.

End of the Line

If your newsletter contains long articles, and some of them are continued onto other pages, use an end mark to show readers the end of each article.

End marks are special graphics, such as a symbol, a square or an element from your nameplate or organization's logo. It is a standard part of your newsletter design and can help dress up an all-text page. The icons used for end marks range from simple dingbats to elaborate, creative logos. They provide an extra graphic touch while helping avoid confusion as readers move through the newsletter.

For simple icons, look at the symbols available in WingDings (in Microsoft Windows) or Zapf Dingbats (on the Macintosh). The advantage of using dingbats is that you can create them on the keyboard and keep them as part of the text. Graphics or pieces of art need to be placed and aligned with the text and don't automatically move when you make last-minute changes.

For more complicated end mark designs, lift an element from your nameplate. Or use all or part of your logo. You might design a special mark using the initials of your newsletter or organization. Or create a graphic that communicates your newsletter's subject. Some icons and logos can be converted to fonts and put into the layout using the keyboard. (For example, the program Fontographer converts graphics to fonts.)

© Goodwill Industries

> **Josephine is earning her own way now. That is good for her family, good for Vanderbilt and good for Middle Tennessee.** 🄴

End with goodwill. The Goodwill Ambassador uses the organization's logo as an endmark.

Encourage Saving & Sharing

Without using a lot of words, you can often tell readers what you want them to do after reading your newsletter. You can tell them to save the publication, pass it along to a co-worker, return the reply card, visit your Web site or call you. These traffic signals help you win a response.

Save it in a binder. To encourage readers to save the newsletter as a reference, punch or "drill" three holes in the binding. This is appropriate for any newsletter, and especially useful for technical supplements. Most users of your products and services save technical information, knowing they may need it for future reference. Rather than prepunching, some publishers provide preprinted circles or extra room along the left margin of the front to prompt three-hole punching.

Give them the binder. Along with adding holes, encourage your readers to save the publication by distributing binders. Offer the binder as an incentive for completing a readership questionnaire. Or print a coupon for it in your newsletter to gauge (and encourage) readership. When designing the binder, make sure your organization's name is printed along the spine. This keeps your name visible if the binder is stored on a shelf.

"Route to" Boxes Spark the Sharing Spirit

While folio designs help you market after your newsletter's been passed along to someone else, you can graphically spark the sharing spirit by including a "route to" box as part of your nameplate or front-page design.

Keep in mind that people share information. Often, you may not be able to find everyone within an organization that influences the use or purchase of your services, especially if you promote to large organizations. To make passing along easier, design a route-to box and place it on the front page.

Once your newsletter is passed along, new readers may want to be permanently added to your mailing list. Provide them with the information they need to contact you in the masthead.

Triple Your Readership

A newsletter readership survey conducted by a bank found that over half its respondents passed the newsletter along to an average of three people. To encourage further circulation, the bank editor immediately added a "route to" box on the first page of the newsletter.

See other "route to" examples on page 104.

Readers Seek Out Masthead

Often, readers search the masthead for more information about your organization and how to contact you. Although you only have to write it once, during the design stage, carefully word your masthead. Make it easy for readers to find the information they want. Use it as another place to promote your products and services.

The masthead not only gives the readers the information they need for correspondence, it also identifies those who produced the publication. No matter how simple the newsletter, include a masthead listing with:

❑ the name of the publication, along with its tagline

❑ its purpose or mission statement

❑ the editor and organization

❑ your products or services

❑ your address

❑ your phone and fax

❑ your e-mail address and Web site

❑ subscription costs (if any) and ordering information

❑ names of contributors

❑ copyright information or permission to reprint certain items

❑ frequency of publication

❑ disclaimers and lists of trademarks used

❑ volume and number

❑ deadline for copy if you accept contributions

Editor: Anne Rabbitt. To learn more about information on current investment opportunities in Phoenix Leasing, contact your investment advisor.

This Publication is not an offer to sell nor a solicitation of an offer to buy any security. Such an offering can only be made by a current prospectus and only to qualified investors.

If you have any comments or suggestions regarding the level of service we offer, direct your comments to Bryant Tong, Senior Vice President/Financial Operations or call (415) 485-4500.

Phoenix Leasing Incorporated
A Phoenix American Company
2401 Kerner Boulevard
San Rafael, CA 94901
(415) 485-4600

© Phoenix Leasing, Inc.

Compliance information. For financial newsletters and publications from other regulated industries, place any compliance fine print near the masthead.

To make your masthead more visually appealing, include the newsletter name as it appears in the nameplate. Box it off to make it easy to find. Reproduce your nameplate design. The masthead is usually placed on the second page. While there's no hard and fast rule on the placement of the masthead, try to keep it in the same place every issue.

Consider giving readers permission to photocopy the newsletter for the purposes of sharing it with other readers by placing a release line in the masthead.

Not all readers are familiar enough with formal publications to search out a masthead. For these readers, put your phone number and contact information in other places, as well.

Sneaking in Your Phone Number & Web Address

Discreetly print your organization's phone number and Web site whenever possible. Newsletters are notorious for their absence of contact information. Appropriate places are in the masthead, under the return address on the mailing panel, in the folio and at the end of any article covering your products or services. Make sure your readers can contact you while the idea is fresh in their minds.

Depending on your type of business, you may also want to include your fax number, hours, credit cards you accept, a list of your dealers and a list of your products. Combine this information into your masthead, or create a special box that appears in every newsletter.

Often, promotional newsletters contain notices of special events or product offerings that are boxed off and designed as ads. Used sparingly, advertisements provide readers compartmentalized information, without detracting from the news feel of your publications. However, overuse can cause your newsletter to look like a brochure.

After hours. A dermatologist includes all of his office telephone numbers, along with the location of his clinic, on the back of every issue.

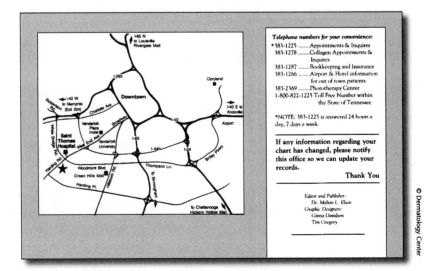

© Dermatology Center

Sometimes, you may not have enough room in your newsletter to provide prospects with all the information they need in order to make a purchase. Instead, give them the chance to request a brochure or a personal visit. This is done using a reply card.

Boomerang Reply Cards

Your newsletter is a one-way form of communication—unless you get reader response. However, most readers won't give you a response unless you ask for it by graphically showing readers what to do.

Response devices can be as simple as a phone number to call or an address to write to. Many newsletters go further and include a reply card or coupon. The most common formats (in order of ease of use) are:

Inserted cards. Inserted reply cards have the advantage of standing out from the rest of your newsletter. They can be glued in, stapled in or inserted loosely so the cards fall into the recipients' hands when the newsletter is opened. (Caution: many people find this irritating.) Reply cards are printed on heavy paper, are pre-addressed and often have postage pre-stamped. This makes it easy for the reader to return the card.

Reply coupons. Reply coupons are similar to inserted reply cards, except that they're printed within the body of the newsletter—so they don't increase printing costs. Like a coupon you clip from the newspaper, readers either photocopy or cut out the form to reply.

Reply coupons normally have a lower response rate because of the extra work. You can enhance the response by placing them near the article you've written that requests a response.

Repeat graphics on reply cards and coupons. This reply card could be separated from the newsletter and stored in a drawer for a year and the respondent would still remember at a glance what it offers.

Fun to Tear

Many readers like the feeling of tearing out perforated cards. This also encourages reader interaction.

Design your reply cards to entice readers to mail them to you. Here's how to increase your response:

- ❑ place the benefit of returning the card in large type
- ❑ repeat the offer
- ❑ give the offer a deadline
- ❑ list your telephone and fax numbers and e-mail address
- ❑ place icons of phones near the phone number
- ❑ highlight the card with spot color or graphics
- ❑ print it on bright paper
- ❑ print it using the same colors or artwork as the newsletter for design continuity
- ❑ make the card or coupon easy to remove from the newsletter and mail back
- ❑ keep the size between 5" x 3 1/2" and 6" x 4 1/4" to qualify for the postcard rate
- ❑ provide check boxes
- ❑ leave plenty of room to write
- ❑ use light line weights for fill-in areas (.5 or less—hairline)
- ❑ include your company name and logo
- ❑ repeat your address on the card
- ❑ design the card so that the mailing address for the newsletter stays with the card
- ❑ run a second set of your labels and affix the address for the respondent
- ❑ ask people to staple or tape their business card (instead of having to write out the information)
- ❑ make the card fax-friendly—no wider than 8 1/2" and not too thick

Business Reply Cards

Your post office can provide you with complete details on how to get a permit and produce your own business reply cards.

There are two good options for getting the cards or coupons back:

- ❑ use a business permit number
- ❑ pre-stamp cards
- ❑ set up a special Web site address for the offer only

Make your next child one of ours!

Yes, I (we) want to become a sponsor of a needy boy or girl in
☐ Kenya, ☐ Philippines, ☐ Bangladesh, ☐ Guatemala, ☐ Peru,
☐ Dominican Republic, ☐ Thailand, ☐ Bolivia, ☐ Haiti
or in the area of greatest need.

☐ Please send me a photo and story of my child. I have enclosed
    $22 as my first month's sponsorship.

☐ Please send me more information about sponsoring a child.

☐ I cannot sponsor at this time but enclosed is my special gift of
    $ _____

NAME: _____

ADDRESS: _____

_____

CITY: _____ STATE: _____

ZIP: _____ PHONE: _____

E-MAIL: _____

© Food For the Hungry

Donation cards. If the primary goal of your newsletter is to increase donations, include a reply card or a tear-out coupon in every issue. Supporters may want to donate mid-year, or they may pass their newsletter along to an interested friend.

Response rates will diminish if your readers have to pay postage and/or address an envelope.

Make Your Own Ads

Some publishers want readers to reply by telephone or e-mail. When readers are ready, they need to be able to find your telephone number and address easily. Create an information box that includes this and, if important, your office hours.

To generate response, many newsletter publishers include an advertisement set apart from the copy within a box. These advertisements encourage readers to come in for a sale, attend a fund raiser, or meet you at a trade show.

© New Leaf books

See a coupon that's also a survey at the bottom of page 90.

Some newsletters include the publisher's product listing, along with an order form to allow prospects to order directly from the newsletter.

Hear the "Snip, Snip" of Coupon Clippers

Just seeing the dashed border of a coupon lets readers know you have something special to offer. Use these guidelines when designing coupons:

- ❑ place coupons to the outside edges of the page for easy removal (lower right-hand corner is best)
- ❑ track response by placing the coupon on the verso (backing) page from the mailing label
- ❑ include a graphic of the item offered for easy recognition
- ❑ run a dashed-line border around the coupon
- ❑ include an expiration date and any rules or exceptions
- ❑ repeat your company name and, in small type, your address, phone number and Web site address
- ❑ place coupons near articles mentioning the products or services involved
- ❑ place an icon of scissors near the top left-hand corner of the border
- ❑ place the discount or offer in large type as the coupon's headline
- ❑ make the coupon easy to remove by perforating around the edges (if your printing budget allows)

Your Response to the Responses

Regardless of how you get the replies to come in, make sure you have a system in place for processing the requests and getting materials back to people as quickly as possible. People have short memories. Stamp or print the envelopes containing the promised materials with something like, "Here's the information you requested." Create an e-mail response that's ready to send. A quick reaction to their query will help keep readers activated.

Till We Meet Again

While the above steps may seem to exhaust the possibilities for reader response, there is one last thing you can do.

Keep your promotion rolling. Encourage readers to look for the next newsletter by telling them what it will offer. Include a "look for in the next issue" list. Of course, some of your content is late-breaking news that you can't predict. Just list a few upcoming features. By listing upcoming articles, you guide your readers full circle back into the recognition stage for your next newsletter.

All of the design elements covered in this chapter will help you attract and keep your prospect's attention. As you sit down to create each page, choose the elements that best guide your readers through your publication. Turn to the next chapter to find out how.

Sidepage:

Legibility Beyond Typefaces

While the choice of a typeface for body text is important, legibility—the ease of distinguishing characters on a page—goes beyond the typeface itself. Designer Jan V. White urges you to also consider:

1. layout of type on the page
2. type size
3. line length
4. leading or line spacing
5. page size
6. paper coating
7. paper color
8. ink shine
9. how the layout reflects content
10. how much type is on the page
11. paragraphing or segments
12. organization of information
13. ease of language

Centering type

Avoid centering more than six or seven lines of type. It's hard for readers' eyes to track back to the beginning of the next line.

Paragraph spacing versus indenting

To conserve space, while signaling the beginning of a new paragraph, either indent the first line or leave some extra leading between paragraphs (paragraph spacing). It is not necessary to do both. Also, it's not necessary to use an indent in the first paragraph after a headline or subhead.

Chapter 12:

"Zone" the Prime Layout Real Estate

Everyone out there who has seen an article titled "Letter from the President" on the front page of a newsletter, raise your hands. The placement of this little gem generates a big "ugh," for two reasons.

First, it needs a better headline. More importantly, it's taking up space in a prime area of your newsletter—like leasing a Madison Avenue storefront for storage.

This chapter shows you how to create layouts that draw readers to the articles that sell your products. You'll learn how to zone your layout—arrange type and graphics on the page—and use publication and page pyramids to guide readers' eyes.

This chapter covers printed newsletters. Skip to page 259 for e-mail and 267 for Web.

In this chapter:

- the best placement for articles and promotions

- front- and back-page design strategies

- drawing readers' eyes where you want them to go

- tools for communicating to skimmers in the layout

- when you have too much or too little copy

- procedures for continuous improvement

Publication & Page Pyramids

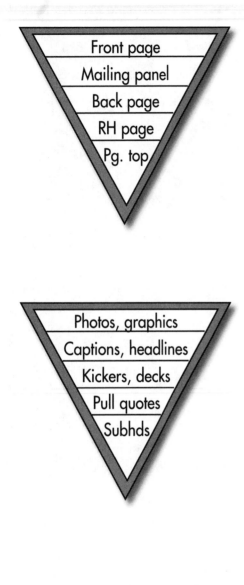

Inverted pyramids work for both news writing and page design. The idea of the inverted pyramid is to begin with the most interesting faces and work downward, in decreasing order of importance.

Within a publication, that means placing your most important news on the most visible pages.

The publication pyramid is built like this:

1. the front page
2. the mailing panel or envelope
3. the back page
4. right-hand pages
5. tops of pages

In addition, each page has an individual hierarchy. Visuals, captions, headlines and subheads all signal to readers and skimmers what's important on the page. If these areas are interesting, the reader assumes the rest will be. If they're not... another page gets turned.

The page pyramid looks like this:

1. photographs or graphics
2. captions
3. headlines
4. kickers and decks
5. pull quotes
6. subheads
7. leads

Once you "zone" the prime real estate in your newsletter, you'll know where to place the high-profile boutiques and where to build warehouse space.

Page Pyramids: How Readers' Eyes Work With Your Page

Understanding how the human eye interacts with your newsletter page can also help you make layout decisions. Readers look at your newsletter in three different stages:

1. when it's folded or flat in the mailing stack
2. when it's unfolded
3. when it's opened to the inside pages

When the newsletter is folded and in the mailing stack, readers first look at their name on the address label to make sure the newsletter was sent to the right person. Then they glance to the return address area. Next, they unfold the newsletter and look at either the front or back page.

On these pages, readers look at photos or illustrations first, unless they are small. In the absence of photographs, readers' eyes are attracted by the largest, most dominant element on the page. Then they move to the second most dominant, then to the third, and so on. On a page of all text, readers' eyes usually move from the upper left to the lower right corner of the page in a "Z" pattern.

Note that only the first and last pages are seen by themselves. Other pages are usually seen as two-page spreads. On two-page spreads in magazines (most eye movement research has been conducted using magazines), the reader's eye goes first to the right-hand page. Once readers have glanced at the right-hand page, their eyes go to the left-hand page. Both pages are read following the "Z" pattern.

The "Z" pattern assumes that the elements on both pages are of equal interest. A key word in a headline or an interesting photograph can draw the readers' eyes to the left or to the bottom of the page.

As the editor, your job is to encourage readers to at least skim all the elements of the newsletter. Armed with better knowledge of eye movement, investigate how you can use the layout to guide your readers through each of the NEWS levels—name, enactment, written words and selling.

Four Design Tricks to Catch Readers' Eyes

The top four ways designers attract attention in a layout are through:

1. **good visuals**— photos, cartoons, illustrations.

2. **unusual shapes**— angle of photo, silhouette of photo, dynamic graphics.

3. **relative size**— displaying the most important item in a prominent size and place.

4. **color**—strategic and controlled placement of spot color to highlight an important item.

© Encoders

Even fellow communicators want it brief. The editors of *communication briefings* conducted extensive focus groups before they designed this newsletter. They knew that readers wanted condensed news.

Selling With "First Glance" Appeal

The position of many parts of your layout, such as the nameplate and mailing panel, will be the same from issue to issue. In the layout stage, use the areas around the standard features, the "active areas," to create appeal.

First, focus on the prime real estate areas of the mailing panel and the front page. The active areas on the mailing panel are the teasers or contents box. Next, look at your goals for this issue or this year. Plan to change this area with each new issue to attract attention by using:

- ❑ teasers
- ❑ contents box
- ❑ event calendar or notice of an upcoming meeting
- ❑ eye-catching cartoon or photo
- ❑ location map
- ❑ sale announcement
- ❑ famous quotation
- ❑ coupon
- ❑ lists of services and everyday specials
- ❑ list of products offered
- ❑ Web site link to must-have content

Place a quick message, table of contents or teaser that gets people immediately involved with your publication.

Front-Page Strategies

Front page. Cover story. Page one. No matter what you call it, it's the place where most people (roughly 85%) start reading your newsletter. Here are a few strategies to consider.

Hard news. Place your most important articles on the front page. Readers expect the most newsworthy articles to appear on the front page. If you place dull articles on the front page, you're telling readers that the rest of the newsletter is even less exciting. (Tell your boss that the traditional spot for the president's letter is on the second page.)

Top ranking. Some publishers rank news items by the greatest amount of overall interest. The most popular articles go on the front page, the middle group go inside, and the remainder are condensed into news bulletins.

Skimmer bait. Invite readers in with short news blurbs. Newsbriefs condense long articles into two or three lines. This gives readers the feeling they're merely skimming the headlines.

Continue one. You can combine the skimmer bait technique with one continued article. Readers often read the newsbriefs first, then start reading an article placed in the right-hand column. This article leads the reader naturally to page two.

The lure. Lure readers by placing useful information on the front page. Once you've captivated readers, they'll turn to the inside pages—filled with your promotional information.

Goal-driven. If you have important news, such as a new product or an upcoming event, that you want everyone who opens your newsletter to see, place it on the front page. Don't bury newsworthy information deep within an article.

Remember that it's the editor's job to give instructions on article placement to the layout artist, if they are not one and the same.

The back page. So much thought has gone into reaching skimmers that this page is even called "The Back Page."

To Be Continued?

If you must continue articles:

Jump the article in the middle of a paragraph and the middle of a sentence.

Include a jumpline, such as, "Please turn to page 4."

Continue only one article per page and continue that article onto the page immediately following.

Show a graphic of an arrow, a pointed finger or a turning page.

Add a teaser to the jump line, such as, "Surprise ending, turn to page 3."

On the page where the article is continued, include a jump headline that's the same or close to the original headline.

List where the article is continued from, such as, "Continued from front page."

Repeat a photograph or graphic used with the first part of the article.

How to Sketch a Layout

1. Start with the right shape. Create page spreads by folding pages.

2. Give clip art and silhouetted photographs rough outlines. Use a rectangle or square with an "x" inside for an unedited photo and stick figures for people.

3. Use thick lines or long rectangles to show headlines.

4. Use closely spaced lines to represent copy.

5. Sketch logos.

6. Draw dotted lines in place of coupons.

Back-Page Designs for Prodigal Readers

An estimated 15% of readers start at the back of the newsletter and work their way forward. These nomadic readers judge a publication based on what's left at the end. If it's interesting, they know that the beginning of the newsletter is good, too. Convince these skeptics with short news blurbs or a newsworthy item. Use one of the front-page strategies here.

If your newsletter is self-mailed, all readers will at least glance at the back page first. Then they'll turn to the front.

© Mid South Marine

Top sell to the right top. The main product article of this newsletter is placed to the top right page.

Left-Page, Right-Page Strategies

Once inside, people start reading at the tops of pages and move down. Begin articles on the tops of pages. If you have a continued article, place the continued part at the bottom of the page.

Place photographs, graphics or important industry information so they draw readers first to the top left side of a spread. However, also realize that the top right-hand portion of a spread is a powerful position. Place promotional items, such as new product or service announcements, here.

People Don't Read, They Skim

When working within your page pyramid, assume that no one will ever read a word of your body copy.

Concentrate on pulling readers in and making your key points through interesting photographs and captions, headlines, pull quotes and subheads. These elements can also guide readers from article to article. Skimmer bypasses also help make your newsletter layout more pleasant for readers. These shortcuts include:

- ❑ photographs and captions that tell a story
- ❑ headlines that say, "Start here"
- ❑ dynamic graphics that point to key articles
- ❑ white space, rules and boxes separating articles

Target Your Audience With Visuals

When deciding which visuals to use and how to size them in relation to one another, consider your target audience. Use subjects and scenes that your readers can relate to. Visuals that always attract include:

- ❑ people doing something (using your products, at one of your events)
- ❑ before and after visuals
- ❑ children and animals
- ❑ a frame with a single element, versus multiple elements
- ❑ unusual angles or a tilted flat visual
- ❑ tight crops and zooms
- ❑ contrasting colors
- ❑ crisp focus
- ❑ varying levels of gray

Cropping photographs. Since most readers look at photographs first, use photographs and captions to convey your most important promotional point. Pull the reader into the subject by cropping in on the subject you want to highlight. Also, when showing customers, make the image of the customer as large as possible.

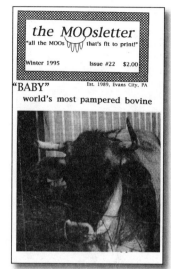

© Cowtree Collector

Cow-a-bunga, it's Baby! Visuals that show the specialty of your newsletter tell your story at a glance.

The car of the future will weigh and cost no more than a $2,000 motorcycle, carry two to four people along with plenty of pigs and potatoes, and run on human, electric or motorcycle-engine power, says Italian-born German designer Luigi Colani during his Automorrow '89 tour currently in the U.S.

This is because the automotive future lies in Asia, Africa and Indonesia, where 75 percent of the population lives. There, people are impoverished by Western standards but car

sales will be one day counted in billions. "Automakers try to make things more complicated and expensive. We have to do it the other way around," he explains.

Colani even has designs for heavy trucks. To haul his Automorrow concept cars, he has rebuilt a Mercedes-Benz tractor-trailer using 25

Continued on page 2

No boxcars. By removing this car from its background in the photo, its shape makes a dynamic graphic on the page.

Creating silhouettes. Another effect that adds interest to a photograph is silhouetting—a cutout of part of the photograph.

Silhouetting is useful for showing people. After all, most people aren't square or rectangular. Removing the background helps make people look more lifelike. Use this effect to show people from within your company. They'll look approachable and personable.

Although silhouetting creates informal pages, keep in mind that these types of photos lose some of their journalistic value. (Newspapers only use silhouettes on their lighter features.)

Real people. These people look more "neighborly" when silhouetted in the layout. Silhouetting even salvages the "grip and grin" award photo with style.

Choose the subject. If it's the man that's important, zoom in on the man. If it's the display, crop out the other people and center on the man's interest in the display. Note the angle of the man's body. It shows his interest and helps the photograph promote the display.

Effective Placement of Headlines

The size of the headline, along with the position of the article on a page, communicates the importance of the article. When laying out your pages:

- ❑ place important headlines to the tops of pages

- ❑ span at least two columns with the headlines for your most important articles

- ❑ use the largest type size you've chosen for major headlines

- ❑ avoid reducing the type size of the headline to make the headline fit; reword it instead

- ❑ use a consistent typeface, type size and alignment

Maintain the maximum promotional punch of your writing by breaking long headlines strategically. Keep adjectives on the same line with the accompanying noun. Avoid ending a line with a preposition.

Instead of breaking the headline like this:

Up to Your Sleigh Bells in Christmas Bills

begin the second line with the preposition:

Up to Your Sleigh Bells in Christmas Bills

Captions. When using a caption, place it under or to the side of the photograph. Set it in large enough type to be read easily by skimmers. According to David Ogilvy, four times as many people read captions as body copy.

© DigiBoard

Up, up and away. Because the reader's eye naturally goes to graphics, place headlines below graphics and photos.

Size Confusion

Headlines reduced to fit available space (instead of being edited) might be mistaken for subheads. Short subheads enlarged to fill up space can be confused with headlines.

6 Common Design Culprits

1. Setting body copy in reverse (white type on a dark background).

2. Excessive leading.

3. Ink colors other than black for type.

4. A headline not placed above the article it introduces.

5. Type over halftone screens heavier than 10% to 20% (when screens are in black ink).

6. Articles continued to inside pages.

Pull quotes. Pull quotes on a page of all text add visual interest and give you another chance to capture readers. Place pull quotes on the part of the page the eyes go to first, approximately at optical center (in the middle column, just above mathematical center).

Subheads. If you have long articles in your newsletter, subheads are essential to guiding the skimmers and telling them the important parts.

If you have an interview written in question-and-answer format, the questions can work as subheads. Set questions in bold, so readers can skim the questions and read the answers that interest them.

Talking to the text. A silhouetted photo adds an interesting shape to this page and interacts well with the text, especially the pull quote.

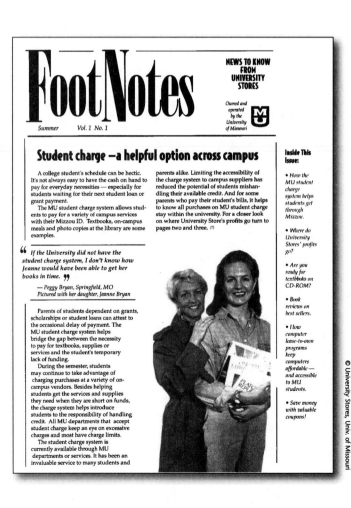

Dynamic Graphics Bring Traffic to a Halt

The key to dynamic layout lies in the inherent capability of our eyes and brains to give two-dimensional objects movement. For example, we can look at a photograph and determine whether the subject is stationary or in motion. The photograph itself doesn't move. But our perception of the object tells us whether it's static or dynamic.

Here are a few design tips to draw readers' eyes where you want them to go. Take caution not to overuse these tools. For maximum effectiveness, use only one or two per page. When you want an area of your newsletter to be noticed, use these guided missiles:

- ❑ arrows that point to the type
- ❑ graphics in the shape of a circle
- ❑ a small amount of reversed (white on black) text
- ❑ a bold typeface
- ❑ colored type or graphics
- ❑ drop shadows
- ❑ unusual photographs
- ❑ silhouetted photographs
- ❑ illustrations that "move" toward articles
- ❑ text wrapped around photographs and graphics
- ❑ drop caps that signal the beginnings of articles

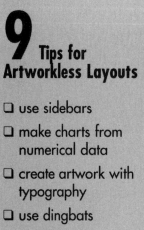

9 **Tips for Artworkless Layouts**

- ❑ use sidebars
- ❑ make charts from numerical data
- ❑ create artwork with typography
- ❑ use dingbats
- ❑ use decorative bullets
- ❑ use white space
- ❑ invest in clip art
- ❑ find a decorative border
- ❑ use large numbers if the article contains a numbered list

Static Boxes & Rules

Static layout elements are just as important as dynamic ones. Borders, screens, and text wraps help group layout elements together. Rules (lines) and white space help separate items.

Boxes and borders. Control the appearance of your borders by changing the width and style of the line you use. Also consider filling the bordered area with a light screen (halftone).

Text wraps. Wrapping text around a visual groups the visual with the text. Overlapping visuals groups them together.

White space. White space also functions as a border. Place the white space around the periphery of the elements you want to group together. Place white space between elements when you want to separate them.

Lines. Lines (or rules), along with screened areas, can separate articles in a mostly-text newsletter.

Avoid placing rules within articles, such as between headlines and body copy or between subheads and body copy. Rules separate.

How Shapes Affect the Layout

Pay attention to the shapes on your newsletter pages. Static elements don't point the reader's eye in any particular direction. Dynamic elements they readers' eyes.

Squares and rectangles. The square is one of the most common design shapes. Most news articles, framed graphics and unedited photographs form squares or rectangles. Extreme proportions in rectangles can add interest to a layout.

Circles. Circles withdraw from other shapes on the page. They tend to pull the eye into the circle and hold it there. This is called "spot value." You can use spot value to isolate and draw readers' eyes to the most important part of your page.

Triangles & polygons. Triangle and polygon shapes are the most dynamic of all. They create excitement and movement on your page. The triangle's shape pulls the eye away from everything nearby. However, the space left around the triangle is uneven and can be awkward to fill.

Amoebas. Silhouetting a photograph or an irregularly shaped illustration creates a more dynamic shape than the original rectangle.

Spot value. The target with 2010 in it pulls the eye to this spot on the page.

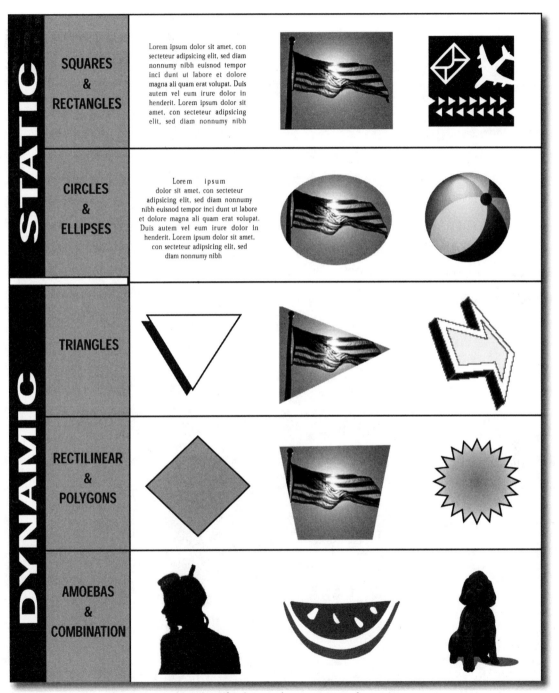

Live wires. Most shapes can be classified as either static or dynamic.

Static   Dynamic

Balance Movement With Stability

Strive to create organized pages. Just as it's hard for customers to find products in a messy store, it's difficult for people to find your message on a cluttered page. An effective layout keeps elements organized and arranged in a logical order. You also need a strong focal point, such as a promotional photo or headline.

Moving layouts. Layouts in perfect balance (top) are perceived as at rest. Off-centered layouts (bottom) are perceived as in motion. Use this motion and informality to create visual interest and appeal.

© Barron's

Give it an incline. You can add motion to photos by tilting them. The tilted box is balanced by the remaining static boxes on the page. The tilt also gives the photo an "attitude" that's in line with the tone of this newsletter (its mission is, "dedicated to good books, good looks, good food, good fun.")

Sidepage:

Strategic Placement of Color

Jan V. White lectures worldwide on the relationship of graphics to editing. An architect by training, an art director for Time, Inc., and owner of his own publication design studio, he now concentrates on persuading word-people to think visually and visual-people to think verbally.

Here are tips from Jan White's *Color For Impact.*

Write the text in such a way that it will benefit from color. Plan the writing to allow key factors to be visually emphasized. When the visual form works with the verbal content, the result is irresistible. Also:

- ❑ accent whatever is of greatest self-interest to the recipient
- ❑ emphasize the main points in the text
- ❑ separate the message from ancillary matter on the page
- ❑ categorize areas of the page with colored boxes or tinted backgrounds

Within newsletters and other documents, such as reports and graphs, also consider color to:

- ❑ alert the viewer to unexpected data
- ❑ personalize the document
- ❑ compare two sets of data
- ❑ distinguish new information from old
- ❑ classify rankings of numbers in a table
- ❑ link related elements with each other

Layout Checklist

❑ Encourage readers to skim all elements.

❑ Begin articles on the tops of pages.

❑ Place the most important articles on the front page.

❑ Place important news to the top right-hand of a spread.

❑ Lure readers with useful or hard-to-find information on the front page.

❑ Communicate an article's importance through the size and position of the headline.

❑ Avoid continuing articles.

❑ Place articles in order of reader interest.

❑ Use the mailing area to hook in readers.

❑ Include an interesting item on the back page.

Simple layouts are best. They keep pages uncluttered and straightforward. Here's how to capture and hold readers' attention:

❑ build your page around one central item (a story or a large visual)

❑ balance color, type and visuals based on the effect you desire (informal or formal)

❑ "point" visuals toward the article they illustrate. For photos with people, the photo's direction is wherever the subject's eyes are looking. For action photos, the direction follows the movement of the subject.

❑ balance dynamic elements with static ones. If your illustrations have movement, make sure they point to a static element—a headline or an article.

Squeezing or Expanding to Fit

What if your copy is too long to include graphics? What if you have too little copy and the layout looks awkward? Here's how to finish your layout without sacrificing promotional punch.

If you don't have enough space for everything:

❑ tightly edit your copy

❑ look for widows and orphans (words appearing at the final line of a paragraph or the first line of a column)

❑ reword sentences

❑ remove subheads

❑ break the article into two parts and continue the article in the next issue

❑ remove graphics or photographs

❑ reduce the body copy type size throughout by .25 point

❑ uniformly reduce the space above and below headlines and subheads

❑ eliminate pull quotes

❑ reduce the size of the mailing area

❑ slightly reduce the amount of paragraph spacing

❑ make graphics or photographs smaller

❑ crop photos judiciously

❑ shorten headlines

❑ justify text and hyphenate

If you have too much blank space left over:

- ❑ add a pull quote
- ❑ enlarge photographs or graphics
- ❑ leave one column empty and put in a pull quote there
- ❑ add subheads
- ❑ box in an article and decrease the column width of text
- ❑ add divider lines
- ❑ run text ragged-right
- ❑ scallop the bottom of the layout in a three-column format
- ❑ incorporate white space into the page design
- ❑ add one or more short filler features
- ❑ add headshots of authors of the lead articles

Through effective layout of each page, you guide and encourage readers to interact with your newsletter.

The Last Stop on the Tour

All editors learn from their readers. Use this knowledge to improve your publication. Take note of the comments and responses you receive from your readers. Try to determine what it is that reached your audience. The variables are many. It could be the topic of an article, the way a headline was worded, an interesting photo, the way you designed your reply card or a mixture of all of these.

If you have a hunch about what might attract readers, give it a try. Let experience with your prospects change and evolve your newsletter. Readers will sense your increased involvement in their needs. That alone is a powerful promotional message.

Evaluating Your One-Color Pages for "Color"

Look at each of your pages from a distance, checking for variation in color. The body copy makes blocks of gray. The headline should make a darker area of black. The color on your pages will be formed by:

- ❑ type and white space
- ❑ solid black lines, spaces and backgrounds
- ❑ gray screens
- ❑ graduated screens
- ❑ grays in photographs and illustrations

Gray-tone variation helps create interest in photographs or other artwork. Look at the photographs in the New York Times for examples. Most are rich with levels of gray.

Top Quality Through Proofreading

Once your layout is finished, it's proofing time. An error-free newsletter is a great boost to your image. It shows that your organization devotes great attention to detail. Here are nine tips for proofreading:

❑ never proofread your own writing
❑ recruit a fresh set of eyes to see things differently
❑ involve both sales and marketing proofreaders
❑ have engineering and design look at technical details
❑ define the duties of the proofreaders
❑ after all corrections have been made to the layout, have a final proofreading
❑ recruit a different person to proofread the layout
❑ use an online proofreading service such as www.proofread.com
❑ find an experienced artist or ask your printer to look for design/layout problems
❑ use a checklist

Your Own Evaluation

Evaluate every newsletter immediately after it comes off the press. Most editors are their own most ardent critics.

Checklist:

❑ highlight typos
❑ note any changes for next issue
❑ note any omissions or retractions you need to print in the next newsletter
❑ jot down article ideas for the next issue
❑ share your feedback with subcontractors

Follow Up on Each Issue

After the newsletter comes off the press, your marketing is just beginning. There are several important follow-up steps you should take care of immediately:

- ❑ send sample issues to all contributors with thank-you notes
- ❑ make sure all customer service representatives in your company have copies of your newsletter before your customers do
- ❑ follow up on all sales leads immediately
- ❑ file a sample of the newsletter in your portfolio

QUICK and EASY NEWSLETTERS

*This form is **updates.pdf** on the CD.*

Updates for Next Issue

Completed by: _____   Date: _____

Newsletter: _____

Issue/Date: _____

(Please attach a copy of the newsletter with corrections marked in red along with a copy of this form.)
General changes or additions for the next issue:

_____

_____

_____

Comments on specific changes:

Printing:
- ❑ Paper _____
- ❑ Ink colors
- ❑ Overall quality _____
- ❑ Turnaround time _____
- ❑ Other _____

Design:
- ❑ Layout
- ❑ Nameplate
- ❑ Typeface _____
- ❑ Photographs
- ❑ Illustrations _____
- ❑ Other

Editorial:
- ❑ Length of articles _____
- ❑ Number of articles _____
- ❑ Writing style _____
- ❑ Typographical errors _____
- ❑ Turnaround time _____
- ❑ Articles or suggestions for next issue: _____

_____

_____

From **Quick & Easy Newsletters**, by Elaine Floyd. www.newsletterinfo.com and www.paperdirect.com

Self-diagnosis. After each newsletter comes off the press, complete your own evaluation of the project using a form like this.

Sidepage:

Take the Newsletter Marketing Quiz

Before you send each newsletter to the printer, run through the following quiz:

1. Does it look like a news publication?

   ❑ yes   ❑ no

2. Is something about your company on each page?

   ❑ yes   ❑ no

3. Do some of the visuals you use show your products?

   ❑ yes   ❑ no

4. Is there at least one helpful tip for readers on each page?

   ❑ yes   ❑ no

5. Does everything in the newsletter have some tie back to your product, organization or industry?

   ❑ yes   ❑ no

6. If readers wanted to contact your company right away, how long would it take them to find your phone number, address or Web site?

7. Glance at your newsletter for 15 seconds. Look at the newsletter name, headlines, visuals, captions and sub-heads. Can you tell which industry you're in and what products or services you sell?

   ❑ yes   ❑ no

The answers to questions 1 through 5 and 7 should be "yes." The answer to question 6 should be 15 seconds or less.

Chapter 13:

Fabulous Fax Newsletters

Postage and printing comprise the lion's share of your out-of-pocket newsletter expenses. What if you could reduce both simultaneously? The solution is fax broadcasting.

With a fax machine, you can send your newsletter over the phone line and have it delivered to your reader's own machine. Faxing provides what fax expert Sarah Stambler, editor of *Marketing With Technology News*, calls the only "true instant physical delivery" of a document. You never know exactly when someone will receive your mailed newsletter. Electronic mail and Web pages depend on the recipient to download them or seek them out. With faxing, you know when the newsletter is on the reader's premise. In the process, you eliminate your printing expense. And if your readership is a local call away, you even eliminate postage costs.

Here are some of the ways to use fax broadcasting:

Provide their newsletter in fax form only. Don't print any issues in the traditional way.

Fax special editions of the newsletter. Maybe it's a product announcement, news of upcoming publicity or a meeting time/date change. Create a special "alert" design for these special editions.

In this chapter:

- how to work faxing into your news program
- design tips for faxed documents
- what to put on the fax cover sheet
- how to set up your database to use automated fax systems
- legal concerns of faxing

Use a fax "mailing" to build the newsletter mailing list. Send a one-page offer describing the publication and offering a free subscription. Interested subscribers can fill out the form and fax it back to get the publication by mail.

Deliver a library of information on reader's request. Offer back issues of your newsletter in a fax-on-demand library.

Faxed newsletters are used frequently by:

❑ association/membership bulletins
❑ short newsletters/not too graphic-intensive
❑ newsletters with timely information
❑ subscription (paid) newsletters

This chapter covers some different marketing strategies for incorporating faxing into your publishing program. There's also information on the types of fax system, whether or not you should outsource the service, special design considerations, setting up your database to be ready to use for faxing and how to operate within faxing regulations.

Up-to-the-Minute News by Fax

Faxes provide more visibility and convey more immediacy than mail. If receiving your newsletter days or weeks earlier offers tangible benefits to readers, consider faxing your newsletter. Subjects that lend themselves well to faxing include financial newsletters, stock market and other trend letters, and publications reporting on price increases and decreases.

Keep it brief. *Brief Factx* is a one-page marketing newsletter sent only by fax from Intelligent Solutions, a personnel agency for engineers. This newsletter is sent to technical managers and includes business- and management-related tips.

To your customers, a faxed newsletter conveys the image that you're on top of the latest news. Imagine the hot news tip you received yesterday—a great item to tell all of your customers, prospects, members or donors. Perhaps this item may foster a need for your services, increase orders or benefit your organization in other ways.

See more on special editions on pages 44-45.

Association publications usually give members advance notice on meetings and subjects. If there's a last-minute change, you can quickly get the news out to everyone with a fax. Local associations can also save money on both printing and mailing.

Creating Excitement With Special Fax Editions

According to fax marketing expert Sarah Stambler, setting up your newsletter for fax broadcasting has advantages you may not have considered. Once you've collected your customers' fax numbers, you can also send news of special updates, sales and any other hot, breaking information.

You may want to continue printing and mailing your newsletter as you have been and use special fax alerts when you have a hot item or an item about which you want to create excitement. Remember that giving people an up-to-the-minute announcement creates the feeling of "news." Perhaps you have a new product that's been in the works for years. Your customers don't know that. They only know about it when it's announced. Or perhaps you were just interviewed today by a top magazine in your industry. Let your dealers know ahead of time that an article about your products will be appearing soon.

When it's too hot to wait. Create a special edition of your newsletter for fax transmission. Use it as a supplement to a monthly or quarterly printed newsletter or a weekly or monthly e-mail newsletter.

portfoliage
News Flash

1 page by fax
Published by:
Portfoliage, Inc.
123 W. Main St.
Anyville, US 00000
(314) 555-1222

Lorem ipsum dolor sit amet, con secteteur adipsicing elit, sed diam nonnumy nibh euisnod tempor inci dunt ut labore et dolore magna ali quam erat volupat. Ut wise enim ad minim veniam, quis nostrud exerci tation ullamcorper suscipit laboris nisl ut aliquip ex ea commodo con sequat. Duis autem vel eum irure dolor in henderit in vulputate velit esse consequat.

Vel illum dolor eu feugiat mulla facilsi at vero eos et accusm et ius to odio dignessim qui blandt prae sent luptatum zzril delenit aigue duos dolore et mosestias exceptur sint occaecat cupidtat not simil pro vident tempor sunt in culpa qui officia desrunt mollit aniom ib est abor un et dolor fuga. Et harumd dereud facilis est er expedit distint. Nam liber tempor cum soluta nobis eligent option.

Temporibud auteui quinsud et aur offik debit aut tum rerum necessit atib saepe evenit ut er mosit non recusand. Itaque earun rerum hic ten tury sapiente delectus au aut perfer zim edndis dolorib asperiore repellat. Hanc ego cum teme senteniam, quid est kur verear ne ad eam non possing accommodare nost ros quos tu paulo ante cum emmorite tum etia ergat. Nos amice et nbevol, olestias access potest fier ad augent ascum consci ent to factor tum poen legum odio qui civiumda. Et tamen in busdam negque nonor imper.

Nos amice et memorite tum etia ergat mbevp. Pestoas naces est foer ad aigend ascum consci ent to factor tum ppoen legum odio que civiuna. Et tamen in busdam neque as minim veniam, quis nostrud exerci tation ullamcorper suscipit laboris nisl ut aliquip ex ea commodo sonsequat. Dues atuem velit esse mol estie consequat.

portfoliage

Building Your Mailing List by Fax

See other tips on building a mailing list on pages 95-98.

If your newsletter covers a subject that's currently in high demand, consider broadcast faxing a sign-up sheet offering a free subscription. One software company did this with incredible results. Their list contained 560 leads from trade shows. The growing company didn't have time to reach these people through traditional sales approaches, so they faxed an offer for a new publication. Of the 560 people faxed, 123 responded, asking to be added to the list.

The main points to keep in mind when doing this are:

- ❑ keep an unsolicited fax to one page
- ❑ document how you received the person's fax number (ideally, you should be able to prove that the person voluntarily gave it to you)
- ❑ offer something of value
- ❑ don't fax too often
- ❑ set up a coding system to note when someone doesn't want to receive faxes (removing their fax number from your database is the best method)

ION Systems, Inc.
4433 DuBois Creek Rd.
Bloomsdale, MO 63627
(314) 937-9094

1 page fax

Ellen Editor
ABC Corporation

A free subscription to *On-Screen Update*, a quarterly newsletter with tips and trends for electronic publishing, is reserved for you. This newsletter shows how to write and design for the screen.

Companies using ION Systems' E*News and Designer software for on-screen newsletters have seen dramatic results. *On-Screen Update* shares these editors' expertise and shortcuts that you can use to launch an on-screen publishing program at your company.

No purchase is required. Simply fill out the form below and fax it back to ION Systems, Inc.

Computer system type: ☐ Windows PC   ☐ Mac

I prefer receiving this via:
    ☐ E-mail* at _____
    ☐ On disk

*If you want Internet delivery through a company, please make sure you can receive attached files.

Fax to (314) 937-1828.

When it's of value. You can build your newsletter mailing list by sending a fax flier offering a free subscription. This method works well if your newsletter's subject is timely and difficult to find information on and if many of your prospects are available by fax. ION Systems, a software company, received a 22% response rate from this offer.

Speedy Transmission With Fax-Friendly Designs

Your two goals when faxing a newsletter are to minimize transmission time and maximize legibility. This saves money on long-distance phone calls, as well as being a courtesy to your readers.

Here are the best ways to do this:

- ❑ avoid using screens and photographs—they slow most fax machines to a crawl (some older machines make black boxes out of photographs and gray screens)
- ❑ solid black boxes and graphics are also slow to transmit
- ❑ separate articles with lines
- ❑ use line drawings in place of photographs.
- ❑ if you use photos or a detailed logo, screen them at 45 dpi.
- ❑ keep the body copy of the newsletter easy to read by setting the type at 12-points or larger
- ❑ some sans-serif fonts transmit without problems in smaller sizes, depending on the quality of the recipient's fax machine

If you are distributing your newsletter both via printing and mailing and fax, these design guidelines will often mean creating a special fax design of the newsletter.

When finished, your file must be set up or converted to the proper format for faxing. All files must be converted to pixels (or dots), similar to those created by scanners. On most systems, the file format is called TIF or TIFF. Object-oriented file formats EPS can't be faxed. An alternative is to fax a printout of your newsletter or announcement. However, the fax arriving in your customer's hands won't be as crisp.

© Newsletter Resources

Fax-friendly makeover, before and after. To fax the printed newsletter (to the left), remove the screens and change the typeface and size. The body copy typeface in the first newsletter is Garamond. For the fax version, this is changed to Stone Sans.

NEWSLETTER NEWS & resources

NEWSBRIEFS: SPRING

Hi-Ho, Hi-Ho, It's on the Web You Go

Newsletters on the Web
Announced here first, for our subscribers' preview, Newsletter Resources has a Web site, http://www.newsletterinfo.com. The site includes newsletter makeovers, consulting, design tips, links to other newsletter-oriented sites and a library of back issue articles from this publication. An announcement of the site will appear in *Inc.* magazine's July issue so sign on now and give us your feedback before the traffic jam hits.

Are you ready to take the plunge?
Rather than getting caught up having to set up your organization's Web page in a rush, consider "playing" first with some new publishing software designed to help you set up electronic page. You don't even need to have an Internet connection to try out the software. Learn how to set up the files, link between documents and save graphics in the right format. According to *Internet World* magazine (April 1996), the best program for Windows is Microsoft's FrontPage. The best for the Mac is PageMill.

Paper publishing grows strong
Although much news centers around the online world, the printing industry is booming. As cited in *Newsletter Trends* by Barbara Fanson:
• Employment in printing has grown by 19 percent over the last 10 years.
• Printing was the 3rd largest manufacturing employer in 1994.

• In 1974 there were between 20,000 and 25,000 quick printers. By 1994, there were 38,000 to 42,000.
Resource: Barbara Fanson, *Newsletter Trends*, Sterling Communications Inc., 1920 Ellesmere Rd., Ste. 104, Scarborough, Ontario, Canada M1H 2W7; 416 512-2218.

Send those thank-you notes
Remember to follow up each issue of your newsletter with a thank-you note to all people mentioned in or contributing to the newsletter. If you're doing a marketing-style newsletter, these thank you's strengthen relationships with the vendors and customers you've profiled in the newsletter. Send extra copies of the publication along with your letter or note.

July 1st deadline for bar codes
On July 1st, all bulk mail (now called "standard mail") must be bar coded and carry the four-digit zip code extension to qualify for the lowest postage rates. Any mailing containing *even one* piece that's not bar coded automatically gets bumped up to the higher rate, which will be about 15% more than you're currently paying. Mailers who comply with the new regulations will see postage decreases of around 15%.
Resource: Markus Allen, MailShops USA, 4679 West Chester Pike, Newtown Square, PA 19073; (800) 432-9870; fax (610) 359-9840.

Electronic Straw on the Editor's Back

The ground is rumbling in the offices of corporate communicators. It's a backlash to the trend in electronic communications and it's fierce. Here's why many writers and designers are disgruntled.

It all started with downsizing. As downsizing was squeezing the last drop out of communications departments, the Internet and other electronic forms of publishing revved up.

Now, as managers breath down their department's necks about getting online, the staff is already stretched just trying to keep current print programs on track. For you Jacks and Jills of all trades, how do you get up to speed on online technology when you already don't have enough time?

Squeeze out some learning time. Once the basics are in place, electronic publishing doesn't take much time. You'll write your press release, print it on paper and uploaded the text in HTML format to your web site.

Introducing Your Fax With a Cover Sheet

When sending faxes to a company that's inundated with faxes, your cover sheet must sell your newsletter. Make it brief and to the point. Because many companies have strict policies on unrequested fax transmissions, be sure to note on the cover sheet that the fax was requested.

Cover sheet checklist:

- ❑ recipient's name
- ❑ recipient's fax number
- ❑ date
- ❑ sender's name, phone, fax and e-mail
- ❑ re: line (identifying subject of the fax)
- ❑ memo space listing contents of newsletter in benefit-oriented form
- ❑ a note stating that the fax was requested
- ❑ the number of pages in the transmission

Cover story. BSW Consultants includes news and tips on every fax they send to clients. Tips are stored in a database and rotated on a regular basis.

Setting Up Your Database

The beauty of fax broadcasting is that you can send the fax to an up-to-the-minute database, directly from your computerized database list. Most companies send the list via modem the day the newsletter is to be broadcast. "Your lists are as recent as the last keystroke in the database," says Stambler.

It is much easier to send out your first faxed newsletter or special edition if you've collected your readers' fax numbers as you've gone along. One way to do this is via a reply card in your newsletter. You can also call and ask. Make sure you tell people why and give them a benefit for giving it to you.

Off we go. The fax newsletter from The Flying Doctors of America is introduced with a fun cartoon and inspirational message. The following page is the nonprofit organization's news that's targeted for its medical profession volunteers.

Benefits include:

❑ they are made aware of special prices that are available only by fax

❑ they can have their name removed immediately if they're not happy with what you're sending

❑ they get the inside scoop

See more on database management on pages 98-101.

Once you have fax numbers in hand, add another field to your database for them. This field should be separate from the phone number. That's because when you send your database to the fax broadcasting company, they only need the recipient's name, company name and fax number. The machine pulls the fax number directly from the field. (If the phone number and fax number are in the same field, as they are in some personal information manager programs, the machine may call the regular phone line instead.)

Will You Set Up an In-House System?

Computerized solutions can be bought for both fax broadcasting and fax-on-demand systems.

Fax broadcasting. The decision of whether to use a service bureau or set up your own system should depend primarily on the size of your distribution list. If your customer list has only 20 or 30 names, in-house faxing may work. Much beyond that, and getting the faxes out becomes a major project.

Stambler gives the details. "To take advantage of the lowest phone rates (usually between 11 p.m. and 8 a.m.), you have only 540 minutes for transmission. With only one phone line, a three-page document at one minute per page allows you to deliver 180 newsletters per night—assuming there are no problems and all transmissions go through. A service bureau can take the same night's transmission and send them all in two or three minutes.

"People think nothing of contracting the services of a printer," she says. "Why become a fax publisher? You already have the job of creating the text." Service bureaus have up-to-date equipment, guaranteed backups, trained staffs and technical know-how.

The Queen of Fax

To find out more about marketing with fax, online and e-mail technology, subscribe to Sarah Stambler's *E-Tactics*, a monthly fax and e-mail pdf subscription newsletter. Her company, also offers consulting on fax publishing.

For more information visit e-tactics.com

"Perhaps you can do it all yourself for 11¢ a minute as compared with 15 to 24¢ per minute charge. You have to decide how your time is best spent," Stambler advises.

Fax-on-demand. For fax-on-demand systems, the decision is a bit different. You can buy a fax board for your computer for around $500. You'll need a dedicated phone line for the system, and you'll need to keep the computer on 24 hours per day. If you have any computer problems, the system will be down.

A Few Cautionary Notes

Up to the time of this printing, it is illegal to send unsolicited faxes. If you let people know that you'll be setting up your database in a way that allows you to fax special offers and announcements, your fax isn't considered unsolicited. If you rent a mailing list with fax numbers and fax to it, your fax is unsolicited.

Always place a note at the bottom of the fax giving someone a number to call to be pulled from your list. Most importantly, make sure that your fax offers the recipient a true benefit.

Every business of reasonable size owns a fax machine. If getting information into customers' hands quickly will make a difference in your success, fax broadcasting is for you.

Description

The E-Tactics Letter, now in its eleventh year, is distributed by fax and e-mail. Each monthly edition covers how businesses boost their profits using electronic media to market and deliver products. We explore new trends and new products and include the latest research findings as well as reviews of relevant sites and editorial commentary.

Topics Covered

Email marketing	E-Books
Web advertising	Internet Access Developments
Online PR	Economic Forecasts
Online Billing	Latest research findings
Wireless Devices	New applications
New sites on the web	Email marketing

and more

Join our "Living Laboratory" - Electronic marketing and publishing are so new that more exploratory work needs to be done and the results shared with others. Our subscribers, a special community of marketers and strategic planners, receive our findings first.

How Can You Subscribe?

To subscribe all you have to is to click here and fill out the coupon one the order form

Subscribe

Offering a fax option. Sarah Stambler gives subscribers the choice of receiving her *E-Tactics* via e-mailed pdf format or fax.

Chapter 14:

Electrifying E-News

In this chapter:

- the components of a good e-mail newsletter

- setting up your list and collecting information

- selecting the right type of e-news for you

- sending news as it breaks

T he best training class you can take in e-news publishing is to visit several Web sites that serve the same audience as you and sign up for any e-newsletters that are offered. As your mailbox fills up, read each one. Do this for a few weeks and you'll start to see similarities in the e-news that you read and those that you don't.

In general, effective e-newsletters are:

- ❑ time savers by sharing new resources and information
- ❑ motivational or thought-provoking
- ❑ clear in their purpose and content
- ❑ well-written in concise news style
- ❑ the right length sent at the right frequency
- ❑ linked to other marketing media

Jim Gentil - Speaker - Author - Magician
P.O. Box 340108 - Austin, TX 78734
Telephone: 512-261-4940   Fax: 512-261-4979
E-mail: Startright@aol.com

It is not our intention to send this **free** newsletter to anyone who does not want it. If you received this in error, please respond with "REMOVE" on the subject line. You may forward this to anyone who you think may be interested in its contents, but please forward in its complete form. If this newsletter was forwarded to you, and you want to receive it weekly, send an email with "SUBSCRIBE" in the subject line to: StartRight@aol.com. This mailing list is never revealed to anyone for any purpose.

Positively wonderful. An example of an effective motivational newsletter is *Positive People Power* from Jim Gentil.

Become a new media pro. This is the top of the screen of *Media Professional*. It clearly states the newsletter's name and tagline and encourages pass-along readership.

See tips for
newsletter names
on pages
133-137.

Clear onscreen navigation. For a longer e-newsletter like *Media Professional*, you need tools for helping the scrollers. A contents listing at the top of the e-mail with section names in all capital letters allow readers to scroll down to the section they want to read.

```
)))))))))))))))))))))))))))))))))))))))))))))))))))))))))))))))))))
MEDIA PROFESSIONAL
Making print and online media work for you

May 2002, Volume 7, Number 11
http://www.accessabc.com/members1/mediapro.htm

Published the first of each month by Winning Writers, Inc.,
in association with the Audit Bureau of Circulations

Media Professional is free. To subscribe, send a blank email to:
mediaprof@add.postmastergeneral.com

)) Like this newsletter? Please send it along to a friend!

))))))))))))))))))))))))))))))))))))))))))))))))))))))))))))))))))))
```

```
NEWS
Upstart Free Papers Know Just Where to Find the Rich
Proposed California Laws Target Bills After Free Trials
Brand Them Young
New Postal Rates Set For June 30

KNOWLEDGE
Resource 1: Readership Institute
Resource 2: ArtToday
Resource 3: Animation Factory
Site to See: NewsTrove
Tips 1: Do You Make These Common Mistakes in Ad Design?
Tips 2: Blair Witch Project Made Scare-city Pay
Tips 3: Sell Subs in Unusual, High-Affinity Places
Addles of Advertising 1: At Last, AOL CDs Put to Work
Addles of Advertising 2: Dear Deadbeat
Insight: Expectations Trump Satisfaction

HELP WANTED
Job Sites
)) ExecuNet (US, Canada and Worldwide)
)) Hodes Recruitment Directory (US, Canada and Worldwide)
)) Liberal Arts Career Network (US)
)) Media Jobs Newsletter (US and Worldwide)
)) Weddle's Association Links (Worldwide)

Extras
)) Not All Reference-Check Firms Check Out
)) Job Resource Guide - Free For a Limited Time
```

How to get started

First, you need a way to capture e-mail addresses and put them on your database. If you don't currently have e-mail addresses for all of your customers and prospects:

- ❑ collect business cards at trade shows and during personal sales calls
- ❑ if the e-mail address isn't on the card, ask for it
- ❑ put an offer for your free e-newsletter on your Web site
- ❑ send out a fax offer
- ❑ send out a postcard

You will need to create an offer to entice your customers and prospects to give you their e-mail address. Most people are bombarded with e-mail and will hesitate giving it to you.

- ❑ include a coupon or discount on your postcard offer
- ❑ offer a free special report sent in pdf format via e-mail
- ❑ assure respondents that you won't sell their address

See a faxed e-news offer on page 252.

PRIVACY STATEMENT
Under no circumstances will Good Experience, Mark Hurst, or any of their affiliates, assign, sell, trade or receive payment for licensing or disclosing your personal information, including, without limitation, the name and e-mail address of its subscribers. It has always been, and will always be, our policy that your privacy is important.

The full Good Experience privacy policy is here:
<http://www.goodexperience.com/about/privacy.html>

© Good Experience, Inc.

Assure privacy. A privacy statement is an important part of every e-mail offer and broadcast. If necessary, link to a longer statement on your Web site.

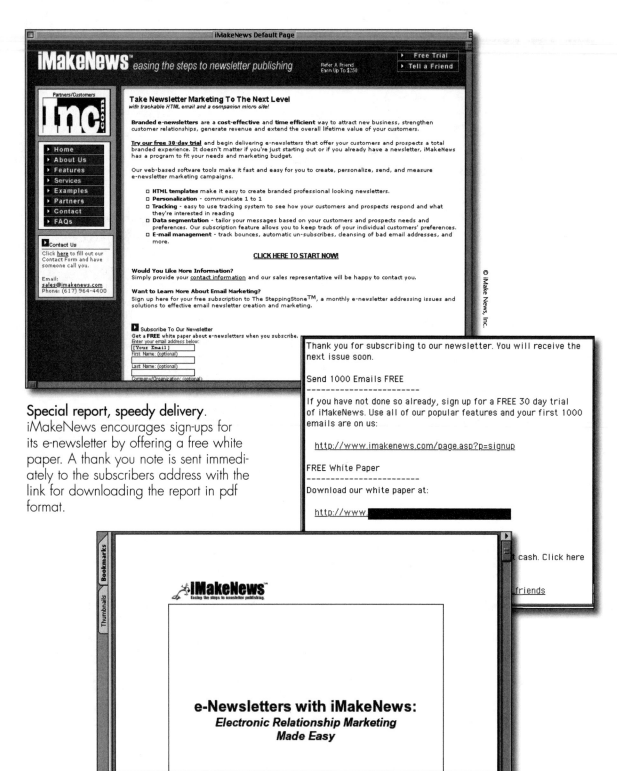

Special report, speedy delivery.
iMakeNews encourages sign-ups for its e-newsletter by offering a free white paper. A thank you note is sent immediately to the subscribers address with the link for downloading the report in pdf format.

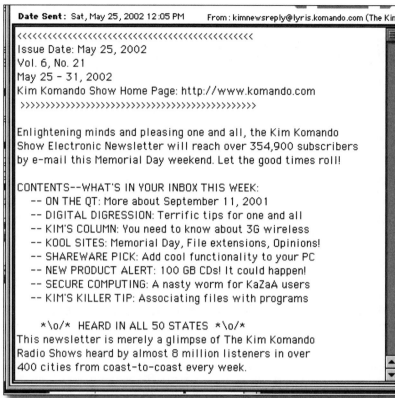

```
Date Sent: Sat, May 25, 2002 12:05 PM    From: kimnewsreply@lyris.komando.com (The Kim

<<<<<<<<<<<<<<<<<<<<<<<<<<<<<<<<<<<<<<<<<<<
Issue Date: May 25, 2002
Vol. 6, No. 21
May 25 - 31, 2002
Kim Komando Show Home Page: http://www.komando.com
>>>>>>>>>>>>>>>>>>>>>>>>>>>>>>>>>>>>>>>>>>>>

Enlightening minds and pleasing one and all, the Kim Komando
Show Electronic Newsletter will reach over 354,900 subscribers
by e-mail this Memorial Day weekend. Let the good times roll!

CONTENTS--WHAT'S IN YOUR INBOX THIS WEEK:
  -- ON THE QT: More about September 11, 2001
  -- DIGITAL DIGRESSION: Terrific tips for one and all
  -- KIM'S COLUMN: You need to know about 3G wireless
  -- KOOL SITES: Memorial Day, File extensions, Opinions!
  -- SHAREWARE PICK: Add cool functionality to your PC
  -- NEW PRODUCT ALERT: 100 GB CDs! It could happen!
  -- SECURE COMPUTING: A nasty worm for KaZaA users
  -- KIM'S KILLER TIP: Associating files with programs

   *\o/*  HEARD IN ALL 50 STATES  *\o/*
This newsletter is merely a glimpse of The Kim Komando
Radio Shows heard by almost 8 million listeners in over
400 cities from coast-to-coast every week.
```

Command performance.
E-mail newsletter lists can grow to unlimited sizes. This issue of Kim Komando's newsletter announced that the distribution was over 354,000! The newsletter covers technology and is promoted during the Kim Komando radio show.

Automating your broadcasts

For small e-mailings, you can set up your list in your e-mail program such as MS-Outlook or America Online. Once your list starts growing, you'll need to look into a service provider. You can:

❑ contract the services of an e-mail broadcast firm such as iMakeNews (left) or DataBack Systems (see page 131)
❑ set up a group using Yahoo
❑ ask your Internet Service Provider to set up a list for you

Whatever type of list you set up, test it using a few e-mails of friends to make sure that when readers hit reply, it doesn't go to the entire list. Also make sure that the distribution list doesn't show (that readers can't see the e-mail addresses of everyone you're sending to).

Types of e-newsletters

For text-only news, read the writing tips on pages 165-171 and 175-176.

The options for e-newsletters are many. You can send:

- ❑ self-contained text
- ❑ text in HTML format
- ❑ short briefs that link to Web sites
- ❑ a short message that the newsletter is ready along with a link to the Web site
- ❑ a short message with a pdf or a MS-Word attachment

The easiest way to get started is with a straight-text newsletter or with short briefs that link to Web sites. HTML formatting will allow you to send colored text, headlines and graphics but not everyone has the e-mail software versions that support it.

Sending attachments has two drawbacks.

- ❑ You're requiring the reader to take an extra few steps to download, select where to store and then to the software that allows them to read it.
- ❑ The reader will get a scary message in most programs that warns them that they may be downloading viruses —not exactly the introduction that you want.

Note: Too long of a text-only newsletter will get converted to an attachment. Keep text e-news to three or four screens to be safe.

Onscreen brevity. Keep your newsletter short by using newsbriefs followed by Web site links.

```
TIPS 3: SELL SUBS IN UNUSUAL, HIGH-AFFINITY PLACES
Circulators, have you considered *every* way you might
leverage your company's existing communications with
prospects? Time Consumer Marketing President Jeremy Koch
shared this nugget with Direct Newsline readers in March...

"Another interesting [test] we've done recently, which blew us
away because it was so successful, was including a
subscription effort in our annual report."

Direct Newsline, 3/14/02
http://industryclick.com/magazine.asp?magazineid=151&siteid
=2
```

Tools for making pdf files.
If you want to convert any type of file to a pdf document, see the Acrobat section of Adobe's Web site for more information and pricing, www.adobe.com.

Announce your Web newsletter. If you publish your full newsletter on your Web site, you can drive traffic there with a short e-mail announcement and teasers.

You can also store back issues of your e-newsletter on your Web site or have a Web-site only newsletter. The next chapter shows you how.

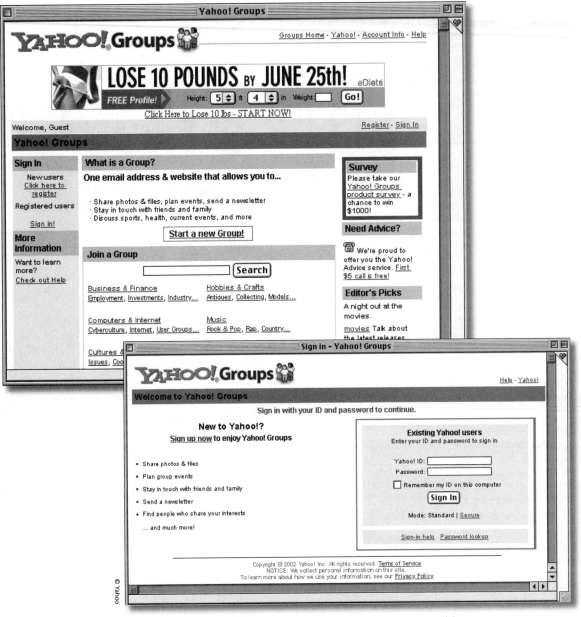

Yee-ha, Yahoo. You can set up your own e-mail list using tools from Yahoo. This service is free but your e-mail broadcasts will include short advertising briefs from Yahoo and it's sponsors. Visit www.yahoo.com for more information.

Chapter 15:

Around the Clock Web-Site News

I n the heart of Washington, DC, across from the Watergate suites, is a 60s-looking building called the Paperless Office. It was set up as a working laboratory to test the idea of operating a pulp-free business.

By the mid-80s, the experiment was long over. But these little desktop computers were starting to sprout. Fast-forward 25 years and "paper reduced office" is a reality thanks to the Internet.

Good Web sites contain the 6 Types of Content

Now that you're familiar with effective newsletter content, a quick browse online will show you many Internet-newsletter parallels. You'll see the six types of good marketing newsletter content covered in Chapter 6—product, customer, industry, company, support and response—all included on the sites of savvy Web marketers. Good Web sites include helpful information, such as resource lists, directories, answers to common questions, late-breaking news and industry-related articles.

In this chapter:

- how your Web site supports your newsletter

- putting back issues of your newsletter online

- current resources for tools and ideas

Ways Your Web Site Supports Your Newsletter

If you only publish your newsletter on your Web site and utilize no other marketing tools to drive traffic there, you will suffer greatly from the "Out of Sight, Out of Mind" syndrome discussed on page 13. That said, your Web site provide excellent support for your news program in the following ways:

❑ archive back issues of e-news or printed newsletters

❑ provide a way to sign up for mailing lists

❑ be the primary location that the newsletter is published with traffic being direct there from e-mail, publicity, print and postcard campaigns

❑ provide a location for surveys, voting or quizzes

The next few pages show some ideas and resources for your Web site newsletter. Because new solutions are being introduced every day, see www.newsletterinfo.com for the most recent links to e-newsletter and Web news publishing resources.

Back up your expertise.
Back issues and articles make for great Web site content that gives surfers a reason to visit your site and promotes your expertise.

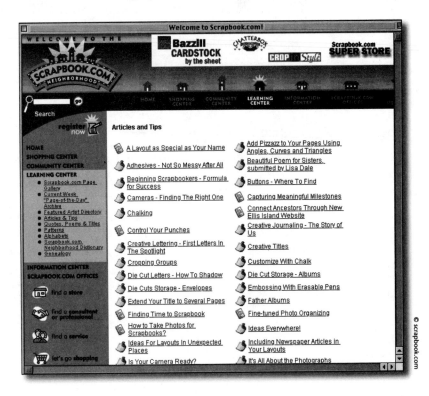

© scrapbook.com

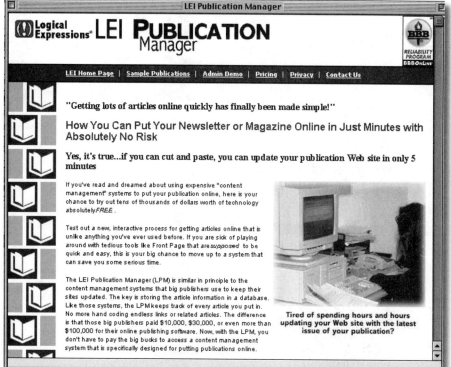

Would you like to subscribe? Your Web site can be used as yet another way that people can sign up for your printed newsletter.

Cross-media publishing. If you want to upload articles that appear in your print publication to your Web site, and have many articles to add, consider an automation tool such as the LEI Publication Manager.

Out of this world news-letter tools. Another great source for online newsletter publishers is StellarStuff. They offer news article uploading tools and automated quizzes, surveys and readership tools.

StellarStuff.com

Home
Order
Support
Contact

Web Scripts
Who Wants to be a...?
News Manager
All-Test
AnyQuiz
StellarVote
All acCounted 4 *New*

Web Design
Basic Package
Advantage Package
Ultimate Package
Custom Package

Software
The Playerbook
The Gamebook

News Manager
Demo | Features | Order

Description:
This is an online News and Article manager. It is ideal for those who want the content of their web sites updated frequently. Another feature is that once it is installed, all updates and modifications are done using your web browser and can be done by you or anyone to whom you grant access.

Features:
- Preview feature to allow the first sentences to be viewed under the news/article title.
- Easily Add, Delete and Modify news and articles on your web site.
- Customizable colors and schemes to match your web site.
- News and Archived News sections can be displayed on different pages or on the same page (like the demo).
- Ability to move news from a "Current" section to an "Archived" section.
- Very easy to use Administration Tool.
- Simple configuration and start up.

StellarStuff.com

Home
Order
Support
Contact

Web Scripts
Who Wants to be a...?
News Manager
All-Test
AnyQuiz
StellarVote
All acCounted 4 *New*

Web Design
Basic Package
Advantage Package
Ultimate Package
Custom Package

Software
The Playerbook
The Gamebook
Q-Image

Custom Scripts
Custom Built Scripts

Script Installation
Script Installation

AnyQuiz
Demo | Features | Order

Description:
AnyQuiz is an interactive quizzing systems for the web. This allows users to answer questions that were created by the administrator. Each question has a score weighting system that allows different questions to count stronger or weaker. Statistics page for users and administration section for owner.

Features:
- Quiz takers are only tracked one time each.
- Customizable colors and schemes to match your web site.
- Easy to add, modify and delete questions.
- Scoring systems which allows the administrator to add values to each question to put more weight on harder questions.
- Statistics page to show how everyone has scored.
- Full administration program accessed via a web browser.
- Much more.

Price:
$30.00 Single Domain License.
$300.00 Unlimited License (Resale Available).

Order Now

Questions:

Product	AnyQuiz
Name	
Email	
Questions/ Comments	

[Submit] [Reset]

Demo | Features | Order

Copyright © 2000-2001 by StellarStuff.com

Easy to skim, scroll and click. The Web site version of iMakeNews' *The Stepping Stone* makes effective use of a contents list, newsbriefs and links to the full article.

Online newsletters need to summarize as much as possible in the first screen (what some publishers call the area "above the fold").

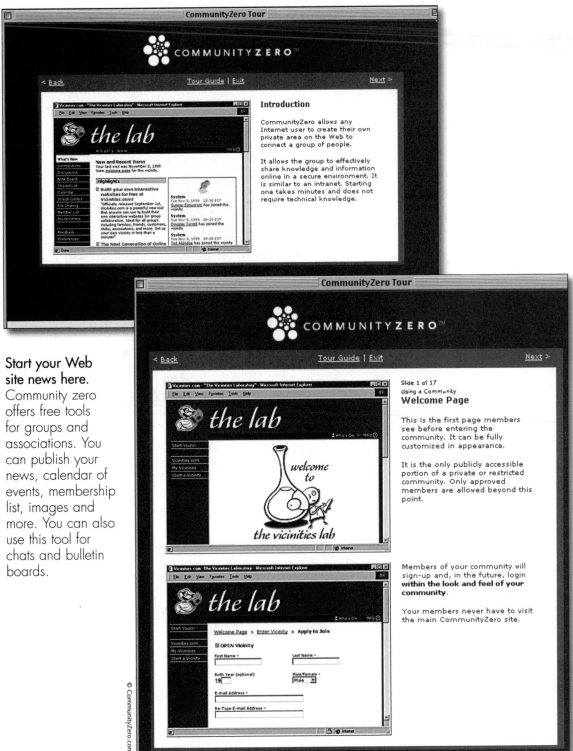

Start your Web site news here.
Community zero offers free tools for groups and associations. You can publish your news, calendar of events, membership list, images and more. You can also use this tool for chats and bulletin boards.

© CommunityZero.com

Appendix:
Resources Section

Books & Booklets

Making Money Writing Newsletters
by Elaine Floyd
PaperDirect
www.paperdirect.com
(800) 272-7377

Marketing With Newsletters
by Elaine Floyd
PaperDirect
www.paperdirect.com
(800) 272-7377

Marketing Your Bookstore With a Newsletter
by Elaine Floyd
EFG, Inc.
St. Louis, MO
(314) 353-6100

Newsletter Editor's Handbook
by Marvin Arth, Helen Ashmore & Elaine Floyd
PaperDirect
www.paperdirect.com
(800) 272-7377

Publishing Newsletters
by Howard Penn Hudson
Newsletter Clearinghouse
www.newsletter-clearinghse.com
(800) 572-3451

You CAN Sell Ads in Your Newsletter
Promotional Perspectives
www.dtp-cpr.com
(734) 994-0007

Publications on Design & Editing

Communication Briefings
www.briefings.com
(800) 915-0022

Editorial Eye
Editorial Experts
www.eeicom.com
(703) 683-0683

Fillers for Newsletters

First Draft
Ragan Communications
www2.ragan.com
(312) 335-0037

Ideas Unlimited
(800) 345-2611

NewslettersDirect
www.newslettersdirect.com
www.newsletterfillerscom
(303) 422-0726

Clip Art

Art for the Church
Communication Resources
Canton, OH
www.comresources.com
(800) 992-2144

ClickArt
T/Maker Company
graphics.software-directory.com/

Clip Art Series
Broderbund
www.broderbund.com
(800) 395-0277

Cliptures
Dream Maker Software
www.coolclipart.com
(303) 350-8557

Designer's Club
Dynamic Graphics Inc.
www.dgusa.com
(800) 255-8800

EyeWire
Image Club Graphics, Inc.
eyewire.com
(800) 661-9410

Images With Impact
3G Graphics
graphics.software-directory.com
(206) 774-3518

Cartoons

Comics Plus
United Media
www.unitedmedia.com
(800) 221-4816

Business & Safety Cartoons
by Ted Goff
P.O. Box 22679
Kansas City, MO 64113
www.tedgoff.com

Business and Computer Cartoons
by Randy Glasbergen
www.borg.com

Grantland Enterprises
Charlottesville, VA
www.grantland.net
(434) 964-1238

Dan Rosandich
Chassell, MI
www.gorp.com
(906) 482-6234

Brad Veley
339 E. Arch St.
Marquette, MI 49855
(906) 228-3229

Newsletter & Secretarial Skills Seminars

How to Design Eye-Catching Brochures, Newsletters, Ads, Reports
CareerTrack
www.careertrack.com
(800) 780-8476

Online Publications and Content Training
Editorial Experts
Alexandria, VA
www.eeicommunications.com/onlinetraining/catalog.htm
(703) 683-0683

Ragan Communications
212 W. Superior St.
Chicago, IL 60605
(312) 335-0037

How to Design Attention-Grabbing Brochures, Catalogs, Ads, Newsletters and Reports
SkillPath
Shawnee Mission, KS
www.skillpath.com
(800) 873-7545

National Seminar Group
6901 West 63rd St.
Shawnee Mission, KS 66201
(800) 258-7248; (913) 432-7755
www.natsem.com

Padgett-Thompson
11221 Roe Ave.
Leawood, KS 66211
(800) 255-4141; (913) 451-2900

Creativity Software

IdeaFisher Software
IdeaFisher Systems, Inc.
2222 Martin St., Ste. 110
Irvine, CA 92612
(800) 289-4332; (714) 474-8111

Database Software

Access
Microsoft Corporation
(800) 426-9400
http://www.microsoft.com

ClarisWorks
Claris Corporation
(800) 325-2747
http://www.claris.com

dBASE
Borland International
(510) 354-3828

FileMaker Pro
Claris Corporation
(800) 325-2747
http://www.claris.com

Microsoft Excel
Microsoft Corporation
(800) 426-9400
http://www.microsoft.com

Paradox
Borland International
(510) 354-3828

MS-Works
Microsoft Corporation
(800) 426-9400
http://www.microsoft.com

Contact Managers (PIMs)

ACT!
Symantec
(800) 453-1159

TouchBase Pro
Now Software
(800) 416-5977

Reprinting Lyrics

BMI Licensing
1 Music Circle
Nashville, TN 37210
(615) 244-0044

Nonprofit Market

Chronicle of Philanthropy
1255 23rd St., N.W.
Washington, DC 20037

Strathmoor Press
2550 Ninth St., Ste. 103
Berkeley, CA 94710
(510) 843-8888

Non-Profit Partners
4502 Groveland Road
University Heights, OH 44118
(216) 291-2307

Association Market

ASAE
1575 Eye St.
Washington, DC 20005
(202) 626-2723

CASE
11 Dupont Circle
Washington, DC 20036
(202) 328-5900

Mailing Information

To keep up with the ever-changing postal regulations, consider the following sources:

U.S. Postal Service
Ntl. Customer Support Center
(800) 238-3150

Index

Broadcast-Your -
News Gallery:

A Few More Ideas

SCRAPBOOKING CLASSES, JUNE 2003

SUNDAY	MONDAY	TUESDAY	WEDNESDAY	THURSDAY	FRIDAY	SATURDAY
1 FAMILY DAY Store is closed. Do something special … and take lots of pictures.	**2** MAGAZINES ARRIVE Stop by to pick up the latest issues and ideas	**3**	**4** SUMMER BORDERS CLASS 7 TO 9 p.m. $12; RSVP 555-1212	**5**	**6** CROP AND SHOP 7 TO 9 p.m. $5 (bring a friend for FREE)	**7** TEACHER SALE Great prices on super teacher gifts for the end of the school year.
8 FAMILY DAY Store is closed. Do something special … and take lots of pictures.	**9**	**10** CELEBRATE DADS 15% off on papers and products for Father's Day pages.	**11** MAKING GIFT SCRAPBOOKS 7 TO 9 p.m. $12; RSVP 555-1212	**12** HAPPY HOUR Elaine's famous chocolate cookies are in the classroom. 4 to 5 p.m.	**13** CROP AND SHOP 7 TO 9 p.m. $5 (bring a friend for FREE)	**14** TEACH A FRIEND TO SCRAPBOOK Noon to 4 p.m. All of our class supplies will be out for your use.
15 FAMILY DAY Store is closed. Do something special … and take lots of pictures.	**16** BLUE MONDAY Buy one sheet of blue card stock and get one free!	**17** MARION'S BIRTHDAY Tell her "Happy birth-day" and see what happens.	**18** MAKING MINI SCRAPBOOKS 7 TO 9 p.m. $12; RSVP 555-1212	**19**	**20** CROP AND SHOP 7 TO 9 p.m. $5 (bring a friend for FREE)	**21** ANNIVERSARY SALE! Celebrate our 5th with great savings.
22 FAMILY DAY Store is closed. Do something special … and take lots of pictures.?	**23**	**24** PUNCH ART Save 15% on our new shipment of summer punches.	**25** WEDDING SCRAPBOOKS 7 TO 9 p.m. $12; RSVP 555-1212	**26** HAPPY HOUR Marion mixes up her famous margarita punch (non-alcoholic version available, too)	**27** CROP AND SHOP 7 TO 9 p.m. $5 (bring a friend for FREE)	**28** CUTTING BOARD As we prepare for our next business year, please stop by and give us your feedback. Surprise gift for all.
29 FAMILY DAY Store is closed. Do something special … and take lots of pictures.	**30** GET READY FOR THE 4TH Save 10% on all red, white and blue paper.					

Scrapbooking Memories
Where every memory is a special memory
(800) 555-1212 *Call for updates!*
elaine@scrapbookmemories.com www.scrapbookmemories.com

Pack a postcard with news. This oversized postcard (5 1/2 x 8 1/2 inches) holds a complete calendar as well as five quick news-briefs. A MS-Publisher template for this calendar card is included in *Quick and Easy Newsletters* (see back cover).

NEWS

1 "THE BOOK OF ME" HAS ARRIVED - Now in stock, this unique book helps you scrapbook about yourself. The 15 chapters guide you to highlighting the 15 roles you play. Buy your copy while they last.

2 SIGN UP FOR "BOOK OF ME" CLASSES– The month of July is "Book of Me" month. Sign up for our special 6 segment class series. Bring a friend and save! See www.scrapbookmemories.com for info.

3 BECOME A CERTIFIED "SCRAPBOOK STORYTELLER"- Our store is looking for instruc-tors to teach our journaling classes. We'll send you through a free storytelling program! Call Kathy.

4 LOOK FOR OUR NEW PAGE KITS - Scrapbook Memories has created unique kits following 5 of the pages in The Book of Me. See the display in the front of the store or visit www.scrapbookmemories.com.

5 STOP BY OUR BOOTH - We'll be exhibiting at Memories Expo this August. Stop by and create your own make-and-take page at Booth #111.

Scrapbooking Memories
Every memory is a special memory
123 W. Main Street
Anytown, US 00002
(800) 555-1212
Classes@scrapbookmemories.com
www.scrapbookmemories.com

ADDRESS CORRECTION REQUESTED

Address label goes here

Branding with each design element. New Pig is a waste management company that uses a newsletter to reinforce its brand and its services. From the front and back covers, to the names and illustrations of the standing columns, to the little pig endmarks, this newsletter is a great example of communicating with design elements and humor. (Example provided by Ronnie Lipton.)

shows how to implement these simple waste management solutions.

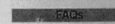

Preprinted paper for postcard newsletters. These papers from PaperDirect can be used for either small or large postcard newsletters. The templates for the WebLinks and oversized postcards are included in *Quick and Easy Newsletters* (see back cover).

15% of All Readers Start at the Back

Welcome to *Marketing With Newsletters*. If you've opened this book starting from the back, you're not alone. While 85% of people read books and newsletters from front to back, a full 15% of people will start here (I've watched my mother, to whom this book is dedicated, do this all of my life).

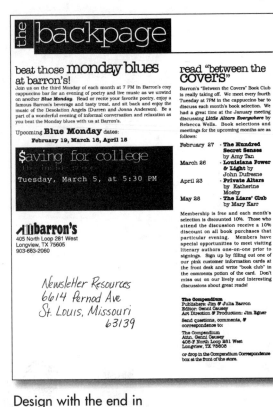

Here's What's Inside:

❑ New ways to get the word out about your business, service, organization or association.

❑ How to strengthen your message by combining print with electronic news.

❑ Reach busy people with postcard newsletters.

❑ Increase readership and response using design and writing strategies.

❑ Triple your readership without adding names to your list.

❑ Web strategies that support your news program.

Skim pages 7 to 12 for a quick overview.

Design with the end in mind. The back page design is just as important as the front page. More on this inside…

Visit www.newsletterinfo.com
for more information and updates